5443 8527

The Best American Short Plays

2012–2013

D1444018

WITHDRAWN
BEAVERTON CITY LIBRARY
BEAVERTON, OR 97005
MEMBER OF WASHINGTON COUNTY
COOPERATIVE LIBRARY SERVICES

The Best American Short Plays

2012–2013

edited with an introduction by
William W. Demastes

APPLAUSE THEATRE & CINEMA BOOKS
An Imprint of Hal Leonard Corporation

The Best American Short Plays 2012–2013
Edited with an intoduction by William W. Demastes

Copyright © 2014 by Applause Theatre & Cinema Books (an imprint of Hal Leonard Corporation)

No part of this publication may be reproduced or transmitted in any form or by any means, electronic or mechanical, including photocopy, recording or any other information storage or retrieval system now known or to be invented, without permission in writing from the publishers, except by a reviewer who wishes to quote brief passages in connection with a review written for inclusion in a magazine, newspaper, or broadcast.

Note: All plays contained in this volume are fully protected under copyright laws of the United States of America, the British Empire, including the Dominion of Canada, and all other countries of the International Copyright Union and the Universal Copyright Convention. Permission to reproduce, wholly or in any part, by any method, must be obtained from the copyright owners or their agents.

Published in 2014 by Applause Theatre & Cinema Books
An Imprint of Hal Leonard Corporation
7777 West Bluemound Road
Milwaukee, WI 53213

Trade Book Division Editorial Offices
33 Plymouth St., Montclair, NJ 07042

Printed in the United States of America
Book interior by UB Communications

ISBN 978-1-4803-6174-4
ISSN 0067-6284

www.applausebooks.com

contents

introduction

"Hot Tempers and Cold Decrees"

William W. Demastes

Humans love to think of themselves as rational beings well in control of their lives from sunup to sundown and dusk to dawn. We learn to follow rules of proper behavior and more than happily issue out advice to those who just can't get a handle on their rash behavior. Restraint and order, after all, are the cornerstones of human society and civilization. The problem is that human nature bucks and bridles at every attempt to socialize and civilize, even when we and our best intentions do everything we can to keep a lid on it. Shakespeare perhaps best captured this sentiment when he had his youthful Portia observe, "The brain may devise laws for the blood, but a hot temper leaps o'er a cold decree." In those few words he has managed to capture precisely why it is so difficult to be human; if it were okay simply to let our hot tempers prevail, life would be so much easier.

Or so we think. Portia speaks these words in *The Merchant of Venice* with all the confident authority of youthful inexperience. It's the kind of fantasizing that obsesses us all to one degree or another, that wish to chuck it all, take that job and shove it, live on love, and head out for the great unknown with little more than a toothbrush to encumber us. Wouldn't life be grand if our impulsive inclinations could overthrow the compulsory duties that actually make living possible though not always enjoyable? Sad to say, blood's hot temper may pave a seductive path for us all, but sooner or later we all come to realize that cold decrees are what prevent those hot tempers from spiraling us all out of orbit.

What we all eventually discover—even Portia discovers this—is that life involves a constant struggle between blood and brain, temper and decree. If either gets the upper hand for any extended period of time, the result is invariably catastrophic, what Robert Frost once described as an end by fire or ice and T. S. Eliot described as either bang or whimper. While the former (fire and bang) are far more dramatic, the latter (ice and whimper), sadly, are far more common.

But then there's the life spent somewhere between the two extremes, that temperate zone of sustainability neither too consuming nor too stultifying. This is the place most of us are searching for. And what we learn on those occasions when we find it is that we can never really just settle down and enjoy it; rather, we find that keeping in that zone remains a lifelong challenge of slipping in and sliding out of that place of contentment, getting sometimes too hot-blooded, sometimes too cold-decreed.

What is exciting about theater and drama is that we can experience this struggle between hot tempers and cold decrees from the relative safety of a theater seat or living room lounge chair. While poets may like talking about this struggle, playwrights go the step beyond and bring the struggle to life for us to witness in all its ever-dynamic detail. It's a struggle we can watch someone like Shakespeare's Portia grow to understand because theater at its best brings a pulse to the many ways we test our boundaries. And it presents the results of this struggle in living color, fortifying us to face the unending challenges that confront us all on a daily basis. That's what theater does. That's what the plays in this volume do.

They capture the struggle between hot tempers and cold decrees, reminding us of the many resulting complexities we all experience in our lives, from the most trivial to the most consequential. The push-pull of this human struggle is captured with almost mythic intensity in Frank Higgins's comic farce *The True Death of Socrates*, which puts an earthy spin on Socrates's stoic embrace of otherworldly idealism. In Higgins's version, flesh-and-blood Socrates balks at the stoically noble suicide that will make him immortal in the annals of Western philosophy, begging the question: How many among us are really willing to die for an idea? For this Socrates, at least, the warm-blooded needs of the individual outweigh the cold-blooded attraction of history.

Then there are those cases when the heat of life goes out long before existence comes to an end, demonstrating the sad—and sometimes even tragic—truth that cold decrees often *do* obstruct a leaping hot temper, if for no other reason than that habit and routine ultimately encrust our lives, and comfort and conformity effectively extinguish the heat of our once warm blood. To many, that has become the definition of modern life. Murray Schisgal's *Existence* provides a comic snapshot of an arrogantly self-contented couple celebrating twenty-seven years of conformist life. Steve Feffer's *The Origins of a Drink They Named After Me* distills the sentiment of regret and captures it in a high-ball glass. Feffer himself describes the play as an illustration of hot passions being fueled by cold drink. If bars are venues for confessions of regret, so are reunions at weddings, which Crystal Skillman captures so well in *Rise*. Lisa Soland's *Spatial Disorientation* rather boldly dramatizes such reflections in a local airport just prior to John F. Kennedy Jr.'s last tragic plane flight, capturing an all-too-brief lifetime of action filled with moments of joyful exhilaration and others demanding extensive self-exploration and confessions of imperfection. Amber Marcoon's *Between the Lines* dramatizes the anxieties that attend youthful relationships and that invisible hand that so often prevents us from following our youthful inclinations. *The Rainbow* by James Armstrong brings together two lost souls who eventually agree to try to dump their lonely pasts and jump-start their futures together. Kevin McFillen's *Subtraction* unites an elderly man and young woman, engaging them in a game of memory and loss, demonstrating one way that regret is dealt with: by subtracting the pain from the narratives that are our lives. Recovering what has been subtracted may be painful, but it also helps heal. Generally speaking, that is a message embedded in most works in this volume.

Flare by Edith Freni offers a dialogue between two strangers, John Patrick Bray's *Blue, Blue Moon* brings together brother and sister, and David Rusiecki's *Kid Gloves* presents a termination interview between an employee and a "personnel expert." In different ways, each presents episodes of loss and missed opportunities. Daniel Guyton's *The Grim Raper* takes its own comic barroom scene, but chillingly reverses all audience allegiances by transforming an abstraction of Death into a commonplace but horrific vision of evil. What rhythms and patterns of life, one might ask, can possibly lead a person willfully to harm another, especially if one does harm without remorse? *Hurt* by Saviana Stanescu follows just such a downward spiral and ends with chilling results of the sort that is increasingly documented on television news.

Cell by Cassandra Medley and *Abandoned in Queens* by Laura Maria Censabella are family dramas in the classically American realist tradition. *Cell* nicely captures the joy of life that can at times overwhelm the fear of living, while *Abandoned in Queens* is a gritty dialogue in which a son faces an uphill battle as he struggles to avoid duplicating his father's bloodless, empty life.

Free Will by Billy Aronson presents a Shakespearean menagerie and brings home the point that love is the greatest power on earth, tantalizing in its promise of bliss but a threat to life itself because of its frequently devastating aftermath. Aronson points out also that freedom can be a terrifying commodity, one which leads his newly liberated characters to learn to improvise or perish. Reina Hardy's fanciful *Dark King Kills Unicorn* rings with the fearsome observation that "love makes meat of us all." But in this, as in most of the plays of this volume, the question that hovers above everything is: Should we abandon our pursuits of love for more comfortable, less disturbing, existences? Is it even humanly possible to abandon thoughts of love? And if so, what would our lives be like?

Maybe it would be like what we see in *Deer Haunting: A Far Side Cartoon* by Andréa J. Onstad. She turns the tables on a group of lifelong recreational hunters in a comic turn that captures the dulling, deadening effects of a life of routine in the great American heartland.

Two futuristic plays conclude the volume, each playing with human nature's many paradoxical urges. *2nd Anniversary Near Taurus Major* by Gene Kato creates an extragalactic nightmare that even technological wonders like sensory duplicators can't overcome. None of the flash and show of this play can outperform the simple power of the humans' closing words: "I love you." And in *The New Models* by Rory Leahy angels are tasked with creating sentient beings capable of maximally experiencing life. The male and female subjects do feel the momentary rush of freedom and companionship. With freedom and companionship, however, comes responsibility, and the age-old struggle between the two poles of hot blood and cold decree emerges yet again.

Portia learns—and so do we—that cold decrees work best when they manifest at least some recognition of the hot tempers they are presumably created to control. Feeling a sort of empathy for the failings that accrue through youthful passion, for example, has the potential to generate greater justice in the controls designed to minimize hot-temper's damage. What theater—and these plays—offers us is the opportunity to consider the human condition and, with greater consideration, to try to embrace both fears and temptations—checks and urges—as necessary and even complementary components of a life worth living.

The Best American Short Plays

2012–2013

The True Death of Socrates

Frank Higgins

The True Death of Socrates by Frank Higgins. Copyright © 2014 by Frank Higgins. All rights reserved. Reprinted by permission of the author.

CAUTION/ADVICE: Professionals and amateurs are hereby warned that performance of *The True Death of Socrates* is subject to a royalty. It is fully protected under the copyright laws of the United States of America, and of all countries covered by the International Copyright Union (including the Dominion of Canada and the rest of the British Commonwealth), and of all countries covered by the Pan-American Copyright Convention and the Universal Copyright Convention, the Berne Convention, and of all countries with which the United States has reciprocal copyright relations. All rights, including professional and amateur stage performing rights, motion picture, recitation, lecturing, public reading, radio broadcasting, television, video or sound recording, all other forms of mechanical or electronic reproduction, such as CD-ROM, DVD-ROM, information storage and retrieval systems, and photocopying, and the rights of translation into foreign languages, are strictly reserved. Particular emphasis is placed upon the matter of readings, permission for which must be secured from the author's agent in writing.

Inquiries concerning rights should be addressed to Penny Luedtke, The Luedtke Agency, 1674 Broadway, 7th Floor, New York, NY 10024, 212-765-9564.

Frank Higgins

Frank Higgins is the author of *Black Pearl Sings* and *The Sweet By 'n' By*, the latter produced with Blythe Danner and Gwyneth Paltrow. His other plays include *Miracles*, *Gunplay*, *The Taste Test*, *WMKS: Where Music Kills Sorrow*, and *Carnality: 6 Double-Shots of Desire*. His work has been seen across the country at the Williamstown Theater Festival, the Old Globe Theatre, Ford's Theater in Washington, D.C., Northlight Theatre in Chicago, San Jose Repertory Theatre, Kansas City Repertory Theater, and other places. He has also written several plays for young audiences, including *Anansi the Spider and the Middle Passage*, *The Country of the Blind,* and *Born Blue: The Diary of the Blue Cat*. He teaches at the University of Missouri-Kansas City and is a member of the Dramatists Guild.

··· production history ···

The True Death of Socrates appeared at the Living Room in Kansas City, Missouri, in December 2013 as part of *Carnality: 6 Double-Shots of Desire*. The cast:

SOCRATES Forrest Attaway

PLATO Coleman Crenshaw

DOOFUS Tosin Morohunfola

Directed by Frank Higgins

characters

SOCRATES

PLATO

DOOFUS a young student of PLATO

set

A simple jail cell in ancient Athens.

synopsis

PLATO arrives at a jail cell to record the last words of the great SOCRATES and to administer the hemlock. But when SOCRATES balks at being executed, PLATO must take drastic action in order to create good history. Will SOCRATES succeed in avoiding death?

[SOCRATES *sits in his cell with his back to the audience.* PLATO *and his student* DOOFUS *enter at the side.* PLATO *carries a cup.*]

PLATO Ah, here we are outside the prison cell of the great man. Blue sky, bright sun. And yet a dark day. The gods like to dick us around with dramatic irony.

DOOFUS Tell me, master, why is Socrates sentenced to death?

PLATO For the most serious crime of all: subverting the minds of young people.

DOOFUS How'd he do that?

PLATO He taught them to ask questions.

DOOFUS You can be executed for that?

PLATO Authority doesn't like questions. We must distinguish between what is *real*, and what is *comforting* to *believe* is real.—Doofus, I'm a great philosopher; you might want to take notes when I speak.— When the thing you question is the state, you become a danger to the state. And Socrates has been sentenced to the harshest penalty of all.

DOOFUS Death?

PLATO No book contract. If people in the future are going to know about Socrates, it will depend on my report of his heroic life, and death. Sniff.

DOOFUS Wine flavored with parsley. Can I have a sip?

PLATO Stop. It's hemlock. This will be the means of the great man's death.

DOOFUS You'll kill your former teacher yourself?!

PLATO By custom the guard gives the poison to a friend or family member. That person then gives the drink to the condemned.

DOOFUS And he drinks freely?

PLATO Yes, for not to do so is dishonorable. It is time. Socrates, it is I, Plato. On this your final day, what are your words of wisdom?

SOCRATES Aieeeeeeeeeeeeeeeeeeeeee!!!!!!!!!!!!!!!!!!!! Get that away from me!!

PLATO Calm down, O great teacher.

SOCRATES Plato, I beg you, help me escape! Smuggle me out under your toga!

PLATO What?

SOCRATES You're right; won't work. I'll leave in his clothing; we leave him here in my clothing. The guards won't find out for hours. I'll be on a boat before anyone knows.

PLATO This is no way to leave this world.

SOCRATES But it's a way to leave this cell.

PLATO This lacks honor.

SOCRATES Honor? What is honor? I want to study honor for another ten years.

PLATO I will not be part of this.

SOCRATES   You won't help your old teacher escape?

PLATO   Never.

SOCRATES   But I taught you everything you know.

PLATO   And what I know is the importance of honor. And of leaving a legacy that will inspire people for thousands of years.

SOCRATES   [*Blows a raspberry.*] If you help me escape, I'll give you all my money.

PLATO   You have no money. You're a teacher.

SOCRATES   Please don't kill me. I have a wife and daughter—kill *them*.

PLATO   Get a hold of yourself. You've often spoken of the underworld, and what things might be like there. Now you'll know.

SOCRATES   But I don't want to know *yet*. Please! Help your old friend and teacher get out of here.

PLATO   I can not.

SOCRATES   You're right. I should not have expected you to help me.

DOOFUS   Should I still be taking notes?

PLATO   No. The world can't know about this. Socrates, how can you behave in this ignoble way?

SOCRATES   Because I want more life. Is that a crime? I have questions that I haven't found the answers to yet. Why do we have earlobes? Why do men have nipples? What's that all about? Do you know?

DOOFUS   So we'll know where to pierce our flesh and be hung from the ceiling during orgies?

SOCRATES   No, in *addition* to that. And tell me this, Plato. What year is it?

PLATO   Three ninety-nine, B.C.

SOCRATES   Yes! And last year was four hundred B.C. Why are the numbers counting *down*? And counting down to what? And what is this *B.C.*? I want to know!

PLATO   None of us will live that long to find out. What matters is a noble death. People need you to die in a way that is *meaningful*.

SOCRATES   Why? Let's question that assumption over wine.

PLATO   No. I'll prove that life has meaning in the book I write. The book about your heroic death. You'll inspire people for all time.

SOCRATES   Sounds good. Let's drink a toast.

PLATO   No. You must drink *this* wine. Drink and become a legend.

SOCRATES   No thank you.

PLATO   Doofus, help me convince Socrates to die a great death.

DOOFUS   Uh, question first, master, since we're supposed to ask questions?

PLATO   Yes, yes, what is it?

DOOFUS   It's about, well, free will?

SOCRATES   Brilliant boy!

PLATO   The voluntary death of Socrates embodies free will.

DOOFUS   But if it's not true—

PLATO   Then people won't be inspired, will they? Human beings need heroes. Now do you help me or not?

SOCRATES   Don't do it. He's being selfish. If he doesn't have a hero and a heroic death, he won't even be able to outsell a cookbook. Ask him! Question authority!

DOOFUS   Master?

PLATO   If I can't sell books, I can't give free scholarships to needy students, can I?

DOOFUS   As you wish, master.

SOCRATES   You traitor to the Truth.

PLATO   Hold him down.

SOCRATES   No, no! Get back! Let go of me! Let go!

[DOOFUS *holds him down.* PLATO *tries to pour the hemlock into his mouth.*]

PLATO   Be noble! This is not painful. A tingling and then numbness.— Stop spitting.—Doofus, give me that parchment.—A sad thing, Socrates. The notes of your final moments must be used as a funnel.— Hold his mouth open!

SOCRATES   Argh! Argh!

PLATO Be noble! Be noble!

SOCRATES Argh!

PLATO There. All done. You could have made things easier for us.

SOCRATES My legs! They're numb!

PLATO Fear not. Do you have any final words?

SOCRATES I can't feel my dick!

PLATO Won't do. How's this? "How little does the common herd know of the nature of Truth."

SOCRATES My heart! There's no feeling in my heart! Arrg, arrg!

[SOCRATES *gives the death rattle and dies.*]

PLATO Farewell, noble old friend.

[PLATO *covers* SOCRATES *with a blanket.*]

DOOFUS I've learned a lot today, master.

PLATO But we must never speak of it. Humanity would be damaged by too much truth. Reality—and history—will be what we tell them it is.

[PLATO *drinks from the other goblet.*]

DOOFUS Can I have some too master?

[PLATO *hands the wine goblet to* DOOFUS, *who is about to drink when* SOCRATES *jumps up.*]

SOCRATES Stop! You like questioning things? You might want to question the wine, Doofus.

PLATO Did I not give you enough poison?

SOCRATES This morning I told the guard to put parsley, not hemlock, in the wine that he'd give to you.

PLATO But the guard knew he had to give you hemlock.

SOCRATES He did. In the wine he gave to me.

PLATO But why?

SOCRATES Always have a Plan B. Let that be a lesson, Doofus.

DOOFUS Noted, *master.*

PLATO   But that means you've poisoned *me*: Plato, your greatest student!

SOCRATES   Life's a bitch.

PLATO   My legs!

SOCRATES   And then ya die.

[PLATO *collapses*.]

PLATO   My groin! My groin!

SOCRATES   See, I wasn't willing to give up my groin just yet. There's too many good-looking girls. And guys. And goats.

PLATO   You mean orgasms are more important to you than honor?

SOCRATES   Why should you be noble, when you can be orgasmic?

PLATO   Knowing this about you, it's better that I be dead.

SOCRATES   Plato, you've been dead for a long time. If your dick is dead, you're dead and don't know it.

PLATO   Argh! Argh!

SOCRATES   Hey, if there's orgasms in the afterlife, come back and let me knooooow.

PLATO   Argh!

[PLATO *dies*.]

DOOFUS   Are you going to kill me now?

SOCRATES   You're not really very bright, are you?

DOOFUS   I'm a witness to murder. You can't let me live.

SOCRATES   Think. The guards saw two men come in. They could see two men go out, carrying a body.
[SOCRATES *advances toward him with the goblet*.]
I'm offering you life. That's more than Plato gave you.

DOOFUS   How can I live knowing the great Plato was willing to lie? And the great Socrates was willing to kill?

SOCRATES   You'll get over it. Life?
[*He grabs his crotch*.]
Or death? Choose.

PLATO   Don't do it!

SOCRATES   Plato, you are a pain the ass.

PLATO   You'll never get away with it. They'll come after you both.

SOCRATES   Actually, no. "Necessity is the mother of invention." I will take on the identity of Plato. Human beings need a hero? I'll give 'em one. And I say, "Socrates died a noble death."

PLATO   No!

DOOFUS   If I go along with this, then I want something more than just life. I want a better name.

SOCRATES   Yeah, you can't attract the really quality lovers with a name like Doofus.

PLATO   This is wrong.

SOCRATES   I'll need you to be loyal. To remind you of that, I'll give you the same name as my loyal dog: Aristotle.

DOOFUS   Agreed.

PLATO   This is wrong!

SOCRATES   We need to shut him up. And Socrates needs some famous last words. What Plato said I said? That's good; write that down.

PLATO   Wrong!

SOCRATES   And hold him down.

[SOCRATES *pours more wine down* PLATO*'s throat.*]

PLATO   No! No! Argh.

SOCRATES   Y'know, Aristotle, you're . . . kind of a good-lookin' guy.

PLATO   *Flirting? Here? Now?*

[*While they are over* PLATO, SOCRATES *touches* ARISTOTLE*'s face.*]

SOCRATES   "How little does the common herd know of Truth."

[PLATO *sees this and dies for good.*]

PLATO   Argh!

• • •

Existence

Murray Schisgal

Existence by Murray Schisgal. Copyright © 2014 by Murray Schisgal. All rights reserved. Reprinted by permission of the author.

CAUTION/ADVICE: Professionals and amateurs are hereby warned that performance of *Existence* is subject to a royalty. It is fully protected under the copyright laws of the United States of America, and of all countries covered by the International Copyright Union (including the Dominion of Canada and the rest of the British Commonwealth), and of all countries covered by the Pan-American Copyright Convention and the Universal Copyright Convention, the Berne Convention, and of all countries with which the United States has reciprocal copyright relations. All rights, including professional and amateur stage performing rights, motion picture, recitation, lecturing, public reading, radio broadcasting, television, video or sound recording, all other forms of mechanical or electronic reproduction, such as CD-ROM, DVD-ROM, information storage and retrieval systems, and photocopying, and the rights of translation into foreign languages, are strictly reserved. Particular emphasis is placed upon the matter of readings, permission for which must be secured from the author's agent in writing.

Inquiries concerning rights should be addressed to Zachary Schisgal at 212-782-8337 or zach@theschisgalagency.com.

Murray Schisgal

Murray Schisgal has an extensive career writing plays, screenplays, and fiction, and as a producer/executive producer. Broadway: *Luv* (Tony nomination for best play), *Jimmy Shine*, *All Over Town* (Drama Desk nomination for outstanding new play), *The Chinese and Doctor Fish*, *Twice Around the Park*, and *An American Millionaire*. Off and Off-Off Broadway: *The Typists and The Tiger* (Vernon Rice Award, Outer Circle Award), *Fragments & The Basement*, *The Flatulist*, *Walter*, *The Pushcart Peddlers*, *The New Yorkers*, *74 Georgia Avenue*, *Sexaholics*, *Extensions*, *The Consequences of Goosing*, *What About Luv?* (a musical based on *Luv*), *Road Show* (revised, 2007, as *Murder in the Drugstore*), *Playtime* (revised as *Wall Street Fandango*), *Angel Wings* (Off-Off Broadway Award for Excellence). Film: Co-screenwriter credit: *Tootsie* (Oscar nomination: Best Screenplay; New York Critics Circle Award: Best Screenplay, Los Angeles Film Critics Association Award: Best Screenplay, National Society of Film Critics Award: Best Screenplay.) Member: The Academy of Motion Picture Arts and Sciences, The Writers Guild of America; The Dramatists Guild; The Actors Studio Playwrights and Directors Unit, Ensemble Studio Theatre.

···production history···

Existence had its premiere at Ensemble Studio Theatre (William Carden, artistic director; Paul Slee, executive director), in EST's 34th Festival of One-Act Plays Marathon 2013. The play was directed by Peter Maloney with the following cast:

IZZY   Richmond Hoxie

LULU   Kristin Griffith

Rehearsal Stage Manager: Angel Emerson; Set Design: Nick Francone; Costume Design: Rachel Dozier-Ezell; Lighting Design: Greg MacPherson; Sound Design: Daniel Spitaliere; Production Stage Manager: Eileen Lalley

scene

The living room in an Upper East Side high-rise apartment building: spacious, expensively furnished, with long, sheer curtains covering floor-to-ceiling windows upstage, overlooking an imposing cityscape.

The entrance to the living room is downstage right. At the rear of the stage are exits to the kitchen, up right, and bedrooms, down left.

The living room has a floral-patterned armchair angled on the right side of a maroon covered settee, which faces downstage. An end table is at the right end of the settee. A bar is to the right, upstage. There is a fireplace in the left wall.

The actors will imagine a large mirror on the fourth wall, left, and picture windows overlooking Central Park, center.

time

Fall, late afternoon.

[*SOUND: Carl Orff's "O Fortuna," the opening section of Carmina Burana. Simultaneously, the sound of loud thunderclaps.*]

[*Howling winds rage through the living room, blowing the long, sheer window drapes violently into the room. Other fabrics covering furniture, papers on the end table, all these things blow like sails on a sailboat during a storm.*]

[*During the above, flashes of lightning illuminate the dim room. As the sound of thunder and wind diminish and "O Fortuna" quiets to a chant, the lights rise and the room returns to normal, the curtains hang still.*]

[*Sound of apartment door opening, closing.*]

[IZZY *enters. He is in his fifties, wearing a dark, pin-striped suit with a crimson silk tie and a matching handkerchief in his breast pocket. His shirt is blue with a white collar. He carries a bouquet behind his back, a dozen roses. Satisfied that no one is in the room, he hides the flowers on a shelf of the end table, covers it with his* Wall Street Journal. *He looks at himself in the mirror on the fourth wall, adjusts his tie. He sits in the armchair. He removes a small pocket mirror from his jacket pocket, looks into it as he pats down his hair. Licking a finger, runs his finger over his eyebrows. He crosses his legs, showing off his garish argyle socks. He wags his leg up and down.*]

IZZY   Hello? Anyone home?

LULU   [*Offstage.*] I'm in here, sweetheart.

IZZY   What are you doing in the kitchen?

[*He stops wagging his leg.*]

LULU   Getting everything ready.

IZZY   Ready for what?

LULU   Stop being a tease. Wall Street's still open, why are you home so early?

IZZY   I wanted to see you. I wanted to hold you. I wanted to tell you how much I love you and how much I need you and worship you and desire you for every moment of my life.

[LULU *enters, carrying a tray on which there are dishes of canapés, nuts, and berries.* LULU *is a few years younger than* IZZY, *still svelte, coiffed, and preened to perfection. She wears a stunning red silk evening dress. Do we see a hint of theatrical makeup on both their faces?* IZZY *rises, moves toward* LULU. *With the tray between them, unable to embrace, they both lean over and make exaggerated noises of kissing without touching each other.*]

[*Note: All their emotions, evidenced in their dialogue, their attitudes, and physical gestures, are excessive, but they must not go beyond the bounds of credibility.*]

[*Finally,* LULU *puts the tray on the end table.* IZZY *sits in the armchair, crosses his legs, wags his leg up and down.* LULU *sits on the settee.*]

Is everything ready?

LULU   Everything. Unfortunately, I have some awful, terrible news to tell you.

[IZZY *stops wagging his leg, uncrosses his legs, leans toward her as she stands and turns away from him.*]

IZZY [*Apprehensive.*] What is it?

LULU I had to fire Minnie this afternoon.

IZZY You had to fire Minnie?

[LULU *nods solemnly.*]

How could you have fired her? She's been with us for sixteen years. What in God's name could she have done to cause you to fire her?

LULU When I asked her to squeeze a pitcher of orange juice for breakfast tomorrow morning, she told me to go fuck myself.

IZZY [*Shocked.*] Really?

LULU [*Sniffling, handkerchief to nose.*] Really! She actually said that vulgar, horrible word twice.

IZZY [*More shocked.*] Twice?

LULU Yes, twice! As she was leaving, she said...
[*Mimics Minnie.*]
"And tell your husband to go fuck himself too!"

IZZY [*Even more shocked.*] Really?

LULU Really! I had no choice but to fire her. I'm afraid we'll have to make do until we can find another woman to wash our toilet bowls, mop our floors, and prepare our dinners of stir-fried chicken thighs and Idaho fingerling potatoes or bay scallops with Middle Eastern couscous.

IZZY Under the circumstances, I agree, wholeheartedly and unreservedly!

[LULU *sits on the settee, pulls up her evening dress to show off her lovely legs before crossing them and wagging her leg up and down.*]

LULU And I thank you, sweetheart, dearest. I knew you'd understand. And in passing, may I ask how your day went?

IZZY Oh, I was busy, busy, busy. In fact the whole city was busy, busy, busy until... I'd say about three-thirty this afternoon.

LULU What was going on?

IZZY Trading, banking, buying, selling, polishing, packing, filing, typing... The usual hullabaloo.

LULU And Wall Street?

IZZY The numbers went through the roof.

LULU I'm sorry I missed it.

IZZY Didn't you go to work today?

LULU I did, but I came home early.

IZZY You're not ill, are you?

LULU No, no, nothing like that. I needed time to prepare everything for our celebration this evening.

IZZY Of course. How thoughtless of me.
[*Leans toward her.*]
And now, I have some wonderful news to tell you.

LULU What be it?

IZZY Guess.

LULU Guess what?

IZZY I said the numbers on Wall Street went through the roof. I wasn't exaggerating. Our Demco Petro shares are now worth...four million ninety-nine thousand four hundred and twenty-two dollars!

LULU Really?

IZZY Really!

LULU And how much did you pay for the shares when you originally bought them?

IZZY I bought them precisely three years, four months, and nineteen days ago, and I paid...eleven thousand one hundred and eighteen dollars!

LULU [*Gasps.*] Noooo.

IZZY [*Pinches her cheek.*] *Au contraire, ma petite cheri.*

LULU So did you cash in and sell all the shares?

IZZY Nope, not yet. As I said, when I left this afternoon the market was going through the roof. Demco can still go higher. I plan to sell all the shares first thing in the morning for much more than four million ninety-nine thousand four hundred and twenty-two dollars!

LULU I can't believe any of this!

IZZY Believe it. It's the truth.

LULU Does this mean that during our mutual lifetimes we will never, ever, ever, ever have to worry about being poor again?

IZZY That is positively, absolutely what it means. The only question remaining is this: Will we live long enough to spend all the money we'll have by tomorrow morning, or will we have to leave millions of dollars to our children, who will never have to work for a living?

LULU I am so, so...so very, very proud of you!

[*She rushes into his arms.*]

IZZY Isn't life wonderful?

LULU We are blessed with every minute of every hour of every day.

[*She recites a fragment of a poem.*]

"...and for you I make an offering of a white goat."

IZZY Come again?

LULU Sappho. That's the whole of it. "...and for you I make an offering of a white goat."

IZZY Delightful. To think, we've been married twenty-seven years and it's like I'm holding you in my arms for the first time.

LULU It's better than the first time you held me in your arms.

[*No matter the size of the actress's breasts, the lines are to be played as written.*]

IZZY It is better. Your body is slimmer and firmer and your breasts are unquestionably larger.

LULU [*Pushing her breasts forward.*] My breasts are unquestionably larger than they were when I married you.

IZZY [*Appraising her breasts from several angles.*] Hmm. Hmm. Uh-huh. Uh-huh. Hmm. They are! They are! In fact, your breasts are quadruple the size of the breasts you had when I married you, no question about it.

LULU No question at all.

IZZY When I first married you, you had these two little pimples on your chest, but now...now you have these two enormous pumpkins on your chest. Darling...

LULU Yes, dearest?

IZZY May I kiss your two enormous pumpkins?

LULU [*Pushing her breasts even further toward him.*] Please, please, do it, promptly and precipitously, kind sir! [*And with a long, drawn-out, gushing, sucking sound, he kisses each breast repeatedly.*] You like kissing my two pumpkins, don't you?

IZZY I love kissing your two pumpkins. My only wish is that you had four of them.

LULU Four enormous pumpkins?

IZZY Minimally.

LULU That is so lovely of you to say. But I'm afraid two will have to suffice for now.

IZZY Two there are and two there will always be.

[*IZZY continues kissing her breasts, noisily.*]

LULU You don't find them or any part of me less exciting than you did twenty-seven years ago, do you?

IZZY [*Taking offense.*] Less exciting? Don't provoke me. Don't percolate my temper. I find every part of you infinitely and abundantly more exciting than I did twenty-seven years ago!

LULU I am more exciting. I know I am. My sexual appetite has grown exponentially over the past twenty-seven years.

IZZY It has! It has! Your sexual appetite has grown even more exponentially than your breasts have grown!

LULU I'm like an animal in bed now, aren't I?

[*She snarls and shows him her "claws."*]

IZZY [*Fervently.*] Oh, this is exciting. This is really exciting. I was hoping we'd have a bite to eat first, but I don't know if I can keep control of my . . . my bellowing, bursting, burgeoning desire for you. You are an animal. You are a primitive, savage, lustful, concupiscent animal, no question about it!

LULU May I ask you what specific kind of animal I remind you of?

IZZY [*Grimacing.*] You? You remind me of a . . . of a . . . of a gorilla!

LULU In bed when the lights go out, I am like a gorilla, passionate and primitive and yet...feminine, fragile...and ultimately submissive.

IZZY Positively, absolutely feminine, fragile...and ultimately submissive! [*Humbly.*] May I ask, sweetheart, what kind of animal you think I'm like in bed when the lights go out?

LULU [*Glancing at him from head to toe.*] I'd say you're like...a turkey!

IZZY [*Shocked.*] A turkey?

LULU Or a guinea hen.

IZZY [*Crestfallen.*] I'm not losing my virility, am I?

LULU No, no, darling, dearest, it's quite the opposite. Turkeys and guinea hens are incredibly virile. Why, if the truth be known, you're indisputably more virile today than you were twenty-seven years ago!

IZZY [*Brightening.*] I am more virile today, aren't I?

LULU Unquestionably and unreservedly!

IZZY Close your eyes and don't move, don't move.
[LULU *closes her eyes. On his feet,* IZZY *whips out the bouquet of yellow roses from its hiding place.*]
You may open your eyes now.
[LULU *opens her eyes.* IZZY, *bowing, extends the bouquet to her.*]
These are for you.

LULU [*Taking the bouquet.*] How beautiful they are. And how thoughtful, how romantic, how utterly Victorian you are!
[*She starts to move toward the kitchen.*]
I'll be right back.

IZZY No! Don't leave! Stay with me.

LULU The roses will die without water.

IZZY If they die, they die. That's life.

LULU That is life.

IZZY We're born, we grow old, we die.

LULU It could be worse.

[IZZY *sits in the chair, speaks as* LULU *puts flowers in water pitcher on bar, then sits on the settee.*]

IZZY It certainly could be. This morning I saw a man on the street who appeared to have a huge tumor on his head. He looked like he had two heads, one on top of the other.

LULU Yesterday I saw an elderly woman with an astonishing vivid pistachio-green face.

IZZY Oh, I've seen her many times. She sells apples near the Eighty-sixth Street subway.

LULU Have you seen the newspaper man on Lexington Avenue who has three nostrils?

IZZY Oh, yes, quite often. If I'm not mistaken, he has an older brother.

LULU [*Surprised.*] Really?

IZZY Really! He's a teller at the Chase Manhattan bank on Madison Avenue. He has two sets of eardrums. One set of eardrums are way up here...
[*Points to his own ears.*]
and another set of eardrums on either side of his neck are way down here.

[*Thumb and forefinger press sides of his neck.*]

LULU I've never seen...

IZZY [*Interrupting.*] Perhaps you've never seen...something as lovely...as this.

[*Grinning,* IZZY *slowly pulls a pearl necklace from his jacket pocket.*]

LULU [*Breathless.*] Sweetheart, you didn't have to...

[IZZY *rises, puts necklace around* LULU's *neck as they regard themselves in the mirror.*]

IZZY I did, and I'm proud to say it cost more than we both earned during the first fifteen years of our marriage.

LULU It's positively, absolutely gorgeous.

IZZY Happy anniversary, darling.

LULU I'll cherish this for the rest of my life.
[LULU *goes to the bar, opens a drawer, removes a small box, hands it to* IZZY.]
And this is for you, precious darling.

IZZY May I open it?

LULU I insist you open it.

[IZZY *removes a small item from the box.*]

IZZY [*Puzzled.*] What be it?

LULU An eighteen-karat-gold money clip.

IZZY [*Play-acting.*] A money clip! Of course!

LULU You don't like it?

IZZY Don't like it? I love it! I've dreamt of owning a money clip my entire life! I beg you, don't tell me how much it cost. Let me enjoy it for a few months before I have to buy insurance.

LULU We have been so, so...so fortunate.

IZZY We've been incredibly fortunate. Twenty-seven happy, glorious years of marriage.

LULU Three lovely children.

IZZY A son happily married to a practicing cardiologist.

LULU Two daughters in the graduate program at Harvard Law School.

IZZY A co-op on the Upper East Side.

LULU A country house in the Hamptons. We have been blessed.

[*As* LULU *speaks,* IZZY *rises and crosses to bar. He mixes two Bombay Gin martinis: dry, stirred, not shaken, filled to the brim.*]

How many men do you know who have achieved as much as you have in so brief a period of time?

IZZY Offhand?

LULU Offhand.

IZZY None.

LULU Especially when one considers your provenance.

IZZY Which wasn't much different from your provenance.

LULU That goes without saying. After all, our fathers were once partners in the coconut business.

IZZY That's right. They sold slices of coconut from a pushcart on Blake Avenue.

LULU Until a truck arrived selling frozen yogurt with rainbow sprinkles that sent them into bankruptcy.

IZZY Neither of them ever got back on his feet.

LULU We children paid for our fathers' failure. You were born in a ghetto.

IZZY In Brownsville, Brooklyn, to be precise.

LULU Your parents struggled from the get-go to make ends meet.

IZZY My father could barely read or write.

LULU Your mother was no taller than a midget.

IZZY My mother *was* a midget. It ran on her side of the family.

LULU And yet you, the son of a midget and an illiterate pushcart peddler, were driven to forge ahead, shrugging off poverty and anorexia to reach the pinnacle of success in the treacherous labyrinth of Wall Street.

IZZY I hated the thought of anonymity. I always had the feeling that if I were to grow old without having a substantial, government-insured bank account earning at least six percent interest, I would die of humiliation.

LULU You also hated the thought of being second-best.

IZZY [*Handing her a martini.*] More than anything. But you have to remember, when I started out, America was the land of endless opportunity and upward mobility.

LULU In those days you could achieve something extraordinary in this vital, vigorous country of ours.

IZZY [*Raising his glass.*] To the America that once was.

LULU [*Raising her glass.*] To a nation that was once top banana.

IZZY [*Speaking the first words of "America" to her.*] "Oh beautiful, for spacious skies...

LULU [*Singing the next phrase to him.*] For amber waves of grain...

IZZY For purple mountain's majesty...

LULU Above the fruited plain...

LULU and IZZY [*Both turning front.*] America, America, God shed his grace on thee. And crown thy good with brotherhood, from sea to shining sea."

[*They toast each other, clinking glasses, finish off their drinks, turn together and throw their glasses into the fireplace.*]

IZZY When I think of what I've achieved, I can't help thinking of what you've achieved.

LULU You taught me to be me, sweetheart.

IZZY Your background was as poverty-stricken as my own.

LULU Hell's Kitchen, Tenth Avenue and Forty-fifth Street. My next-door neighbors were bookies and hoodlums and two-dollar scabby-faced hookers.

IZZY But as a young girl, your head was filled with dreams.

LULU [*Regarding herself in mirror.*] I was terribly butch as a young girl. In the sixth grade I had a crush on my gym teacher, Miss Brenda Schwarzenegger.

IZZY You studied far into the night and tried again and again to break out of your environment. At eight years of age you started taking tap-dancing lessons from a black shoeshine man.

LULU Rufus Washington. He was my mother's lover.

IZZY Your mother had many lovers.

LULU She certainly did.

IZZY Your father resented your dancing career.

LULU His wooden leg had a lot to do with it.

IZZY As I remember him, a humorless man.

LULU He begged me to take a job as an FBI agent.

IZZY The son he never had.

LULU But once I met you, in my freshman year at college...

IZZY I invited you to join me in an after-school phonetics club, where we learned how to articulate Super—

[*Stammers, embarrassed.*]
Super... Supercali... frag... Supercalifragi... Super... Supercal...
Supercalifragi...
[*A big breath.*]
Supercalifragilisticexpialidocious!
[*He beams, happily.*]

LULU I bloomed and blossomed when I met you.

IZZY On your own you went to night school.

LULU To get my bachelor and master degrees.

IZZY And you became a respected, much envied, and emulated editor at Simon and Schuster.

LULU [*She kisses his hand.*] I couldn't have done it without you, sweetheart.

IZZY [*Putting his arm around her shoulder.*] The achievement was yours, though. To be a mother, a wife, a housekeeper, an editor at Simon and Schuster, and chief executive officer of the Osprey Rescue Fund in the Hamptons is nothing to sneeze at.

[*He sits in the chair, she sits on the sofa. They both cross their legs and bounce their legs up and down.*]

LULU We've been blessed.

IZZY We have been blessed.

LULU So much could have happened to us during these past twenty-seven years.

IZZY I could have had a heart attack, like my deceased brother-in-law John Herman Modigliani. One evening we could have been sitting here, chatting amiably, and... and suddenly...
[IZZY *grimaces, grabs at his chest, can't breathe.*]
Lu... Lu... LULU!

LULU [*Rising in a panic.*] What? What is it? What's wrong?

IZZY My heart... it... it's... heavy!

LULU Do you...?

IZZY [*Nodding.*] Yes! Indigestion! Heartburn! Nausea!

LULU The signs of a heart attack!

[*Running to phone on bar.*]

I'll phone the doctor!

IZZY [*Waning.*] It...It won't help. It's...too late, much...too...much...
too...late.

LULU [*Rushing back to him.*] My precious darling. Don't leave me...
please, please...

IZZY [*A whisper.*] Shhh. Shhh. I...I have strength for...only...a few
words. I truly...thank you...for giving me...a life...of fulfillment
and...happiness. I love you...forever and...

[*IZZY's head falls forward. He appears to be dead.* LULU *takes his handkerchief from
his breast pocket, pulls his head back, wipes his brow.*]

LULU [*Hysterical.*] Darling, darling, don't leave me, not yet, not yet,
please, I beg you! Give me a minute, one more minute...nanosecond.
There's something I must tell you...confess, acknowledge...

[*Turning away from him.*]

and ask for your eternal forgiveness.

[IZZY's *eyes pop open. He sits up abruptly, shocking* LULU.]

IZZY What are you ranting about? Can't you see I could have just died?

LULU Listen, please, you have to know this before anything terribly bad
really happens to you!

[*Inhales, softly.*]

I've been unfaithful. I've been having an affair...with Arnaldo...
Carlos...Rodriguez.

IZZY [*Perplexed.*] Who is Arnaldo Carlos Rodriguez?

LULU [*Head bowed.*] The service elevator man.

IZZY [*Shouts.*] I am not interested in hearing any of this. I did *not* ask you
and I do *not* want you to tell me anything!

LULU It's true. Nothing will change that. The affair has been going on
now for...it'll be...

[*Counts on her fingers.*]

fourteen years on the fifth of September.

[LULU *sobs, puts* IZZY's *handkerchief to her eyes.* IZZY *is in anguish.*]

IZZY Why, Lulu, why in God's name would you have done anything as cruel and stupid as having an affair with the service elevator man, who, I would remind you, is not even a member of the elevator man's union:

LULU I don't know, I don't know. Except...every time I answered the kitchen doorbell, Arnie would be there, waiting for me to bring out the garbage.

IZZY Arnie?

LULU He'd be grinning from ear to ear with his gold-capped teeth and his bristling mustache and I...I couldn't...control myself!

[*A burst of sobs.*]

IZZY [*Emphatic.*] You actually fornicated with him?

LULU In the service elevator.

IZZY The service elevator?

LULU Somehow the sight of him in the midst of all those large, heavy-duty, drawstring, plastic garbage bags that sell for seven-eighty-nine in the supermarket turned me on. I was...helpless.

IZZY [*Imploring.*] Lulu, Lulu, we have had sex on an average of twice a week, every Wednesday and Saturday at nine-thirty in the evening for twenty-seven years! *Twenty-seven years*, wasn't that enough for you?

LULU Enough?! Twice a week every Wednesday and Saturday at nine-thirty in the evening for twenty-seven years enough for me? [*Breaks out in a maniacal laugh, then stone-faced.*] Sorry, dear. I...I got carried away. [IZZY *turns, strides away.* LULU *follows him, goes down on one knee.*] All I ask is for your forgiveness. I won't ever be unfaithful to you again, whether it be twice a week or twice a year. I give you my sacred word, my...

IZZY [*Angrily interrupting.*] No! It's too damn late for that! Forgive you for fornicating with the service elevator man on those large, heavy-duty, drawstring, plastic garbage bags that sell for seven-eighty-nine in the supermarket? Never! Never! I'll pack my things and be out of here before you can say...Supercalifragilistic—expialidocious!

[*He beams happily.*]

LULU Izzy, please, listen to me...

IZZY I don't want to discuss it further! I've said I'm leaving and I'm leaving. To think you could have actually have done such a thing. No more, please, I beg you. I am human, perhaps all too human, but human nonetheless.

[*Staring off into space, he recites a favorite poem.*]

That strange flower, the sun, / Is just what you say, / Have it your way. The world is ugly, / And the people are sad. That tuft of jungle feathers, / That animal eye, / Is just what you say. That savage of fire, / That seed, / Have it your way. The world is ugly, / And the people are sad.

LULU "Gubbinal" by Wallace Stevens.

IZZY Yes.

LULU Will you ever forgive me for what I've done?

IZZY I don't know. At the moment I feel nothing for you, neither forgiveness nor enmity, neither...

[*He is interrupted by the ringing phone. He goes to bar, snaps receiver to his ear, answers.*]

Yes...Yes, Winterbottom. What is it? Speak slowly. I can't understand a word you're saying...Demco Petro is...what? What?...It's plummeting at a precipitous rate?...Go on, go on...What was that?... It's not worth four million ninety-nine thousand four hundred and twenty-two dollars any longer? How much...What? What?...You're not serious. You can't be...Will you please speak slower! I can't understand a word you're saying...Nothing? It's worth nothing?...I do not believe you, not a word you said. This is a joke, a scam, a travesty. I'll sue you for every penny you...Don't you hang up on me, Winterbottom! Don't you dare!

[*Sound: we hear the sound of a dial tone. IZZY, stunned, puts receiver back in its cradle on the bar.*]

He hung up on me.

[*Slowly turning to LULU.*]

We're...we're broke, flat...I blew it. I...I lost everything we had.

LULU The co-op we live in?

IZZY [*Shaking his head.*] No more.

LULU Our country home in the...

IZZY I said everything! Everything! Why do you have to torture me? Does it give you pleasure? We're wiped out, bankrupt, destitute! The suit on my back has to go back to Dolce and Gabbana first thing in the morning!

LULU [*Numb.*] So it's come to this.

IZZY I am so, so...so very sorry. I shouldn't have gambled. I was a fool, an arrogant, irresponsible fool!

[*On his knees, he rests his head in* LULU's *lap. She strokes his head.*]

LULU We were both fools. We took our wealth for granted. We thought it was a bottomless well from which we could make continual withdrawals without making adequate deposits.

[*A beat;* LULU *stops stroking* IZZY's *head.*]

I wish what you just told me was the worst that has happened to us.

[*A beat.*]

It isn't.

[*She rises and moves away, her back to* IZZY.]

IZZY [*Rises.*] I don't want to hear it.

LULU You have to hear it.

[*Solemnly.*]

I just found out from Emily's advisor at Harvard that she...that our Emily...is pregnant.

IZZY Pregnant? You're sure?

LULU Positive. It was confirmed by Doctor Pipashinski.

IZZY Is it the son of the Republican senator from South Carolina who's responsible for her pregnancy?

LULU No. It's her professor of torts.

IZZY But he must be...

LULU Seventy-four on the eighth of October. I had it verified. I told Emily she had to abort, but she refuses. She plans to have the baby and live with the professor in an assisted living facility.

IZZY [*Inconceivable.*] No.

LULU Yes.

IZZY I don't believe it.

LULU Believe it; it's the truth. They've already made reservations to move in on the first of the month.

IZZY Won't she at least discuss it with us?

LULU She told me, explicitly and unequivocally, that she hates our guts.

IZZY [*Wearily.*] I suspected as much.

LULU She also told me that…
[*A lump in her throat.*]
her brother, our son, left his cardiologist wife a week ago.

IZZY What about his job as accountant with the Bettenheimer Company?

LULU Yesterday's news. He now stands on a street corner in Harlem selling amphetamines to schoolchildren.

IZZY [*Sighs.*] If only that was the worst of it.

LULU [*Distress.*] What else could there possibly be?

IZZY When I spoke to Doctor Pipashinski…

LULU [*Interrupting.*] You spoke to Doctor Pipashinski?

IZZY This afternoon.

LULU About Emily?

IZZY No, about Caroline.

LULU Is there anything wrong with Caroline?
[*No reply from IZZY. LULU shouts.*]
Tell me!

IZZY [*Stammering.*] It's…It's…

LULU Oh no. Oh noooo.

IZZY She…She has…

[LULU *runs to IZZY, puts her hand over his mouth.*]

LULU Don't tell me! Don't tell me, please! I don't want to know. I don't want to know!

[*Sobbing, LULU embraces IZZY, who holds her tight. After a moment, they break apart and instantly resume speaking normally, casually.*]

IZZY So much worse could have happened to us.

LULU So much that didn't.

IZZY We're alive and healthy.

LULU And still madly in love with each other.

IZZY We've been blessed.

LULU We have been blessed.

IZZY Would you care for another martini?

LULU I'd love another martini.

[IZZY *goes to bar, pours two more martinis from the pitcher.*]

IZZY It's been quite a life we've shared together, sweetheart.

LULU It's been a wonderful life.

IZZY Twenty-seven years today.

LULU Twenty-seven marvelous years on this very day.

IZZY [*Moving to her.*] When you get right down to it, we were lucky to be born at the right time in the right place.

LULU I know what you mean: while it was still possible to achieve something concrete and substantial in this country of ours.

IZZY [*Hands her martini.*] To the America that once was.

LULU To a nation that was once top banana, second to none.
[*Turning front, she sings.*]
"America, America..."

IZZY [*Turning front, sings.*] "God shed his grace on thee ..."

LULU and IZZY [*Singing together, glasses raised.*] "And crown thy good with brotherhood, from sea to shining sea."

[*They turn to each other, clink glasses, drink their martinis down, turn together, and toss their empty glasses into the fireplace.*]

[*SOUND: Of glasses loudly breaking over fireplace speaker, followed immediately by...*]

[*SOUND: Thunderclap, as sharp and loud as possible over house speakers. At the same time...*]

[*SOUND: "O, Fortuna," the ending of the first movement of Orff's Carmina Burana, played as loudly as possible.*]

[*There should be no break between these sound effects. One should follow the other: Bang! Bang! Bang! Add more thunderclaps over the music as lightning flashes into the room through the windows overlooking Central Park. At the same time, the long, sheer curtains hanging from the floor to ceiling windows upstage are blown violently into the room, creating the same effect as was achieved at the top of the play.*]

[*After the first flash of lightning, the light within the room flickers and grows dim, as if the power in the whole building has suddenly been weakened.*]

[*Lightning flashes continue, coordinated with the sound of thunder, throughout the final sequence.*]

[*IZZY and* LULU, *meanwhile, are shocked by the lightning and thunder and by what is happening to the light in their home. They look up and around in the direction of the usual light source, whether it be a chandelier hanging in the middle of the room or whatever, then out front as if looking through the large windows opening onto Central Park. They are "seeing" a sudden storm of apocalyptic proportions. It is the end of the world for them, just when they thought they had adjusted to the previous disasters and were looking forward to a bit of a respite. They are like "deer caught in the headlights" and they gravitate toward each other in the shattered room, hold on to each other as they stare out of the room, terrified. At the final crashing chord of "O Fortuna," all lights blackout.*]

• • •

The Origins of the Drink They Named After Me

A Short Play for Drinking and Crying

Steve Feffer

The Origins of the Drink They Named After Me by Steve Feffer. Copyright © 2014 by Steve Feffer. All rights reserved. Reprinted by permission of the author.

CAUTION/ADVICE: Professionals and amateurs are hereby warned that performance of *The Origins of the Drink They Named After Me* is subject to a royalty. It is fully protected under the copyright laws of the United States of America, and of all countries covered by the International Copyright Union (including the Dominion of Canada and the rest of the British Commonwealth), and of all countries covered by the Pan-American Copyright Convention and the Universal Copyright Convention, the Berne Convention, and of all countries with which the United States has reciprocal copyright relations. All rights, including professional and amateur stage performing rights, motion picture, recitation, lecturing, public reading, radio broadcasting, television, video or sound recording, all other forms of mechanical or electronic reproduction, such as CD-ROM, DVD-ROM, information storage and retrieval systems, and photocopying, and the rights of translation into foreign languages, are strictly reserved. Particular emphasis is placed upon the matter of readings, permission for which must be secured from the author's agent in writing.

Inquiries concerning rights should be addressed to Steve Feffer at steve.feffer@wmich.edu.

Steve Feffer

Steve Feffer's *And Yet...* was published in *The Best American Short Plays 2010–2011*, and his *Little Airplanes of the Heart* was published in *The Best American Short Plays 1997–1998* and in *Plays from the Ensemble Studio Theatre 2000* (Faber and Faber). Dramatists Play Service publishes his play *The Wizards of Quiz*; Heinemann Books and New Issues Press publish additional plays and performance pieces. Steve's plays have been produced or developed by theaters that include the O'Neill National Playwrights Conference, Ensemble Studio Theatre, Stages Repertory Theatre, Playwrights Theatre of New Jersey, Ruckus Theatre, and Untitled Theatre #61. Steve has won a number of national playwriting awards, including the New Jewish Theatre Project Award from the National Foundation for Jewish Culture and the Southwest Plays Award for a Play for Young Audiences. He is a professor in the creative writing program at Western Michigan University (Kalamazoo), where he directs the graduate and undergraduate playwriting programs. Steve has served as a regional chair for the National Playwriting Program of the Kennedy Center American College Theatre Festival.

···production history···

The Origins of the Drink They Named After Me was first developed and staged in the Cafe Ypsilon Theatre in Prague, Czech Republic, as part of the Prague Summer Program in Creative Writing, 2013.

The song "Chivalry" from the Mekons' *Fear and Whiskey* album was an inspiration for the play.

characters

SAM   twenties, recently had a drink named after him

SHEILA   twenties, a cocktail server, has served the drink

DARCY   twenties, part of the reason the drink was named after Sam

PETER   twenties, a bartender, named the drink

time and place

The present. A bar in Chicago.

[*At rise, a bar in Chicago.* SAM *sits at the bar.* PETER, *the bartender, is behind the bar with an empty glass and a full bottle of whiskey.*]

SAM   [*To the audience.*] The drink they named after me isn't a complicated one. Bartender...

PETER   [*To the audience.*] It's one part whiskey.

[PETER *pours.*]

And one part fear...

[PETER *pours more whiskey. He looks at* SAM. *He pours again. He looks at* SAM *again.* PETER *pours.*]

SAM   Alright. It's equal measures of whiskey and fear. It's not on the menu. But you can step right up and order it like any of the others that have been named after people both famous and...obscure. Tom Collins. Harvey Wallbanger. Shirley Temple.

PETER   Some people like 'em on the rocks.

SAM   I don't.

PETER   I know you don't. But some people do.

SAM I don't think it's a "me," if it's on the rocks.

PETER I think it's a "you"—on the rocks.

SAM To me, rocks are a mixer. And in a "me," the only mixer, is the fear…and the glass.

PETER We all have our own recipes for a "you." Even here, where we named the drink after you. It's like the Bloody Mary. Sure at Harry's New York Bar it was once a very specific recipe named after the actress Mary Pickford or Queen Mary the First of England—depending on whether or not you believe Mary Pickford or Fernand Petiot, the bartender who claims to have invented the Bloody Mary.

[SHEILA, *a cocktail server, enters.*]

SHEILA Others say it was invented right here in Chicago by a waitress named Mary at a tavern called the Bucket of Blood.

SAM A "me"? The Bucket of Blood is claiming they invented a "me"?

SHEILA The Bloody Mary…There's no one claiming to have invented a "you." I sure as hell ain't. I don't even like serving 'em. As far as I'm concerned, that's nothing to be proud of.

SAM You know, it's funny, we're talking about this right now, because I was wearing this very suit the night the drink was named after me.

PETER How do you remember that?

SAM There's a small hole in the knee from when I fell. I've tried to have it patched, but it won't hold. It's too small to patch, but just big enough so I always know that it's there. This suit was once very smart-looking.

SHEILA I'll take your word for it.

[SHEILA *exits.*]

PETER You want another?

SAM Sure.

PETER Another "you"?

SAM Yep. One more "me." And no rocks. That's not a "me." I'm telling you.

PETER I'm not gonna argue with you. You drink your "you"s the way you want 'em, and I'll make 'em the way I want. Don't stifle my creativity.

SAM Yep, the night you named this drink after me, I was sitting right here, wearing this suit. And I saw her across the crowded bar. At least I thought it was her.

[DARCY *enters.*]

DARCY It wasn't *me*.

SAM It wasn't, huh? I had almost convinced myself that it was.

DARCY No, it wasn't me. I was there. But the woman you saw, wasn't me.
[DARCY *sits at the bar.*]
I'll have a "him." Rocks.

SAM It's not a "me," if it's on the rocks.

DARCY Of course it is. I mean, it's still a Bloody Mary if you add horseradish or asparagus...

PETER That's just what I've been telling him. One "him" coming up. On the rocks.

SAM I got hers.

DARCY Forget it.

SAM No, I want to.

DARCY It's too late for that, isn't it?

SAM Is it?

DARCY Yeah.

SAM I was hoping...

DARCY I know what you were hoping. But that ship has sailed.

SAM You better make mine a double.

PETER They only come as doubles.

SAM Make mine a triple.

PETER They only come in multiples of two. They're doubles—doubled. There's no room for variation there. If it's not a double, it's not a you.

SAM Then make it a double. When did making a "me" become so complicated?

PETER We take pride in here for the drinks we serve—even if the drink's namesake may lack that same pride.

DARCY I'll drink to that. Make mine a double.

SAM Well, anyway, it's good to see you.

DARCY Is it?

SAM Yes. It is.

DARCY It sure didn't seem that way on that night.

SAM You just said I didn't see you.

DARCY I saw you. You didn't see me. I had a good look at the whole thing. The way you looked at her. The way your eyes somehow met hers through the all those other eyes.

SAM Really? I don't remember.

DARCY I'm surprised. I mean, from where I was sitting it was almost...

PETER Profound...

DARCY Yes. Profound...

SAM You saw it too?

PETER Oh, quite clearly. I saw the way your eyes caught hers and there was something...

DARCY Profound...

PETER Yes...It was like I could see it through Darcy's eyes and that's when I first thought, you know, there might just be a drink to be named here.

[DARCY *drinks to that.*]

DARCY How can you drink these?

SAM They're named after me.

DARCY Still. Peter, I'm so sorry to do this. Can I have something else?

PETER Not a problem for you, Darc.

DARCY I'll have a Cosmo.

PETER Got it.

SAM A Cosmo instead of a "me"? Really? You've changed.

DARCY Yes, I have. A lot changed for me that night.

[PETER *slides her drink away. As* SHEILA *reenters.*]

PETER [*To* SHEILA.] You want this? I'm just gonna dump it.

SHEILA What is it?

PETER A "him."

SHEILA Dump its ass.

DARCY Hear-hear.

[SHEILA *exits.*]

SAM Don't waste it. I'll drink her "me." As soon as I take the ice out…

PETER I'll put it on your tab.

DARCY Is that all you drink now? "You"s?

SAM Pretty much.

DARCY I'd think after a while you'd begin to get sick of them.

SAM I drank "me"s before they were "me." Certainly I'm going to drink them now that they're named after me.

DARCY I suppose there's a certain obligation there.

SAM I feel it.

DARCY Seems to be one of the few you keep.

SAM I keep telling you I swore it was you.

DARCY You're like Bill Kurtis at Harry Carey's. Bill Kurtis has a meatloaf named after him at Harry's and that's all he ever eats. And I guess he's in there all the fucking time.

SAM How do you know that?

DARCY I'm a news junkie. You see, that's the kind of thing that I would've expected, after all our time together, you knew about me.

SAM That's news? Bill Kurtis's meatloaf?

DARCY He's a news personality. An investigative reporter with a national reputation. I'm less into the news than I am the newspeople.

SAM How does one get meatloaf named after them?

DARCY I suppose one must really love meatloaf. I mean, how does one get a drink named after them?

SAM One must really love...

DARCY ...That drink.

SAM No. *You.* I was going to say *you.*

DARCY I wish you hadn't.

SAM It's funny, it's not really that big in here, and it never really gets that crowded, but that night...you seemed so far away.

DARCY As we discussed, it wasn't me. And it's not going to be ever again.

SAM Then what are you doing here?

DARCY I'd hate to think now that all this is over, I couldn't come here anymore. Is that what happens? We fight over who gets the bar.

SAM I have a drink named after me here. Doesn't that give me some rights?

DARCY I was hoping maybe they were visitation rights—nothing permanent, you know.

SAM Look, I'm sorry. I swear, I thought it was you.

PETER It was interesting to watch the whole thing develop. It was like slow motion. I saw you. And I saw you look at her. Not Darcy. The her you thought was Darcy. I even said to Sheila...

[*As* SHEILA *enters.*]

DARCY Tonight's the night we're going to name that drink after him.

SHEILA I saw the same thing. Like in slow motion. The way you were looking at her. Darcy even asked me...

DARCY Did he ever look at me like that?

SAM I *was* looking at you like that. I mean, I thought it was *you.*

PETER Yes, I remember that, Sam. Because in that moment, you asked—

SAM Is that?

[*Looking across the crowded bar.*]

PETER   But that's not something I could answer.

DARCY   What did you see in her that made you think it was me?

[SAM *looks at* DARCY. *Though she is right next to him,* SAM *appears to search for her through what would be the crowded bar.* SAM *gets off his bar stool and crosses to her. Again, though* DARCY *is right next to him,* SAM *appears to make his way through a significant distance. When he reaches her, there is a beat, and then he kisses her deeply.* DARCY *kisses* SAM *back. There is then a pause as they look at each other with confusion, before they hold each other tight with great need.*]

SAM   Oh my God. I'm sorry...

DARCY   It's okay, really...

SAM   I thought you were someone else...

DARCY   I know. I understand...

[SAM *walks away, looking back at* DARCY *as he begins to leave the bar.*]

SAM   Right after that I left the bar. There were tears streaming down my face. They mixed with the rain. I fell to my knees tearing a small hole in my suit. I felt embarrassed and disgraced.

[SAM *exits.* PETER *watches him for a moment.* PETER *moves to clear* SAM'*s drink off the bar. He tastes it.*]

PETER   Mmmm. Yes, that's it. Tears. I knew it was missing something.

• • •

Rise

Crystal Skillman

Rise by Crystal Skillman. Copyright © 2013 by Crystal Skillman. All rights reserved. Reprinted by permission of the author.

CAUTION/ADVICE: Professionals and amateurs are hereby warned that performance of *Rise* is subject to a royalty. It is fully protected under the copyright laws of the United States of America, and of all countries covered by the International Copyright Union (including the Dominion of Canada and the rest of the British Commonwealth), and of all countries covered by the Pan-American Copyright Convention and the Universal Copyright Convention, the Berne Convention, and of all countries with which the United States has reciprocal copyright relations. All rights, including professional and amateur stage performing rights, motion picture, recitation, lecturing, public reading, radio broadcasting, television, video or sound recording, all other forms of mechanical or electronic reproduction, such as CD-ROM, DVD-ROM, information storage and retrieval systems, and photocopying, and the rights of translation into foreign languages, are strictly reserved. Particular emphasis is placed upon the matter of readings, permission for which must be secured from the author's agent in writing.

Inquiries concerning rights should be addressed to the author at crystalskillman@gmail.com or Abrams Agency, Amy Wagner, at amy.wagner@abramsartny.com.

Crystal Skillman

Crystal Skillman is the award-winning author of *Geek* (produced by Obie Award–winning Vampire Cowboys, earning a *New York Times* and *Time Out New York* Critics' Pick); *Cut* (The Management, *New York Times* Critic's Pick; Apollinaire Theatre, Boston); *Vigil or The Guided Cradle* (ITG/Brick; New York Innovative Theatre Award for Outstanding Full-Length Script); *Birthday & Nobody* (Rising Phoenix Rep in NYC; UK Premiere with Kibo Productions; Chicago Premiere with Side Project); and *Wild*, with director Evan F. Caccioppoli (Chicago Premiere with Kid Brooklyn Productions, NYC Premiere with Sanguine Theatre Company). Skillman's work is published by Samuel French, Applause Theatre & Cinema Books, and Smith and Kraus, and is available on www.indietheaternow.com.

···production history···

Rise was produced as part of *The Beach Plays* which were commissioned and produced by Rising Phoenix Rep (artistic director, Daniel Talbott) and Kid Brooklyn Productions (artistic director, Evan F. Caccioppoli) on July 13–14, 2013, Ocean Beach in San Francisco, California.

Director Evan F. Caccioppoli

JAIME   Sam Soule
JOY   Addie Johnson
ANA   Jelena Stupljanin
SALLY   Lila Coley

characters

ANA
JAIME
JOY

Ages for the three ladies can be open, but they would be at least late twenties. Diversity in casting is encouraged.

time

Now.

place

A beach in San Francisco.

NOTE : The moment with the small girl coming in can be cut if desired. In that case, JAIME would set up the chairs on her own.

[ANA *runs onto a beach. She is wearing a flowing green dress. Her enthusiasm is infectious. She kicks up sand as she runs. She stops near the water. Dances a bit.*]

ANA   Yes! Yes! Yes!

[*She takes out her phone. Attaches some portable speakers. She puts on Pink's album* The Truth About Love. *She dances around in a circle even more excited. She runs, takes her stick, and draws in the sand. She creates two sections of lots of little circles. Then between them, one line, then the other. She faces the water. She*

*walks down this "sand aisle." She reaches out—pretending her partner is there to
go down the aisle with her. She goes down once. Shakes her head; she isn't sure.
Then runs back and starts over. She keeps practicing, but it's never right.*

*Too bratty, or fast or slow but she is enjoying trying. JAIME appears. She
watches this for a while. She looks hot and sweaty and has a huge roll-y bag and is
holding wilted flowers. ANA finally spots her—is this who she thinks she is?]*

Hey.

JOY Hi. Is this—I'm looking for a wedding…a reception…

ANA Joy?

JOY Yes.

ANA This is…

[ANA *runs up to* JOY *and kisses her.*]

JOY Yes. Okay! Thanks!

ANA Jaime is gonna love this.

JOY Where is…

ANA Parking the car. The traffic getting here. Of course always traffic.
Everyone decided to get married today. Isn't that crazy?

JOY Right.

[*Holds out wilted flowers.*]

These are for you. The two of you. I got them before I got on the
plane—I wasn't thinking. They died on the way. I don't think that
means anything.

ANA Hey. Don't be nervous.

JOY I'm not.

ANA All exes are scared to see each other.

JAIME Okay.

ANA Jaime wanted you here. You know what that means? I want you here.

[JAIME, *a woman wearing sunglasses, comes over the hill.*]

JAMIE [*Running to* JOY.] Joy? Ahhhhhhhhhhhhhh!!!! No way?! You
came!!!

JOY I came!

[JOY *gives* JAIME *a hug.*]

Thin! You are too thin!

JAIME   Me? You're...are you eating?

ANA   She eats like a horse.

[JAIME *runs to* ANA, *scoops her up.*]

JAIME   Monkey!

ANA   Monkey? I'm a mermaid. That's the theme. We spent months picking out the theme. I am the goddamn theme!

JAIME   My wife. Excuse me, I love saying that!

[JAIME *and* ANA *kiss.* JOY *stands there.*]

It's just you...? No Sherry?

[JOY *shakes head "no."*]

Tina? How old is she now...? She must be...

JOY   Yeah. I am sorry I didn't RSVP.

JAMIE   You are here! Forget it. You still look twenty-five—like you'd down a thousand fries at the Crispy Critter Hut.

JAIME and JOY   U-Ha!

ANA   What was that again?

JAIME   University of Hartford—Connecticut, where we went for undergrad, told you a thousand times, honey.

ANA   Cold. Connecticut.

JAIME   Only around Christmas.

JOY   The summers get hot.

[*Beat.*]

JAIME   Joy. You should have seen—at the Clerk's office—all afternoon—everyone in tuxes, dresses, flowers, flowers!

ANA   The flowers.

JAIME   Jonathan is bringing them. Monica's getting here with the chairs. Terry's bringing some food. We have—like seven minutes—and then we will be descended upon! "Renegade Beach No Permit Jaime and Ana Reception/Ceremony with Family Post Actual

Marriage Certificate Finally Recognized by the State of San Francisco" is about to begin!

ANA Yay!

JOY Yes.

JAIME Did you come right here? You look…I don't know if you want to put your things.

JOY I don't know where I'm staying actually.

JAIME Oh. Well, I'm sure we'll figure that out.

ANA Before they get here. She should learn the dance. She needs to dance.

JOY I don't—

JAIME What 'til you see! Who needs a wedding planner when you have the great Ana!

ANA I'll walk you through.

JAIME She will blow you away. First burlesque show she took me too—our first date might I add—that she choreographed I was blown away she was so—

ANA I can hear you and if I can hear you you're not listening! You're talking.
[ANA *walks through the "ceremony."*]
So walk, walk, walk. Love, love, love. Vows!
[*Turning to* JOY.]
Will you read my vows actually—

JOY Me?

ANA You're a writer, right?

JOY I'm not even half as talented as this one.

JAIME Oh no, I'm all about the scribbles. Drawing, not writing, please.

ANA I want you to read it.

JOY Okay.

ANA Good! So after all that.
[*Takes off ring and holds it up.*]

The rings. I play the music and it starts like this!

[ANA *plays a song on her iPhone. She starts dancing. The moves get more and more complicated.* JAIME *loves this and claps and she gets into it, jumps in.* JOY *is doing terribly.*]

I taught everybody yesterday. See?

JOY Yeah, no. I don't.

[ANA *and* JAIME *encourage her.* JOY *starts to dance on her own. It's awful.*]

ANA Stop.

JOY What?

ANA You're kidding?

JOY No.

JAIME She doesn't need to dance.

ANA Everyone is dancing at the end. Everyone is wearing some kind of green, there are flowers, we say the vows, and everyone dances at the end the way I've pictured our formal wedding for seven years.

JAIME Baby.

ANA Everyone got the video. Everyone knows this dance.

JAIME Well, we didn't know she was coming.

ANA Who doesn't RSVP?

JAIME We're old friends.

ANA She never calls you.

JAIME Hey. Babe.

ANA [*Gets a text.*] It's Monica. She's here with the chairs.

[ANA *exits.*]

JOY Wow. She's a spitfire.

JAIME She's a redhead. She's right. You couldn't have told us—before you got on the plane—maybe?

JOY I really can't explain.

JAIME That hasn't changed.

JOY Look I'm going, I'm fine.

JAIME   Joy. You're not going anywhere. You look like shit. What is going on?

JOY   It's your day, I'm ruining it.

JAIME   You leave, you'll ruin my day.

JOY   Look, I don't want to fuck this up, okay?

JAIME   So you'll hop on a flight for six hours to just go back?

JOY   Don't be pushy, Jaime. I don't miss you being pushy.

[JAIME *pushes her.* JOY *tries to get around her.* JAIME *starts wrestling with her.*]

JOY   Don't make me hurt a bride.

JAIME   I have been pushing weights for three months to look good for this. I've been boxing my ass off—you cannot get—past—me!

JOY   Fuck! Fuck! Fuck! Ahhhhh…

[*They have both fallen into the sand. They lie there. Beat, then.*]

This morning I woke up hung over in my own vomit. The windows were open. My cats escaped. Or I can't find them. My book has been passed on. That's twenty-four different publishers. That's twenty-four different agents. And I don't even like it anymore. It's not me. I'm just trying to be someone else in it—to sell—sell because I don't know why—I want to write one story that someone opens and just goes— that changed me. That changed my life, but I'm not changing my life. I'm drinking a lot and I tell myself it's the wine that goes with pasta, but it's too much and Sherry has been falling out of love with me for a long time and I've been watching it happen like a TV show where you know it's happening and Tina—we went through such hell to get her. Do you know I got the book you illustrated with all the monkeys. We sit and we count all the monkeys. All the fucking monkeys and I think I should be good for something. I should be such a good mother. My mother was such a good mother, even though I gave her such shit. Are you going to try to have kids?

JAIME   Ana's looking into it.

JOY   Good! Good! See, you'll make a good mother. That's what I was thinking when I saw your invitation in the garbage after Sherry took Tina and left. I got off the floor. I got to the airport. I got on a plane. I followed the invitation—had a driver drop me off to Oakland Beach and I don't know why. I don't know why you fucking invited me in the first place.

JAIME Don't you…ever want to share who you are with your first love?

JOY I was that for you?

JAIME You were that for me. So making the list…I added you. I couldn't explain to Ana why, but even though she acts…she understands. I couldn't have met someone like her without being with you.

JOY Why?

JAIME Oh, honey. You loved me. You made me feel loved.

[JOY *is crying*. JAIME *holds her.*]

JOY Can you do me a favor? Can you roll me? Can you roll me in the water and let the waves roll over me. Let the water rise over me. Let me drown because I'm already drowning.

JAIME You can't drown.

JOY Why?

JAIME You're a mermaid at a mermaid-themed wedding and Ana will kill you if you don't play by the rules and the biggest rule for a mermaid is she floats.

JOY Swims.

JAIME You might float. I think you're a good floater. I think—you'll be fine.

[JAIME *and* JOY *sit up*. ANA *returns with a chair. A little girl enters, holding a chair too.*]

ANA Monica's unloading the chairs. She sent Sally to help. Say hello, Sally. She's shy. You can put that there, sweetie.

JAIME I've it, honey. You take a break, okay?

[JAIME *helps* SALLY *put out the chairs, clean up a bit, decorate some more from* ANA's *bag. Beat with* JOY *and* ANA. JOY *breaks the silence.*]

JOY What about those vows?

ANA I don't have them.

[*Imitates writing.*]

I'm not like you...I'm shit at writing. I have them—

[*Gestures to head.* JOY *nods for* ANA *to go ahead.* ANA *speaks from memory.*]

When I met you I didn't know what love was. I thought I did. I thought I knew everything. The day we met here. The day you wore your silly pink hat and looked up at the sun, but the sun was me. This gigantic creature of a woman with red hair over you on your beach towel. You said I was in the way of the light. You were drawing the waves. But in them you drew mermaids and creatures of the sea and fantastical things. You said you drew for kids and I told you I made dances for adults. I thought looking at you, drawing, looking away from me that I was seeing beyond something. I'd look at the world and see the beautiful stars and think what I saw was what was. But with you. The stars are a chariot. The waves a home. In my heart. We were always married. Now we are wife and wife. But what a wife is with you changes...and I want it to always change. Like the water. Like us. I love this poem:

You will remember that leaping stream where sweet aromas rose and trembled, and sometimes a bird, wearing water and slowness, its winter feathers.

You will remember those gifts from the earth indelible scents, gold clay, weeds in the thicket and crazy roots, magical thorns like swords.

You'll remember the bouquet you picked, shadows and silent water, bouquet like a foam-covered stone.

That time was like never, and like always. So we go there, where nothing is waiting; we find everything waiting there.

JOY You—

ANA It's bad! It is? God! Everyone uses Neruda.

JAIME I'm glad she has you. Will you show me? Again?

[ANA *starts to dance again.* JOY *tries, getting better. The girl runs to them dancing too.* JAIME *jumps in. They get better and better! They turn to the audience. They encourage them to dance with them. They dance until everyone is smiling.*]

• • •

Spatial Disorientation

Lisa Soland

Our feelings, indulged without examination, will kill us. Feelings, intuition, and emotions are inputs that should be fully heard, but they must never govern our behavior. For those of us whose goal is happiness, it is only with the mind that we can see rightly, for what is essential is invisible to the heart.—Eric Nolte, airline captain

We are tied to the ocean. And when we go back to the sea... we are going back from whence we came.—John F. Kennedy

To Flight Safety Academy, The bravest people in aviation because people will only care where I got my training if I crash. Best, John Kennedy.—John F. Kennedy Jr.

Spatial Disorientation by Lisa Soland. Copyright © 2013 by Lisa Soland. All rights reserved. Reprinted by permission of the author.

CAUTION/ADVICE: Professionals and amateurs are hereby warned that performance of *Spatial Disorientation* is subject to a royalty. It is fully protected under the copyright laws of the United States of America, and of all countries covered by the International Copyright Union (including the Dominion of Canada and the rest of the British Commonwealth), and of all countries covered by the Pan-American Copyright Convention and the Universal Copyright Convention, the Berne Convention, and of all countries with which the United States has reciprocal copyright relations. All rights, including professional and amateur stage performing rights, motion picture, recitation, lecturing, public reading, radio broadcasting, television, video or sound recording, all other forms of mechanical or electronic reproduction, such as CD-ROM, DVD-ROM, information storage and retrieval systems, and photocopying, and the rights of translation into foreign languages, are strictly reserved. Particular emphasis is placed upon the matter of readings, permission for which must be secured from the author's agent in writing.

Inquiries concerning rights should be addressed to Lisa Soland at LisaSoland@aol.com.

Lisa Soland

Lisa Soland's plays *Waiting*, *Cabo San Lucas*, *Truth Be Told*, and *The Name Game*, along with the anthology *The Man in the Gray Suit & Other Plays* are published by Samuel French Inc. Her work can also be found in anthologies by French, Applause Books, Smith & Kraus, and Dramatic Publishing. Her children's book *The Christmas Tree Angel* by Celtic Cat Publishing, has become a holiday favorite, and her book *The Writer's Motivation* has inspired countless writers to fill the blank page. She has produced and/or directed over eighty productions and play readings, fifty-five of which have been original, and is the founder of the All Original Playwright Workshop, where she works as artistic director and teacher, producing workshops throughout the United States and online. Ms. Soland is currently writing, teaching, and directing in the theater department at Maryville College in Tennessee.

··· **production history** ···

Spatial Disorientation was first produced in a collection of plays by Lisa Soland, entitled "The Ladder Plays," in the Clayton Performing Arts Center at Pellissippi State College on March 23, 2012. The drama was directed by Lisa Soland, produced by Charles R. Miller, with Andrew Henry as stage manager. The lights were designed by Jessica Goings and the set by Charles R. Miller, with Jeff Delany as technical director. James Francis played JOHN, Katie Alley played LAUREN, and Emily Soleil played CAROLYN.

Spatial Disorientation was again produced, in the same collection of short plays, at Muskingum University Theatre in Thompson Theatre, and opened November 29, 2012. The play was directed by Nathan Lawhun, with Chase Strawser as stage manager. Marcus Correa played JOHN, Emily Brice played LAUREN, and Caitlyn Romshak played CAROLYN.

characters

JOHN   John F. Kennedy Jr., thirty-eight years old, walks with a cane

CAROLYN   John's wife, thirty-three, cocaine-addled

LAUREN   Carolyn's older sister, thirty-four

time

July 16, 1999, at 8:00 p.m.

place

Essex County Airport in Fairfield Township, NJ.

setting

We are in the terminal of the Essex County Airport, on the night of July 16, 1999, at about 8:00 p.m. The moon has just risen above the horizon but barely casts any light onto the ladder, which can be seen off in the distance, upstage left, representing the steps one must take to board JFK Junior's private plane. As the conversation ensues, more and more light is cast onto these foreboding steps.

[*At rise, three chairs sit side by side center stage, facing downstage. Another three chairs are behind them, facing upstage. A trash can sits stage right of them and a small table/chair sits stage left.* JOHN *rushes onto the stage from stage right, carrying a duffle bag and a travel garment bag.*]

LAUREN [*Following close behind, with a weekend bag.*] I'm so sorry I've made us late.

JOHN [*Crosses to stage-left chair.*] You haven't made us late. *She's* late. We got here before she did.

LAUREN Well, we're *all* late.

JOHN How many times did I call her?

LAUREN Too many.

[*She sits.*]

JOHN "I told you I'm getting a pedicure. The more you call me, the longer it's going to take."

[*He sits.*]

LAUREN It's the wedding, the paparazzi…

JOHN We're going to the wedding.

LAUREN It's freaking her out…

JOHN Everything freaks her out these days.

CAROLYN [*Entering from stage right.*] Thank you. Thank you for your kind vote of confidence.

LAUREN [*Rising.*] You made it! Good.

[*She hugs* CAROLYN.]

JOHN [*He rises.*] Sorry.

LAUREN We're all here then.

JOHN [*Hesitant.*] I'm glad you got here, in one piece.

CAROLYN Thank you. For that.

JOHN [*He crosses to* CAROLYN, *greets her with somewhat of a kiss as she offers her cheek to him.*] Well, let's see those 200-dollar nails.
[*Sarcastic.*]
Brilliant. Brilliant color.

CAROLYN They kept screwing it up. It was making me crazy.

JOHN Let's see…do they match the shoes? Do they match? Shoe, please.

[*CAROLYN removes her pump and hands it to* JOHN. *He takes the violet pump from her and compares it to her nails.*] Ahhh…I don't know. Close.

CAROLYN Close enough.

JOHN They'll criticize. They'll judge.

CAROLYN Well, that's what happens when you marry into your family and so I have learned to take great interest in the highly irritating visual details that set one far above the boring masses.

LAUREN You look great.

CAROLYN Thank you, Lauren.

LAUREN So, we're all ready then?

CAROLYN I take it you haven't been listening to the weather?

[*JOHN reacts, "Oh, no. Here it comes," as more light is added to the ladder.*]

LAUREN We had on the traffic report. The roads were a mess.

JOHN [*Crosses stage left and sits.*] It's Friday. I reminded you ladies to leave early.

LAUREN Again, I'm sorry. I had a client I couldn't get rid of.

CAROLYN John, really. Maybe we should think about leaving in the morning.

JOHN Shit.

[*He pulls his duffle bag closer to him, then takes off his ACE bandage and tucks it inside the luggage.*]

LAUREN [*To* CAROLYN.] Really?

CAROLYN They're not advising any flights to leave tonight. I checked with the…

JOHN [*Scratching his ankle.*] So now you're the pilot? You're the champion navigator extraordinaire?

CAROLYN No. I'm not. I'm just saying…

JOHN Give me a rope here. A string. Either of you have a string?

LAUREN [*To* JOHN.] What are you doing?

JOHN I want to measure the difference between my ankles.

LAUREN How did you do that, anyway?

JOHN Paragliding.

CAROLYN I married a risk taker.

LAUREN You married a Kennedy. String…

[*She searches her purse.*]

JOHN Some risks pay off.

CAROLYN [*Sarcastically.*] Yeah, you said that about *George*.

LAUREN Why? What's happening to *George*?

CAROLYN He's had an offer for the money-gulping magazine, so he's thinking of dumping it.

LAUREN I didn't know. I'm very sorry, John.

JOHN I have a new investor. I'm not "dumping it."

CAROLYN Some things gotta go.

JOHN [*Suddenly a bit angry, poignant.*] Yes, that is a very true statement, Carolyn. But the magazine is not one of them.

LAUREN I don't have any string.

JOHN I'll use your necklace. That'll work.

CAROLYN He's not supposed to fly for another ten days, but does he listen?

LAUREN [*She hands* JOHN *her necklace from around her neck.*] I'm guessing not.

CAROLYN Not to the surgeon, not to me, not to anyone.

[*A bit more light is added to the ladder, as they continue their conversation.*]

LAUREN [*She senses the presence of the ladder.*] Listen, John. Where are you staying?

JOHN Stanhope.

LAUREN Why don't we all head over there, get a good night's sleep, and leave in the morning.

JOHN That's a fine idea. That's a dandy idea. Thank you, wife, for instilling fear in your older, more wiser sister, and thank you, Lauren, for your concern, but no thanks. I'm heading out tonight as planned. If you want to go back to Carolyn's and drive up in the morning, that's fine. No problem.

CAROLYN Sounds good to me.

[*She turns to leave.*]

LAUREN [*She rises.*] Wait, wait. I promised. I promised to help. The wedding is tomorrow. His whole family will be there.

[*To* JOHN.]

How dangerous is it, with...uh...weather like this?

JOHN [*He rises and as an aside to* LAUREN.] I tell ya, she does this with everything lately. She turns everything into a goddamn nightmare. It's not a big deal.

CAROLYN Not a big deal.

JOHN No, it's not.

CAROLYN [*She crosses downstage and looks out window, into audience.*] He's not passed his instrumentation flying yet. And the sky looks like Campbell's cream of mushroom soup. I'd say it's a big deal.

LAUREN John?

JOHN [*Hesitating.*] There's a lot...you don't know...about your sister.

CAROLYN John!

JOHN I'll just leave it at that.

CAROLYN What?!

JOHN Nothing.

CAROLYN What were you going to say?!

JOHN Forget it.

CAROLYN Were you going to tell her what you so strategically revealed to our ex-marriage counselor?

JOHN And why is she our ex, Carolyn? Explain that to us!

LAUREN You don't have to...

CAROLYN   No, John, you. Go ahead. Finish what you were going to say…

JOHN   I wasn't going to say *that*.

CAROLYN   What was it then?

JOHN   [*Carefully walking on eggshells.*] Just that it's been very difficult to get you…out of the house…for anything. You've become a bit of a…

CAROLYN   What? What?

JOHN   I forgot the name for them.

CAROLYN   For *them*?

JOHN   That's right. For *them*.

[*Rises.*]

For people like you who are depressed and spend most of their day crying all the time for reasons that don't even exist or for reasons that no one in their right mind can understand. I'm not sure which. I've lost track. I've lost complete track of every fucking little detail of your psychological makeup, Carolyn. Most of which I wish I'd been aware of before we were married.

CAROLYN   [*Opens up stage right and crosses a bit away.*] Where's the paparazzi now, huh? Where in the hell are those tormenting, prying little pricks now? Why is it that they never catch you, the sexiest man alive, in one of your *charming* moods? Why is that?

JOHN   [*Crosses to window downstage.*] They don't like foggy weather. Their cameras don't work.

[*Beat.*]

Reality is negotiable, you know that, Carolyn. Isn't that why you're a cokehead? It makes you feel like you can manipulate reality?

LAUREN   Carolyn?!

CAROLYN   Fucker.

LAUREN   [*Crosses to* CAROLYN.] Carolyn!

CAROLYN   [*Mimicking* LAUREN.] *Lauren.*

LAUREN   [*Grabbing her sister's arm.*] What are you doing?

CAROLYN   [*Pulling away.*] Same as you, hypocrite. Same as everyone. Just trying to get through the next fucking day by whatever means I have at my disposal. And now, I have a lot more at my disposal. Because he's married to me.

[*Crosses to center stage.*]

Because I'm happily married to you, I have the wherewithal to do whatever I damn well please. So screw off, both of you.

[*She crosses upstage right.*]

JOHN   Where are you going?

CAROLYN   [*Stopping in her tracks.*] I have to take a piss. Is that okay with you, control freak?

JOHN   If you have to take a piss, yes. And then we have to leave.

[*Beat.*]

CAROLYN   Fine.

[CAROLYN *storms off.*]

LAUREN   [*Shocked.*] Not sure what to say. I had no idea.

JOHN   I stopped by the flat a couple of months ago and found her coked-out on the floor with a bunch of her gay fashion friends and I'm thinking, where in the hell did all these people come from? She'd given every one of them a key to our apartment and told them they could come and go as they pleased.

LAUREN   What?!

JOHN   [*Crosses to center.*] There was a stash of coke in the freezer that was…huge. I mean, I've been to some parties, trust me, but… Huge.

LAUREN   Oh my God.

JOHN   [*Crosses upstage and sits in stage-left chair.*] I don't know what to do. I gotta tell you. I am at a complete loss.

LAUREN   [*Crosses to chair, stage right, sits.*] Well, at least you're talking now. I couldn't believe it yesterday.

[*She takes Tums out of her purse and eats one.*]

We sat there, the three of us, for over an hour without saying a single word. The olive from my martini is still lying undigested in my stomach, I'm sure of it.

JOHN She doesn't want children. Did you know that? She doesn't want children. Who would have thought?

LAUREN Yeah, I guess I knew that.

JOHN Why didn't she tell me?

LAUREN Oh, I don't know. Probably because she was in love.

JOHN No. That's not love. Withholding information is not love. I don't know what that is. But…I love her. *I love her.*
[*Beat.*]
She's still seeing Michael.

LAUREN You're kidding?

JOHN Nope.

LAUREN No, she's not. She's not, John.

JOHN She told me she was.

LAUREN Well, she lied.

JOHN Why would she lie about something like that?

LAUREN Dear God. She's not seeing him, I promise you.

JOHN Doesn't sound too hopeful, though, does it? I've given her my heart, and now it's become impossible for me to take it back.

LAUREN I don't know what to say.
[CAROLYN *enters with white rings around her nostrils. They stare at her. More light shines on the ladder.* LAUREN *rises.*]
You look like a bull, about to charge.

CAROLYN No. I'm not the bull.

JOHN [*Rises.*] Well, you've got the ring in your nose. I'd say you were the bull.
[*Beat.*]
I'll get the Piper ready and…be back in a minute.
[*He crosses stage left, then turns back.*]
You don't have to come. You don't have to do anything you don't want to.

CAROLYN Go.

[JOHN *continues looking at her and her nose.* CAROLYN *crosses to him, shooing him off.*]

Go, go, go!

[JOHN *defiantly holds his position, then exits.*]

LAUREN What's up?

CAROLYN The sky. Last time I looked.

LAUREN What's up with you?

CAROLYN Welcome to the nightmare.

LAUREN [*She crosses to* CAROLYN.] You're in on it, you know.

CAROLYN You here to screw with me too? That why you're here?

LAUREN You know why I'm here.

CAROLYN You're my sister. Don't forget it.

[*Crosses to chair stage right and sits.*]

LAUREN If I'm your sister, then tell me what's up. Other than the sky.

[*Beat.*]

Last time you looked.

CAROLYN [*She removes mirror from purse and tidies up.*] You know what I hate about this terminal? There's no Starbucks. There's no anything, for that matter. Nothing to fiddle with or bother over, pretending everything's all right. Nothing to distract your mind from wandering on to what's there looking you back in the face—staring at you—slapping you, like a baby that's just been born and needs it's lungs opened up so it can breathe freely again.

[*Puts mirror back in purse.*]

LAUREN [*Crosses downstage to look out window, left.*] What's he doing?

CAROLYN Tormenting me.

[*Rises and crosses downstage to window, right.*]

Oh, you mean out there? He's getting the plane ready. It doesn't take long. He's gotta sign it out, go through his check list, and "all that jazz."

LAUREN Is it true he's not finished with his flight training?

CAROLYN Instrumentation. He doesn't have his instrument rating, I guess. I don't know. He's got his license. We haven't talked much lately. I seem to have lost track of it all.

LAUREN It is kind of a mess out there.

CAROLYN It's always messy. Trust me. Always messy.

LAUREN [*Crosses to* CAROLYN.] What's up with you?

[*Pause.*]

CAROLYN [*Growing lost in thought.*] I was at a bar. I'm ordering a drink and I turn to my right and he's there, lighting some woman's cigarette—an ex-girlfriend...

LAUREN John?

CAROLYN [*Continuing, lost in thought.*] And he's got this look on his face—like some sort of smirky, crooked thing. He does it—this smile. It's a smirky, crooked thing. And I see it there, on his face, and I just want to grab a hold of it with my fingers and rip it off. Rip it off his face.

LAUREN You're talking about John, right?

CAROLYN Such a handsome face. You just want to slap it.

LAUREN Is he still seeing what's-her-name?

CAROLYN No idea. Can't prove it. Makes me crazy. Makes me want to rip off his face.

LAUREN Maybe it needs ripping off.

CAROLYN Thank you.

[*She hugs* LAUREN.]

Thank you, thank you, thank you.

LAUREN What does it take?

CAROLYN I don't know.

LAUREN Why is it that someone like him, with a father like that and uncles and a grandfather...?

CAROLYN Like that.

LAUREN ...I mean, if it were me, I would look at that history and think to myself, "Self? I, uh, don't want to be like that. I want to be different. I want to create something different here, something healthy, lasting. I don't want my handsome face ripped off."

CAROLYN I'm thinking it's genetic.

LAUREN That's bullshit.

CAROLYN I'm thinking it is. All good-looking men.

LAUREN If we were animals, it would be genetic. But we're not. We're humans and humans get to use their brains.

CAROLYN Not these humans. They're above that. They're above using their brains. That's why I get my nails done to perfectly match my dress.

LAUREN You used to do that before.

CAROLYN Not like this, Lauren. Not perfect, like this. Now I have to be perfect and the pressure is tearing me apart.

LAUREN I'm so sorry. Look on the bright side. Now you have the wherewithal to be perfect.

CAROLYN Now I've got the wherewithal to lose my fucking mind.

[*She crosses upstage and sits in stage-right chair.*]

LAUREN [*Crosses upstage with her and sits in chair stage left.*] You can make another choice, you know. You know that, right? You can use your brain and make another choice.

CAROLYN Maybe. Maybe not.
[*Beat.*]
Good-looking men are genetically programmed to be unfaithful.

LAUREN No. They just get away with it easier.

JOHN [*Entering.*] All set. So…what? What have you decided? You coming?

CAROLYN What do you think?

JOHN [*Gets water bottle out of his carry-on while searching for something else.*] I'm thinking you've made a decision that is best for you.

LAUREN [*She rises and gathers purse.*] Well, I promised I would fly with you as far as Martha's Vineyard. And I keep my promises.

[*She glances at* JOHN. *More light is revealed on ladder.* CAROLYN *rises and eerily gathers her things to leave in the opposite direction.* LAUREN *and* JOHN *watch her.*]

LAUREN What, Carolyn? What are you doing?

[*Beat.*]

You said you would attend the wedding with John if I...

CAROLYN I know what I said.

LAUREN We all held hands over a martini!

CAROLYN I know what we did.

[*Sensing something dreadful.*]

JOHN If you're coming, you'd better change your shoes.

CAROLYN [*Half listening, if that.*] What?

JOHN Your shoes?

CAROLYN You don't like my shoes?

JOHN [*Patiently, on glass.*] I love your shoes, they are the perfect color, but last time you complained that the heels got ruined from slipping in between the metal holes when you climbed the ramp.

CAROLYN [*Crosses to chair stage right and sits.*] Yeah. Yeah, that's right.

JOHN [*To* LAUREN.] She's always complaining that I don't look out for her; that I don't listen. But trust me, I listen.

LAUREN I can see that.

[LAUREN *pops another Tums.*]

[CAROLYN *takes off her violet pumps, opens her suitcase, and puts on her violet tennis shoes.*]

JOHN [*Sits.*] Fucking cast. Six weeks and my ankle shrinks and now it itches to beat hell.

[JOHN *puts foot up and scratches his ankle again.*]

They should make casts so you can take them off. How come no one thinks of that? Doctors. It's like they can't think outside the box they themselves created. You would just need to put hinges in the thing and some sort of a latch to lock it on, then when you get a scratch or you have to take a shower...

CAROLYN ...or fly a plane...

JOHN You could just take the damn thing off and then your ankle won't shrink.

CAROLYN [*Absentmindedly.*] Atrophy.

JOHN What?

CAROLYN The word you're looking for—*atrophy.*

LAUREN That's actually a pretty great idea.

CAROLYN He's full of 'em.

JOHN I am?

CAROLYN Yeah. A magazine called *George*. Removable casts.

JOHN I actually thought for one brief moment that you were paying me a compliment.

CAROLYN Nope. Sarcasm.

JOHN Socially acceptable anger.

CAROLYN That's right, John. I've accepted that I'm socially sarcastic.
[*She crosses downstage to the window overlooking the airplanes.*]
We were supposed to take off in the light.

JOHN [*He crosses downstage to window.*] I've flown in the dark.

CAROLYN Not this kind of dark. Not cream of mushroom soup dark.

JOHN You don't have to come. You don't, for the hundredth time.
[*Turning to* LAUREN.]
You, especially, do not have to come. I don't mind flying there by myself. You guys can fly up in the morning.

LAUREN [*She crosses downstage with purse.*] Just tell me. If you tell me that it's fine, I'll believe you.

JOHN It's fine. Carolyn's got this maudlin thing going on. Believe me, it's fine.

LAUREN Okay. Well, do you mind if I quick use the bathroom? There's no bathroom in that, is there?

JOHN Six-seater—that depends.

LAUREN [*Understanding what this means.*] I'll be right back.

[*She exits with purse. Beat.*]

CAROLYN [*Plainly.*] Aren't *you* going to pee? Don't you pee? Ever?

JOHN [*Plainly.*] Yes, I pee. You've known me to pee.

CAROLYN I don't think I have. Come to think of it, no. I have never seen or heard you pee. You do, don't you? You are human?

JOHN I suppose it's possible.

CAROLYN You are, John. You are human, just like everybody else. And someday it'll catch up with you. Someday you're going to wake up, all alone, and wonder how the hell you got there.

JOHN [*He turns and crosses halfway to her.*] I don't want to be alone, Carolyn. I want you to be with me. I want us to get along, like before.

CAROLYN Before I knew you were seeing Daryl again?

JOHN [*Shocked, confused.*] I'm not seeing Daryl.

CAROLYN "America's most eligible bachelor finally meets his match."

JOHN [*Crosses upstage to chair stage left.*] What did you do now? Read all the back issues of *People* magazine?

CAROLYN Lying won't keep you from being human.
[*Crosses stage right.*]
Maybe *she'll* go with you to this wedding. Give her a call, John. Or have you already? Is that's what's going on here? You talk me out of this because she's already agreed to meet you there?

JOHN Let's look at the time, ladies and gentlemen.
[*He looks at watch.*]
Yup, this is about the time you start freaking out. I don't know what to say, Carolyn. How am I supposed to react to this? I'm tired of "crazy."

CAROLYN You make me this way.

JOHN Uh, no. We both know what makes you crazy.

CAROLYN You swaying back and forth, that's what does it.
[*Crosses upstage around the back of the six chairs.*]
Should I be faithful, should I not? Should I be committed…? Ah… no. No, I won't. It's too hard.

JOHN You're damn right it's too hard. "She's on drugs."

CAROLYN [*She kneels on the back chair and leans over to* JOHN.] Wah, wah, wah. You're a big crybaby. That's all you Kennedys are. You cry like a big baby so you can legitimize everything you take. You're takers. All of you...

JOHN [*Under his breath.*] I hate when you lump me in with all of them...

CAROLYN [*Continuing to push.*] You see something you want and you take it. You're not men. Not real men. Men don't take. They earn. Real men earn a woman's love.

JOHN [*Rises and crosses to his bag.*] Carolyn, let's not fight, please. Not today. Please. Not now. I have a headache. I've had it since this morning.

[*Gets Evian water bottle from top of bag.*]

Do you have any aspirin?

[*Without speaking,* CAROLYN *moves to her purse.*]

Do you or don't you?!

CAROLYN I'm getting it!

[*She empties two pills into her hand and holds them out for* JOHN *but does not release them yet.*]

Stop seeing Daryl.

JOHN Carolyn, give me the aspirin.

CAROLYN Stop.

JOHN Carolyn!

[*She releases them and they fall too long of a distance, causing* JOHN *to grapple for them. With eyes on* CAROLYN, *he pops the pills into his mouth then takes the last swig of water to wash them down.*]

We can keep doing this, if you want. We can keep wasting time, instead of trying to make our marriage work—all the while lying about this and lying about that. But the drama is wearing thin, my dear. I can't do it anymore. I can't do "crazy" forever.

[*He takes a step in to* CAROLYN *and angrily throws the Evian water bottle into the trash can.*]

You walk out of a last-ditch-effort to get help; you walked right out of a marriage counseling session because I happen to mention that you are addicted to cocaine. I happened to mention the truth.

CAROLYN You make it sound like such a big deal…

JOHN It is…

CAROLYN Spouting off…

JOHN It is a big deal…

CAROLYN Spouting off every chance you get…

JOHN [*He turns away.*] I give up…

CAROLYN …to *my* sister.

JOHN It's time people know…

CAROLYN And how you love to tell them…

JOHN You need help.

CAROLYN You want me perfect…

JOHN I want you drug-free…

CAROLYN Yes, but that will happen and then it will be something else…

JOHN Yes, perhaps I will ask that you be faithful as well.

CAROLYN I am faithful.

JOHN Faithful to what?

CAROLYN To you.

JOHN No, not to me. To Michael yes, in spite of our marriage, in spite of our vows, which meant something to me! In spite of this, you have remained faithful to him, not me! Not to me!

CAROLYN [*She sits in stage-right chair.*] I lied.

JOHN When you told me?

CAROLYN Yes, I lied. I thought it would help if you were jealous.

JOHN Oh, really? Don't you think that's rather infantile?

CAROLYN Not any more than you.

JOHN So you lied about you and Michael still seeing each other so that you and I would somehow benefit?

CAROLYN Yes.

JOHN That makes no sense. No sense at all.

CAROLYN I don't know what to say.

JOHN How 'bout the truth.

CAROLYN I am.

JOHN You are.

CAROLYN Yes.

[*Quiet.*]

JOHN [*He crosses to table/chair stage left and sits.*] Carolyn, I hired someone to trail you and this person has your many photographically documented visits in film—color, glossy, to his apartment in Greenwich Village. You are still seeing your precious Calvin Klein underwear model, whether you are able to admit it to me now or not.

CAROLYN Who else knows?

JOHN That's what you care about—"Who else knows?"

CAROLYN I think because of the circumstances, yes. That's what I care about.

JOHN [*Sarcastic and poignant.*] Amazing.

[*Shaking his head, lost.*]

You know, everyone thought my father was some great visionary— able to see into the future and claim what human ingenuity could accomplish if we all put our minds to it. After the Bay of Pigs, he conveniently announces that the United States is going to put a man on the moon by the end of the decade and people are shocked. They think he's nuts. But July of 1969 rolls around and Neil Armstrong places his foot onto the surface of the moon.

[*He rises and crosses downstage, looking out window.*]

That moon. What people don't know is that my father had access to special knowledge that could be obtained by someone like my father, in a family, like my family. He knew that the space program was more than capable of putting a man on the moon when he made that speech in May of '61. He had the information, which made him...powerful really. Powerful. He wasn't so much a visionary as he was a man who knew how to acquire truth. And the truth was what made my father powerful. You've kept me from that—the truth.

[*Turns to her.*]

Do you understand how crippling that is? You've manipulated me and lied and…I really don't know what else to say to you, Carolyn. Don't you want this to work? Don't you want to be a part of something important? Something that lasts?

CAROLYN [*She crosses to him and puts her hand on his, then quickly pulls the cane out from beneath him and takes a step back.*] Tell me you're faithful and I'll believe you.

JOHN I can tell you till I'm blue in the face.

CAROLYN I'm okay with blue.

JOHN We're talking about you here.

CAROLYN I read the papers. I'm not dumb.

JOHN If you read the papers, you're dumb.

[JOHN *reaches for cane and* CAROLYN *pulls away.*]

CAROLYN You Kennedys, you're all alike.

JOHN [*Somewhat hopping on one leg.*] Carolyn, please. Throw me a life jacket here—something. I'm drowning.

CAROLYN Tell me you're faithful.

JOHN Stop seeing Michael.

CAROLYN Tell me.

JOHN Carolyn.

[*Reaching out again,* CAROLYN *pulls back.*]

CAROLYN You first.

JOHN [*He gives up and hops to his seat, stage left, and sits.*] I thought you were going to stop reading that crap.

CAROLYN [*She crosses downstage left, on the edge.*] I had to give up my job because of this, because of you. A job that I really enjoyed. And now it's gone and there's nothing. There's not a single place I can go without insufferable harassment, and you, the thing I left my job for…you work night and day, continuously, on and on and on. What do you expect me to do? What do you want me to do with my time, tell me?

JOHN I know we're a unique family…

CAROLYN   [*Crosses upstage behind him and the chairs to stage right.*] *You're* unique!

JOHN   …but you knew before you married me what you were getting into.

CAROLYN   Not entirely. A person can imagine, but really, John, this is impossible. The press is impossible. They followed me to the salon, seven or eight cars, snapping, flashes, riding my tail, trying to get me to falter, show my imperfection, finally getting that priceless photo of me flipping them off. And then the thought came—to take the wheel in my hands and quickly turn it into the oncoming traffic and then they would get to see for themselves, front row center, what they drove me to—photograph me to their heart's content slapping up against an immovable force. I imagined clothes, dinner parties, and lovemaking, romantic nights under the moon with you, my dear love, but not this. Not wanting to veer into oncoming traffic at a tremendous speed and everything suddenly, peacefully finally being over. This is where I am, John. This is where my "lack of imagination" has brought me.

JOHN   Brought us.

CAROLYN   Me. Me, John. I'm afraid I'm alone in this.

JOHN   [*Genuinely, he reaches for her hand across the chairs.*] You're not alone, trust me. I understand these things. I've lived with this from the beginning and it's beyond difficult, I know. But if you can't find it within yourself to trust me, we have no chance of navigating our way through it. No chance, Carolyn. You've got to trust me.

CAROLYN   Trust you.

JOHN   Yes. When all is said and done, I'm just a person.

CAROLYN   [*Crosses behind chairs to stage left of chairs.*] That's right, John. *You're human.* Just like everyone else.

JOHN   Well, I won't admit to that but I am just a person.

CAROLYN   [*Standing left of the chairs.*] You're a self-consumed egomaniac.

JOHN   Yes, I'll admit to that.

[*He quickly and aggressively takes her wrist, turns her, pulls her down across his lap, and kisses her, hard. Out of the kiss and still determined.*]
Trust me.

CAROLYN I'll do my best.

JOHN [*He picks her up off his lap and moves her beside him.*] And stop with the drugs. Really. It's not useful in any way.

CAROLYN It is, though. I can deal with it all better. It helps me, John.

JOHN [*Determined.*] No. It doesn't, Carolyn. It's disorienting. It turns you upside down in such a way that you don't know which way is up anymore. It's not what you think it is.

CAROLYN Nothing is.

JOHN Yes, some things are. We could be. But you have to first give it up, Carolyn. I need you to. *You* need you to, with or without me...

CAROLYN Don't say that...

JOHN I'm just saying...

CAROLYN Well, don't.

JOHN With or without me, it's going to serve you in your life to not be doing that. Okay?

[*Beat.*]

CAROLYN Okay.

JOHN Good. And we're going back to that counselor and we're going to start telling the truth. Otherwise, we're dead in the water, Carolyn. We really are.

CAROLYN Okay. I'll do it. I will.

JOHN Promise?

CAROLYN I promise.

JOHN All right then. All right.
[*He starts to rise to get his cane.*]
You ready to go?

CAROLYN [*She draws him back down to the chair.*] John?

JOHN What?

CAROLYN After this weekend is behind us, can we please just have some time alone—married time. Just us?

JOHN Yeah, you bet.

CAROLYN Really?

JOHN Sure, we need that.

[*Beat.*]

We'll take the Piper and fly down to Cuba, get a few cigars...I'm kidding. I'm kidding. We'll take a few days and head off to Jamaica. How's that?

CAROLYN We could lock ourselves in the apartment, for all I care.

JOHN And never come out. For two days.

CAROLYN Four.

JOHN Four.

[*The deal has been made.*]

Great. If that gets you through this weekend, great.

CAROLYN Love you.

JOHN Love you too.

[*They kiss.*]

What the hell is your sister doing in there?

CAROLYN I think she had to take a dump.

JOHN I guess she's human.

CAROLYN Just like us.

[*She rises and bends over to get JOHN's cane.*]

You looked at my ass, didn't you?

JOHN You are the sexiest woman alive.

CAROLYN Thank you for that.

[*She kisses him then crosses to the window, downstage right.*]

The fog hasn't cleared much.

JOHN [*He rises and crosses downstage left, out window.*] It's cleared enough for me. It's a short flight. Just follow the coastline all the way up.

CAROLYN Okay. You know best.

[*She smiles at him.*]

JOHN You got your bag, there?

CAROLYN [*She crosses to her things. Puts on her trench coat and then pulls the handle up on her carry-on.*] Yeah. All set.

[*She looks at him with intense love and vulnerability.*]

Kiss me. Kiss me.

[*They cross to each other center and kiss passionately.*]

LAUREN [*Enters.*] Sorry it took me so long but I...

[*Noticing the two of them.*]

Oh, this is very good. I should have gone to the bathroom hours ago.

CAROLYN Lauren, the fog. It's cleared a little.

JOHN Just enough.

LAUREN Well, then. If it's enough for you, it's enough for me too. So, what else then? We good to go?

JOHN We're all set. Garment bag? Shoes?

[*He looks down at* CAROLYN's *shoes.*]

CAROLYN Yup.

[*They gather their things.*]

JOHN Ladies?

[*They cross to the ladder upstage left.* JOHN *looks at his watch.*]

8:38. Maybe we'll have time to stop for a drink at the Seaside Pub in Hyannis Port.

CAROLYN That'd be great.

LAUREN Don't you two get swarmed at a bar like that?

JOHN Nah. No one goes there at that time of night. It's too crowded.

LAUREN That's cute.

CAROLYN Nice, John.

[LAUREN *and* CAROLYN *smile as they ascend the laddered stairs onto the plane, with* JOHN *prepared to follow as the lights fade, leaving them halted on the ladder as dark shadows. We hear the CBS broadcast announcing that their plane has vanished off the coast of Martha's Vineyard and the chances of finding anyone alive are fading like the light... blackout.*]

• • •

Between the
Lines

Amber Leanne Marcoon

Between the Lines by Amber Leanne Marcoon. Copyright © 2013 by Amber Leanne Marcoon. All rights reserved. Reprinted by permission of the author.

CAUTION/ADVICE: Professionals and amateurs are hereby warned that performance of *Between the Lines* is subject to a royalty. It is fully protected under the copyright laws of the United States of America, and of all countries covered by the International Copyright Union (including the Dominion of Canada and the rest of the British Commonwealth), and of all countries covered by the Pan-American Copyright Convention and the Universal Copyright Convention, the Berne Convention, and of all countries with which the United States has reciprocal copyright relations. All rights, including professional and amateur stage performing rights, motion picture, recitation, lecturing, public reading, radio broadcasting, television, video or sound recording, all other forms of mechanical or electronic reproduction, such as CD-ROM, DVD-ROM, information storage and retrieval systems, and photocopying, and the rights of translation into foreign languages, are strictly reserved. Particular emphasis is placed upon the matter of readings, permission for which must be secured from the author's agent in writing.

Inquiries concerning rights should be addressed to Amber Leanne Marcoon, 529 Windy Hill Lane, West Chester, PA 19382

Amber Leanne Marcoon

Between the Lines is Amber Leanne Marcoon's first play, which earned her attendance to the National Playwrights' Symposium at Cape May Stage in May 2013. She attributes much of the success of *Between the Lines* to her professors Leonard I. Kelly and Dr. Harvey Rovine. Marcoon graduated from West Chester University of Pennsylvania in May 2014.

···production history···

Between the Lines was first workshopped at the West Chester University of Pennsylvania and premiered there as part of a performance of one-acts in February 2013. The play was revised further after being workshopped with John Pielmeier and other writers at the National Playwrights' Symposium at Cape May Stage in May 2013.

cast

AARON   Derry McDermott

ANNA   Helene DelNegro

LEAH   Stephanie Smith

Director: Jeremiah Bean

characters

AARON   in his mid-twenties. Actor. Easy-going. Struggles to show emotion outside of his roles onstage. Selfish. Impulsive.

ANNA   in her early twenties. College student. Type A. Somewhat codependent. In a relationship with AARON. Wears a crucifix around her neck.

LEAH   in her early twenties. Playwright. Wears a crucifix around her neck.

time

Now.

setting

LEAH's imagination. Small table that functions as both a kitchen table and a desk. One notebook, one pen/pencil. Two chairs at table. Two acting cubes (together representing couch). Two crucifixes. One cell phone.

[*Lights up on* ANNA *and* LEAH. LEAH *sits at table writing in her notebook.* ANNA *is facing stage right, looking into a "mirror," primping. She's wearing a dress and heels.*]

ANNA I mean, I should just stop complaining and be happy, right? I'm being selfish. When you love someone, their happiness is more important than your own.

[*Turning away from mirror.*]

But does that only work if both people feel and act that way? How do you know when that's not working anymore? And where is the line between loving someone and loving yourself? And how do you know when you've crossed that line? Am I just being naive? Maybe the idea of love is better than the thing itself...

LEAH [*Stops writing and thinks aloud.*] You should be an actress.

ANNA Why?

LEAH [*Pushing the notebook away.*] You're so melodramatic!

ANNA I'm just...scared.

LEAH Scared?

ANNA I want to be with Aaron more than anything but part of me isn't—I'm not happy.

LEAH Anna?

ANNA Leah?

LEAH Shut up.

ANNA Ugh—I can't!

LEAH Why not?

ANNA Because no one is listening!

LEAH [*Shaking her head.*] I'm writing down everything you say, you know...

ANNA He isn't listening.

LEAH I'm sure it's just a phase. Long distance is a tricky thing. Be patient.

ANNA You know he went four days without calling me last week. Is it really that hard to call and say good night? Doesn't he want me anymore?

LEAH Sure, but he's a twenty-something guy. He's thinking about himself. Eventually he'll grow out of it.

LEAH and ANNA You're right. We'll figure it out.

LEAH See—you should listen to me more.

ANNA Well, right now I'm listening for Aaron's car—running late as usual. What time is it anyway?

LEAH Whoops, almost 5:30.

[AARON *knocks on door. ANNA smooths her dress one last time before opening the door. AARON enters and kisses ANNA quickly. LEAH looks up and watches them.*]

AARON Hi! Ughhh I'm so hungry!

ANNA Hi! Well, what do you want to eat?

AARON Anything. I'm starved—whatever you want, babe.

ANNA Good, because I already have the pizza bagels and chicken nuggets in the oven.

AARON You know me too well.

[AARON *flops facedown on the couch.*]

ANNA That's because you eat like a four-year-old. Come into the kitchen, they'll be ready in a minute!

AARON [*Face in pillow, voice muffled.*] I'm too sleepy.

ANNA You just got here! And I want to hear about your audition.

AARON [*Unintelligible garbled sound.*]

ANNA [*Walks offstage into the "kitchen."*] Come talk to me!

AARON [*Like a belligerent child.*] Errrmmno!

ANNA Fine. [*Beat. ANNA tosses her high heels onstage one by one. AARON lifts his head to see what the noise is.*]

AARON You're mean.

ANNA You think that was mean?

[ANNA *throws her bra onstage. AARON jumps off couch, runs offstage and returns with ANNA over his shoulder. AARON and ANNA fall onto the couch. AARON begins to kiss ANNA and she starts to laugh.*]

AARON [*Confused.*] What?

ANNA [*Laughing harder.*] It's just—

AARON Anna!

ANNA What is this relationship about anymore? Feed or procreate?
[AARON *and* ANNA *both laugh.*]
Really, though, do you want to be here?

[LEAH *stands and walks slowly around them and begins to fiddle with her crucifix.*]

AARON Yes! I'm just really busy—after the show I have rehearsal for the next show.
[*Beat.*]
I'm doing the best I can. I'm sorry if that isn't good enough.

ANNA You're annoyed.

AARON No.
[*Beat.*]
I'm thinking that I already know how this conversation is going to end—we'll both get upset, you'll start crying, we'll say good night, you'll keep both of us awake all night worrying, tomorrow it'll be awkward in the bathroom for five minutes when we're brushing our teeth and then everything will be fine!

ANNA That's not funny, Aaron.
[AARON *raises his eyebrows at her and suppresses a smile.*]
Okay, maybe it's a little funny.
[AARON *takes* ANNA*'s hands and musses her hair.* LEAH *sits again, still fiddling with her necklace nervously.*]
I'm really, really proud of you, okay?
[*Beat.*]
I love you.

AARON I love you too, pretty girl.

ANNA [*Leaning in to kiss him.*] Then that's enough for m—

[LEAH *pulls too hard and accidentally breaks the clasp on her necklace.*]

LEAH and ANNA Dammit!

[LEAH *stands, examines the broken necklace, holding it up to the light for a few moments, and tosses it on the floor.* ANNA *slowly stands—moving one cube upstage into the shadows and sits.* AARON *sits center stage, head down.* LEAH *rips out the page in her notebook and crumples it. After a few moments, she picks up the phone and makes a call. In the following lines,* LEAH *moves in the space around* AARON *but does not notice he's there.*]

LEAH   Um, hi?

> [*Hurt poorly disguised as anger. Pause, long enough for "response."*]

Why are you so quiet...what's going on?

[*Pause.*]

Hello?

[*Pause.*]

I love you.

[*Pause.*]

Why aren't you saying anything?

[*Pause. Half-enthused.*]

That's great! Congrats, babe.

[*Pause.*]

Of course I'm happy you got the part!

[*Pause.*]

We'll figure it ou—

[*Pause. Not understanding.*]

What guilt?

[ANNA *stands and walks to hover behind* LEAH, *concerned. Pause.*]

Resent me?

[*Pause.*]

I don't know what script you're living in but normal couples fight. And over worse things than this long-distance stuff. I'll come visit you. We'll make it work.

[*Pause.*]

What does that mean?

[*Pause.*]

Are you—are you breaking up with me?

[*Pause.*]

No—say it! Say you're breaking up with me!

[*Pause.* ANNA *backs away, shocked, and is visibly in pain herself.*]

LEAH and ANNA [*Facing opposite directions with* AARON *between them.*] Oh my God, oh my God. You don't want me, you don't want me, you don't want—

ANNA Stop it!

[LEAH *obeys and slowly gathers her notebook and moves upstage, bringing the remaining cube, and sits.* ANNA *and* AARON *move to sit/move around the kitchen table—however, they are not necessarily stationary throughout the entirety of the following scene.*]

So you've been keeping up with auditions?

AARON Yup, I'm getting ready to move upstate for the summer. I'm casted for the whole season.

ANNA That's really exciting. I'm happy for you.

AARON Do you have anything fun planned?

ANNA Just trying to stay busy.

[*Beat.*]

You know, I had all of these things I wanted to say to you—and now that you're here—

AARON It's nice to see you, Anna.

ANNA Can I just—? I need to ask one question.

AARON Okay.

ANNA How could you be calling me your "pretty girl" one night and the next you're just done?

AARON I—I saw myself not trying anymore. And that's when I gave up.

ANNA [*Almost to herself.*] Why?

AARON I—I don't know.

[*Beat.*]

You weren't asking for too much. I'm sorry that I let you believe that. I need to focus on myself before I can worry about someone else.

ANNA I think part of me knew. A few days before that call, I went to church and—

AARON You went to church?

ANNA Well, I just kind of sat there and cried. I don't know if you can really call it praying—but maybe this was my answer.

AARON I never meant to hurt you. I—I still care about you.

ANNA You know, I wasn't perfect either. Part of me wants to tell you all the things I've learned—the things I'd do differently. There's probably nothing I wouldn't do to see your face—to hear you laugh—and have it feel like more than a memory. But even after all this time, when I look at you, I'm home.

AARON Anna, I—I'm sorry.

ANNA It's getting late. You should probably go.

AARON Come here.

[AARON *pulls her close and weaves his hand in her hair. They share a long embrace.* ANNA *nearly kisses him by impulse as they pull away, but takes a step back.* AARON *turns to leave and walks offstage.* LEAH *stands and runs to edge of stage after* AARON.]

LEAH [*Turning and addressing* ANNA.] Go after him! What's wrong with you? You love him, don't you?

ANNA Of course I do. But we both need time to become who we're meant to be. Maybe the lines we're supposed to follow will cross again, but we have to keep living—we have to keep trying because…we have to see how the story ends.

LEAH You mean it's not finished?

ANNA No—you may be writing our story, but someone else is writing yours.

[*Begins to walk offstage.*]

LEAH You're leaving too?

ANNA [*Stops and turns to answer.*] I'll be back. Do you have abandonment issues or something?

LEAH Ha, probably.

ANNA Oh, wait a second.

[ANNA *takes off her necklace and hands it to* LEAH.]

LEAH [*Holding it up to the light.*] Thank you. I don't really pray much, but it's beautiful.

ANNA Have a little faith!

LEAH Faith?

ANNA It's between the lines.

[*Exits.*]

[LEAH *slowly walks back to the desk, examining the necklace in her hand. Puts on the necklace, sits, picks up pen, and begins to write again.*]

• • •

The Rainbow

James Armstrong

The Rainbow by James Armstrong. Copyright © 2012 by James Armstrong. All rights reserved. Reprinted by permission of the author.

CAUTION/ADVICE: Professionals and amateurs are hereby warned that performance of *The Rainbow* is subject to a royalty. It is fully protected under the copyright laws of the United States of America, and of all countries covered by the International Copyright Union (including the Dominion of Canada and the rest of the British Commonwealth), and of all countries covered by the Pan-American Copyright Convention and the Universal Copyright Convention, the Berne Convention, and of all countries with which the United States has reciprocal copyright relations. All rights, including professional and amateur stage performing rights, motion picture, recitation, lecturing, public reading, radio broadcasting, television, video or sound recording, all other forms of mechanical or electronic reproduction, such as CD-ROM, DVD-ROM, information storage and retrieval systems, and photocopying, and the rights of translation into foreign languages, are strictly reserved. Particular emphasis is placed upon the matter of readings, permission for which must be secured from the author's agent in writing.

Inquiries concerning rights should be addressed to James Armstrong, 1443A Fifth Ave., 4th Fl., New York, NY 10035, or e-mail armstrongwrites@gmail.com.

James Armstrong

James Armstrong has had his plays performed by such theaters as the Attic Ensemble (*The Four Doctors Huxley*), the Abingdon Theatre Company (*Foggy Bottom*), the Epiphany Theater Company (*A Christmas Carol*), and Playwrights Forum (*The Metric System*). New York audiences have seen the premieres of a number of his short plays, including *The New Mrs. Jones, Searching for Saint Anthony, When Ladies Go A-Thieving, The Mysteries of the Castle of the Monk of Falconara, Corpse, The True Author... Revealed,* and *Housekeeping*, as well as *The Rainbow*, which premiered at the American Globe Theatre in 2012. He is a member of the Dramatists Guild of America, and you can keep up with him at www.armstrongplays.com.

···production history···

The Rainbow was originally performed at the Turnip Theatre Company & American Globe Theatre's 18th Annual Fifteen Minute Play Festival on April 23, 2012. It was directed by Dev Bondarin. The cast was as follows:

JACK   Christopher Kloko
MEG   Kathryn Holtkamp

characters

MEG, twenties
JACK, twenties

time

The present. Labor Day. Around noon.

place

Bryant Park in New York City. There is a picnic blanket spread on the ground with a knapsack on top of it. Nearby is a metal table with two chairs.

[JACK *stands near a picnic blanket, reading a book. He holds the cover up so that it is clearly visible. The book is* The Rainbow *by D. H. Lawrence.* JACK *keeps glancing over the top of the book, as if looking for someone.* MEG *enters, somewhat disheveled, glancing at her watch. She sees the picnic blanket, looks at* JACK, *and checks the title of the book.*]

MEG   Um…Jack? You're Jack, right?

JACK   Hi there. You must be…

MEG   Meg. Karen's friend. Sorry I'm late.

JACK   No problem. I'm glad you came.

MEG   That was a great idea about the book. I spotted you right away. *The Rainbow!*

JACK   Yes. I figured it would be the easiest way to recognize me.

MEG   And it was. I was just worried I'd come over here and there'd be, like, twenty guys reading *The Rainbow*.

JACK   Ah, yes! The D. H. Lawrence convention in town.

MEG Could happen.

JACK So where's Karen?

MEG Well…this is just a little awkward, but…Karen's not coming.

JACK Oh, I…

MEG She got called away for work. There's always someone having a crisis, she said, even on Labor Day, and they're sending her off to, like, Bloomfield or Ridgewood or wherever, which seems a shame, because it's, you know, the one day you're not supposed to work. But she had to. And she said you wouldn't mind. I mean, that it would be okay, if I still came. So I came. Is that okay?

JACK Karen called me this morning. When I asked where she was, I meant, like, Bloomfield or Ridgewood or wherever.

MEG Oh.

JACK So, yes. I was expecting you. I was just wondering where they sent Karen.

MEG Ah. Newark, I think. Lucky Karen.

JACK Well…shall we?

[JACK *motions toward the picnic blanket.*]

MEG Actually…do you mind if we don't sit on the blanket? I have this thing about…ground.

JACK It's…

MEG I know. It's a picnic. It's just…when I was, like, five, I had this traumatic experience at a picnic out by my grandmother's house.

JACK Did it involve ants?

MEG Uncles.

JACK Sorry to hear that.

MEG I'd still like to join you for a picnic, just not with the whole sitting on the ground part.

JACK Well…there's a table over here.

MEG Would you mind?

JACK No. No. It's fine.

[JACK *picks up the knapsack and blanket.*]

MEG Thanks. I really appreciate your…you know…making accommodations. Especially for a crazy woman you've never met before.

JACK You're a friend of Karen's. Besides, there are a lot of people in this world much crazier than you.

[JACK *folds the blanket and drapes it over the table like a tablecloth.*]

MEG Yeah, I know. And I tend to date them all. Hey…that's really nice.

JACK Table for two, *mademoiselle?*

MEG Why thank you, *monsieur.*

JACK [*He opens up the knapsack and takes out some food.*] We have sandwiches. Potato chips. Fruit. And a couple bottles of water. Would you like the turkey or the ham?

MEG Turkey.

JACK Here you are.

MEG Thanks. I feel so rude. I didn't bring anything.

JACK You weren't supposed to. I said I'd take care of it.

MEG [*She starts digging through her purse.*] Still. I should have brought something. You don't even know me.

JACK I didn't know you. But now I do. Your name is Meg, and you like turkey.

MEG Here! I've got dessert. Emergency chocolate.

JACK You keep emergency chocolate in your purse?

MEG Doesn't everyone?

JACK Well…thank you for dessert.

MEG Thank you for the sandwich.

JACK *Bon appétit.*

[*They dig in.*]

MEG Mmm. This is good. What's on it?

JACK Mozzarella cheese, and pesto.

MEG   Pesto! That's a good idea.

JACK   One of those things I just thought I'd try one day, and I liked it.

MEG   I'll have to remember that. Pesto on turkey. You make your own?

JACK   Out of a jar. The pesto. Not the turkey.

MEG   So how do you like *The Rainbow*? Or have you just started?

JACK   I have just started, but I've read it before.

MEG   Really?

JACK   Yeah. It's one of my favorite books, actually.

MEG   I've never read it. What's it about?

JACK   It's about a lot of things really…Men, and women, and love, and sex, and jealousy, and the coming together of people from different parts of the world, and there's marriages, and struggles, and blasphemy, and faith, and this teacher who has a really creepy relationship with one of her students, but then the girl grows up, and all of these people that you've been following, all these different story lines, they all lead up to this one young woman, and you want, you want so badly for her to find happiness, and there's this guy, and you think, yes, this is it, this is happiness, and everything is finally going to work out, and it doesn't, and it can't, and you know that it can't, so she's left alone at the end, and she looks out over the city, and it's hideous, and it's just sprawling its filth all over, and she looks up, and there's this rainbow. And it doesn't make it all okay. But there's this rainbow. And you think…yes…this…is worth it…Life…is worth it.

MEG   You got all that out of a rainbow?

JACK   I have to. Otherwise…why are we here?

MEG   Wow. This picnic just got really sad.

JACK   It's not sad. Well…it is sad. But it's beautiful.

MEG   You know what my favorite book is?

JACK   If you say *Twilight*, I'm taking back the sandwich.

MEG   Nope. Guess.

JACK   I have no idea.

MEG   I'll give you a hint. The eighteenth century.

JACK Really? Written in, or takes place during?

MEG Both.

JACK I don't know, um... *Gulliver's Travels.*

MEG *Candide.* By Voltaire.

JACK *Candide!* Why *Candide?*

MEG It's short.

JACK You like *Candide...* because it's short.

MEG Not just because it's short, but it packs a lot of stuff into something that's really short, and I think that's cool.

JACK Any other reason you like *Candide?*

MEG Yes. You know how in *Candide* there are all these people and they keep meeting each other over and over in different situations?

JACK Yeah.

MEG Well, that's how life should be. Sometimes people have to leave, and move on, and die in an earthquake, or find El Dorado, or whatever, but you should still get to see them again. It's only fair.

JACK Do you think life is fair?

MEG I didn't say life is fair, I said life should be fair. If life were fair, I wouldn't be spending Labor Day having a picnic with a total stranger.

JACK Oh. Sorry.

MEG No. I didn't mean to be offensive or anything. I like you. I mean, I think I like you, but I don't know you. It's a three-day weekend, and it's hot, and I wanted to get away like everybody else. And I couldn't. But then I thought I was going to see Karen, but she had to work. And it's Labor Day! How can you work on a day that's named for work? Okay, so that actually does make sense, but it shouldn't.

JACK I'm sorry you had to spend your Labor Day... with...

MEG No. No, you're great. You made me a sandwich. With pesto.

JACK From a jar.

MEG It's still pesto.

JACK I just thought a picnic... It seemed like a good idea.

MEG It was. And thank you. Thank you for inviting me. Well, okay, technically, it was Karen who invited me, but you didn't uninvite me.

JACK No.

MEG And you could have. I mean, I was crashing your picnic, right? And you probably weren't thrilled about spending Labor Day with a total stranger either. But you did. Choose to. And that was nice of you. Thank you.

JACK It's…nice not to be alone.

MEG But you didn't just move here, did you?

JACK Going on five years.

MEG So you know people. Right? I mean…right?

JACK I had this…relationship. It lasted for a while. And then it didn't. But it was one of those things where…sometimes you spend so much time with one person that…when they're not there anymore…you just don't know what to do. Because sometimes it was really good… and even when it wasn't good…there was still somebody there. But then they're not. Or not as much. And you get lonely. And you realize maybe some of the other relationships in your life…maybe you didn't tend to them as much as you should have. So it was a while ago… but…I guess I'm still getting over her.

MEG I'm sorry. What was her name?

JACK Karen.

MEG Um…not…?

JACK Yeah.

MEG How did I not know this?

JACK It was more than a year ago. It's okay. We're still friends. Things just didn't work out. She works a lot.

MEG I'm so sorry. And you thought you were meeting her.

JACK But just for a picnic. And things have been over for a while. It's not like this was a date.

MEG No! No, this wasn't a date. No. Of course not.

JACK Did you…think this was a date?

MEG No! I mean...not really.

JACK Not...?

MEG Not a date. I just moved here, like, a few months ago, and...I'm still meeting people, and that's probably why Karen invited me, because...I'm trying to meet people. Not just men. Not that I have anything against men. Men...are...nice...to meet. But so are other people. Who aren't men. But the fact that you are...a man...was a bonus. I admit that. But no. Definitely not a date.

JACK Oh. Too bad.

[*He resumes eating his sandwich.*]

MEG Why? Why too bad? Why did you say that?

JACK It's just you're very...

MEG Very...?

JACK Weird. And I like that.

MEG Okay. I've heard better pickup lines. But you made me a sandwich. So I'm going to ignore it.

JACK Ignore...?

MEG The line. Not ignore you. I wouldn't want to...I mean...Is this a date?

JACK It could be. If we wanted it.

MEG Do you want it? That didn't sound right. Or maybe it did. Why can't I talk today?

[*She gets up.*]

JACK Where are you going?

MEG I'm not good at this. I left Cincinnati because I broke up with my boyfriend, which is the only reason I applied for the job to begin with, but I know nobody here, except Karen, because we went to college together, but we weren't even friends in college, and I'm just not very good at this.

JACK [*He gets up.*] Neither am I. I'm awful at this. I'm so bad, I rely on my ex-girlfriend to help me meet people. How pathetic is that?

MEG What a pair...

JACK Look...how about if we say...not a date...but a picnic...and... two people...who maybe...want to get to know each other. Sound good? Shall we...shall we start over?

MEG Um...Jack? You're Jack, right?

JACK Hi there. You must be...

MEG Meg. Sorry I'm late.

JACK No problem. I'm glad you came.

• • •

Subtraction

Kevin McFillen

Subtraction by Kevin McFillen. Copyright © 2014 by Kevin McFillen. All rights reserved. Reprinted by permission of the author.

CAUTION/ADVICE: Professionals and amateurs are hereby warned that performance of *Subtraction* is subject to a royalty. It is fully protected under the copyright laws of the United States of America, and of all countries covered by the International Copyright Union (including the Dominion of Canada and the rest of the British Commonwealth), and of all countries covered by the Pan-American Copyright Convention and the Universal Copyright Convention, the Berne Convention, and of all countries with which the United States has reciprocal copyright relations. All rights, including professional and amateur stage performing rights, motion picture, recitation, lecturing, public reading, radio broadcasting, television, video or sound recording, all other forms of mechanical or electronic reproduction, such as CD-ROM, DVD-ROM, information storage and retrieval systems, and photocopying, and the rights of translation into foreign languages, are strictly reserved. Particular emphasis is placed upon the matter of readings, permission for which must be secured from the author's agent in writing.

Inquiries concerning rights should be addressed to Kevin McFillen at: kmcfillen@aol.com

Kevin McFillen

Kevin McFillen is a playwright and teacher based in Columbia, Missouri. Originally from Bowling Green, Ohio, Kevin received a BA in theater from the College of Wooster, an MA in theater from Miami University, and is currently finishing his PhD in theater at the University of Missouri. He has previously been a national semifinalist for the John Cauble Short Play Award from the Kennedy Center's American College Theatre Festival, and a finalist for the Heideman Award from the Actors Theatre of Louisville. His full-length play *The Sleepers* was recently developed by WordBRIDGE Playwrights Laboratory, and was a semifinalist for the Eugene O'Neill Theatre Center's 2013 National Playwrights Conference. *Subtraction* is McFillen's first published play.

···production history···

Premiere, Warner International Playwrights Festival, Torrington, CT: October 2013

Staged reading, Mizzou New Play Series (University of Missouri): Spring 2012

Concert reading, KCACTF Region V Conference: January 2012 (regional finalist: One-Act Playwriting Competition, national semifinalist: John Cauble Short Play Award)

Workshop reading, Missouri Playwrights Workshop: Fall 2011

characters

WALTER   sixties
MELANIE   late twenties/early thirties, professional-looking

time

Present day.

setting

A quiet city park. A park bench sits center stage.

synopsis

A strange encounter with a woman from the Office of Subtraction, MELANIE, forces WALTER to re-examine what he believes about memory, loss, and the nature of the universe.

[*Lights up.* WALTER *sits on a park bench, feeding pigeons. After a pause, enter* MELANIE *carrying a briefcase.*]

MELANIE   Beautiful day, isn't it?

WALTER   Certainly is. Beautiful.

MELANIE   I used to love feeding pigeons when I was a kid. My mother used to take me.

WALTER   Yeah? She available? She sounds like my type...

MELANIE   No, unfortunately. She's gone now.

WALTER   Sorry to hear that. You want to give it a whirl?

MELANIE Really?

WALTER Sure, sure, sit a spell. Plenty of bread to go around.

[MELANIE *sits.*]

MELANIE Thanks.

[*They sit in silence, feeding the pigeons for several beats.*]
Say, I really hate to ask this...

WALTER Yes? Don't be shy—I'm an open book.

MELANIE Well...You don't remember me, do you?

WALTER Should I?

MELANIE You might, that's why I have to ask...

WALTER Oh...Well, I'm afraid not, no. I'm sorry—my memory, you know—

MELANIE No worries—I just had to check.

WALTER I don't feel old, but sometimes my brain disagrees. A bit embarrassing—

MELANIE No, no, don't be embarrassed at all. Truth be told, I try very hard to be as unmemorable as possible...

[*They share a laugh.*]

WALTER So, where should I remember you from? Were you one of my students?

MELANIE No—

WALTER We haven't met here before, have we?

MELANIE We have, actually.

WALTER Ah—a pigeon-feeding acquaintance?

MELANIE But you really shouldn't remember it, Mr. Mitchell—

WALTER We've probably sat here dozens of times, feeding the birds, shooting the breeze, and I'm totally at a loss.

[WALTER *laughs,* MELANIE *remains silent.*]
My apologies. You have me at a disadvantage at any rate—what's your name?

MELANIE Melanie.

WALTER *Melanie.* Let's start over: Melanie—a pleasure to meet you. I'm Walter.

MELANIE Walter Mitchell, yes—

WALTER That's me!

MELANIE It's nice to meet you, Walter…Again, I guess…

[WALTER *laughs*.]

WALTER So, Melanie, now that we're reacquainted, how did we know each other the first time?

MELANIE Well, I never know how to say this…I'm your caseworker, Mr. Mitchell.

WALTER My what?

MELANIE Your caseworker…

WALTER Is this about the car insurance?—

MELANIE No, Mr. Mitchell—

WALTER I haven't had a claim on, well, anything—not in years—

MELANIE No, Mr. Mitchell, I'm not from an insurance company.

WALTER Oh…Alright. I'm at a bit of a loss then. Are you sure you've got the right guy?

MELANIE Quite sure—

WALTER No offense, Melanie, but I think I would know if I had a *caseworker* for something—

MELANIE Not necessarily—

WALTER Then what's this all about? What do you want?

[*A beat.*]

MELANIE I'm here about your life, Mr. Mitchell.

WALTER *What?*

MELANIE Oh, sorry, that sounded a bit melodramatic, didn't it? No matter how long you work this job, you never really get used to it—

WALTER Are you threatening me?—

MELANIE   No, no, of course not. You—well, you don't remember this, naturally, but you're a sort of a subject—our—well, *my* subject—

WALTER   This is totally ridiculous—you should be *ashamed*, trying to pull this crap on someone! Where are the cameras, hmm? You might as well stop filming now, because I'll never sign a release—

MELANIE   Mr. Mitchell—

WALTER   I know my rights, and I'm not signing anything, so this is all just a big waste of time—

MELANIE   Mr. Mitchell, *please*—

WALTER   [*Beginning to exit.*] Or maybe this is some kind of scam, hmm? Don't bother—I haven't got anything worth stealing. I'm calling the police.

MELANIE   Mr. Mitchell... Walter Mitchell, age sixty-eight. Married, Brenda Mitchell—deceased, complications from colon cancer. One child, Brittany Anne, age thirty-eight. Married, two children, Walter—after his grandfather—age ten, and Stephen, age six—after his father. They reside in Baltimore—

WALTER   Hey—

MELANIE   Would you like me to continue?

WALTER   *Hey!*

MELANIE   Their Social Security numbers, perhaps?—

WALTER   *Stop!*
[*A beat.*]
What do you want? What do you think you can get out of scaring me, huh?

MELANIE   I'm sorry, I didn't mean to scare you, I just... I need you to stay.

WALTER   Stay?

MELANIE   Stay and talk to me, yes.

WALTER   You need to explain yourself.

MELANIE   I'm from the Office of Subtraction, Mr. Mitchell.

WALTER   The *what?*

MELANIE   Office of Subtraction.

WALTER   I don't understand—that doesn't mean anything to me. Is that some kind of government thing?

MELANIE   Not exactly, we … We're the extra-governmental agency charged with balancing the universal equation.

WALTER   What?

MELANIE   We're the extra-governmental—

WALTER   You can say it again, but it's still horseshit! You're wasting my time—

MELANIE   Mr. Mitchell—

WALTER   No! Joke's over—there's no such thing—

MELANIE   I'm afraid there is—

WALTER   Then why haven't I heard about it? If I walked out to the corner and told the guy at the newsstand that I was just talking with someone from the Subtraction Office, and they're the ones that balance the universal, whatever, what would he say, hmm? "Gee, that's nice"?

MELANIE   He wouldn't say anything—

WALTER   Exactly!

MELANIE   Enormous amounts of time and resources are spent to make sure no one knows about the Office of Subtraction, and if Mr. Cornwall had ever been subtracted, he wouldn't remember it anyway—

WALTER   Who?—

MELANIE   Cornwall, Robert J. The man who runs the newsstand.
[*A beat.*]
Walter, I don't need you to believe me, but I do need just a few moments of your time to talk with you, and then you're free to go.

WALTER   You need a good psychiatrist is what you need—

MELANIE   If you say so.

[MELANIE *removes a large file from her briefcase.*]

WALTER   What's that?

MELANIE   Your file.

WALTER All of that is about me?

MELANIE Oh, well, no, it's *your* case file, but it's mostly about your wife—

WALTER *Listen*, you say a *thing* about Brenda and I'll slap that face right off of you, I don't care—

MELANIE I'm not talking about Brenda—

WALTER She's not—what?

MELANIE I'm not talking about Brenda, Mr. Mitchell. I'm actually here about your first wife.

WALTER My *first* wife? Brenda *is* my *first* and *only* wife…

MELANIE You were never married to anyone else?

WALTER What? No!

MELANIE Oh, good!

[MELANIE *makes a note in the file.*]

WALTER Good? What does that mean, "good"?

MELANIE So how much do you recall from high school?

WALTER No—answer my question—what do you mean, "good"? You said you're here about my wife—

MELANIE First wife, yes—

WALTER But I've only been married once—

MELANIE If you say so—

WALTER *No*, I *know* so, to Brenda…

MELANIE Alright. Am I correct then that you wouldn't be opposed to me asking you a few questions *not* about your wife, Brenda?

WALTER This is the stupidest—

MELANIE Please, Mr. Mitchell—

WALTER You said *first* wife, I've only been married once—you want to ask me questions about another wife? A wife I never had?

MELANIE Would you be opposed to it if I said yes? I mean, let's say for a second that that was exactly what I was asking—what would be the harm?

WALTER I don't know, but that's what I'm trying to figure out...

MELANIE I assure you, Mr. Mitchell, no matter what you might think about this encounter, or might think about me personally, I mean you no harm. Quite the opposite, in fact—

WALTER Oh, I can tell—you're a regular guardian angel.

MELANIE If you like.

WALTER Will you answer *my* questions?

MELANIE Questions?

WALTER If, against my better judgment, I sit here and answer your questions, will you answer mine?

MELANIE Well. I don't see why not. What questions do you—

WALTER How do you live with yourself, doing this to people?

MELANIE Please, Mr. Mitchell, serious questions only.

WALTER How is that not a serious question?

MELANIE How much do you recall from high school?

WALTER High school. My *other* wife?

MELANIE As it were, yes.

WALTER Can you be more specific?

MELANIE No, I can't—

WALTER And why is that?

MELANIE It skews the data.

WALTER What data? What are you doing here that you're interested in what an old man did in high school?

MELANIE I already told you, I work for the Office—

WALTER You didn't tell me *anything*—you spout off this *nonsense* about subtraction, the universal, uh, universal—

MELANIE Equation, yes—

WALTER And just what the hell is the universal equation?

MELANIE As far as I understand it, the universal equation solves for everything—

WALTER   Everything?—

MELANIE   Everything. Everything everywhere, yes. It's an equation that describes the behavior of everything we know, big and small—the tiniest particles all the way up to the shape of the universe.

WALTER   I don't believe you.

MELANIE   What?

WALTER   I don't believe you. Explain to me how that's possible—how does an equation tell you about everything everywhere?

MELANIE   I can't.

WALTER   *Can't?*—

MELANIE   I can't. I'm not a mathematician, nor am I a physicist—I can't—

WALTER   So you go around *harassing* people for the sake of something *you don't understand?*

MELANIE   Are you a religious man, Walter?
[*A beat.*]
I'm sorry. That was rude.

WALTER   Does your family know that you do this, this—whatever this is?

MELANIE   No, they think I'm an accountant.

[*After a beat*, WALTER *starts to laugh.* MELANIE *joins in, in spite of herself.*]

WALTER   Look, Melanie, I'm going now, okay?

MELANIE   No, please—

WALTER   I won't call anybody—I'm just going to chalk this whole experience up to stress, sunstroke, something—

MELANIE   Mr. Mitchell—

WALTER   No, I'm going—and I strongly suggest you find a new line of work, whatever it is you do—

MELANIE   What if I gave you something? Something you lost?

WALTER   Whatever you're selling, pretty sure I don't want it—

MELANIE   Your *other* wife?

WALTER   Now I *am* going to call the police—

MELANIE   Melody. Melody Michaels.
[*A beat.*]
Does that name mean anything to you?

WALTER   Never heard of her—

[WALTER *begins to exit.*]

MELANIE   Michaels was before you two married, then it was Mitchell, of course. Sort of silly either way—sounds like a stripper name…
[WALTER *stops.*]
The alliteration. It became Roberts after she remarried.
[*A beat.*]
It's a strange feeling, isn't it? Realizing that you lost someone like that? I've never been subtracted myself, but our families are when we take the job. An unfortunate necessity—

WALTER   It's not possible…

MELANIE   Sure it is—people lose things all the time—where you parked the car, what your PIN number is—

WALTER   But you can't…You can't just lose a *person!*

MELANIE   What do you remember from high school, Walter?

WALTER   You did something to me—

MELANIE   I haven't done a thing—

WALTER   That name—I have this picture in my head…you did *something*, hypnotized me, or…*What did you do?*

MELANIE   Please, Mr. Mitchell, I need you to calm down—

WALTER   *TELL ME WHAT YOU DID!*

MELANIE   NOTHING! I didn't do *anything*…

WALTER   If you didn't do this, then how did this happen? There was nothing—*nothing*—and then you said that name, and now…You said you subtracted me—

MELANIE   I said I was your *caseworker*, I don't subtract anything. I do my best to manage the *effects* of your subtraction—

WALTER   So *how?*

MELANIE How?

WALTER *How—yes—how?* How did this happen?

MELANIE Well, it's the universe—

WALTER The universe?

MELANIE Making space, yes—

WALTER *Space?* Outer space?

MELANIE *Room*, I should say, not *space*. It's the universe making *room* for other things—

WALTER That's bullshit—the universe is infinite! Every schoolkid knows that!

MELANIE Maybe so, but the stuff in it is *not*—

WALTER *What?*

MELANIE Energy—resources—materials—what do you think planets are made of? Stars? People? Our universe is very, very big, but there's only so much matter out there—only so much to go around—

WALTER This woman was *taken* from me?

MELANIE In a manner of speaking, yes, she was taken away from you, but not by me—

WALTER So she was, what, *abducted?* This is an alien thing?
[*After a beat*, MELANIE *starts laughing.*]
What the hell is so funny?

MELANIE [*Still laughing.*] I'm so sorry—

WALTER *What's funny?*

MELANIE I'm sorry, Mr. Mitchell, this is a very difficult situation—for both of us—

WALTER You? How is this difficult for you? You come out of nowhere, you feed me this ridiculous story, you gas me, or hypnotize me, or—
[MELANIE *begins laughing again.*]
WHAT THE HELL IS SO FUNNY!?

MELANIE I'm sorry, you remind me—

WALTER *What? Of what?*

MELANIE Of my father, that's all.

WALTER Yeah? I bet he's real proud...

MELANIE He was, yes. I'd like to think he still is in his own way.
[*A beat.*]
The problem with the universe, Mr. Mitchell—as far as we
understand it—is us. Everything we know about the universal
equation says that it should be zero-sum. Balanced. Everything comes
from somewhere, right, nothing created, nothing lost? It never quite
works out. We like to try to change things around ourselves. Free will
and all that—

WALTER And what the hell does that have to do with me?

MELANIE Melody—

WALTER What *about* Melody? You said she was my wife—

MELANIE Yes, but she was taken away—a variable removed to help
balance the equation, as it were—

WALTER That's impossible—*impossible!*

MELANIE Why impossible?

WALTER People don't just disappear, that's why! People go missing—
things go missing—that doesn't mean they, what, blink out of the
world? There are traces, signs—things left behind!

MELANIE Yes—there are always bits left behind—

WALTER Photos, documents—

MELANIE Memories, associations—yes, all correct, and that's what the
Office of Subtraction tries to manage. People leave behind a very big
footprint.

WALTER So you, what, help make these people disappear? Sucked up by
the universe?

MELANIE We try to help clean up the mess, that's all. The universe is
going to try to balance itself whether we like it or not—

WALTER So where is she?

MELANIE Where?

WALTER *Melody*—where? Where is she? Dead?

MELANIE   *No*, not dead, just—

WALTER   *Just?* Just what!?

MELANIE   Gone—removed—*reassigned*—

WALTER   *Reassigned?*

MELANIE   Reassigned, yes.

WALTER   What does that mean, reassigned?

MELANIE   It means that she's not *gone*, not *dead*—she's just gone from *you*, from *your* life. You never met, never knew her, never married…

[*A beat.*]

WALTER   [*Quietly.*] That's not possible…

MELANIE   Walter, I have been meeting you here once a week for over a year—

WALTER   No—

MELANIE   I have been meeting you here, this park, this bench—

WALTER   No, no, no—

MELANIE   [*Continues.*] To help you forget about a woman named Melody, a woman who was once important to you, but she has a new life now—a life that, as far as she remembers, never included you. And I'm telling you this now confident that when I leave here, all memory of this ordeal, and what little bit you have left of her, will be coming with me. That's just the way it works.

[*A beat.*]

WALTER   Am I losing my mind?

MELANIE   Hardly, Mr. Mitchell.

WALTER   You expect me to believe all this garbage—why should I believe in any of it?

MELANIE   Why don't you tell me what you remember?

WALTER   I could be on my bathroom floor right now, head dented in from slipping and hitting the corner of the sink—

MELANIE   It's entirely possible, yes—

WALTER   I could be lying in the hospital, tubes everywhere—

MELANIE   Then what difference would it make if you just told me what you remembered? If you don't believe anything I've said, then it shouldn't matter...

WALTER   I can't—

MELANIE   Why not?

WALTER   Because I'm afraid of what it means if you *are* telling the truth.
[*A beat.*]
Why me? Why *her*?

MELANIE   Think of all of the stuff in the universe like a big birthday cake. Some people take bigger pieces, some take smaller, but all the pieces put together still make just one cake, okay? If all the pieces are gone, and someone out there wants more than what they have, it means someone else's piece has to get smaller. You and Melody weren't singled out, you're not being punished, it's just...someone needs a bigger piece, Mr. Mitchell.

WALTER   Who? Who is this person?

MELANIE   There's no way of knowing for sure. It might not be a person at all. Could be an interstate bypass, could be a new star being born...

WALTER   And if I tell you what you want to know, then I won't remember any of this? What's left of her will be gone?

MELANIE   That's the way it's supposed to work, but memory is very complex. Lots of different kinds of memory, associations. It takes a great deal of time to remove all of them, and just when you think a case is settled, something comes popping back.

[*A beat.*]

WALTER   I remember...

MELANIE   Yes?

WALTER   No, nothing—

MELANIE   *Please*, Mr. Mitchell—

WALTER   I can't do this—

MELANIE   *Why?*

WALTER   I don't know if I'm more bothered by what I have rattling around in my head, or what it means when it's gone—when *she's* gone . . .

MELANIE She's in no danger, Walter, but she is out of your life. I just want to help you let her go...

WALTER Was my piece really so big? Did I have so much?

MELANIE I couldn't say.

WALTER What happens if I remember the wrong thing?

MELANIE Wrong thing?

WALTER If I spout off something by accident—something that doesn't have anything to do with her? *Christ*, what about *Brenda*, Brittany's *kids*—

MELANIE It doesn't work like that, Mr. Mitchell, I'm only here about your wife—

WALTER *Melody*—

MELANIE Melody, yes.

WALTER A few minutes ago I didn't remember she even existed, and now you want me to let her go...
[*A beat.*]
What if I refuse?

MELANIE If you refuse. If you refuse, I walk away and we have to start this process over from the beginning...

[MELANIE *begins to repack her briefcase.*]

WALTER What? That's it?

MELANIE What did you expect?

WALTER I don't know...I guess something epic—Jacob wrestling the angel—

MELANIE Sorry to disappoint. Is that your choice then?

WALTER Have people refused to cooperate before?

MELANIE Of course. It's an unfortunate waste of time, but yes.

WALTER And what happened to them? Do they get disappeared? *Reassigned?*

MELANIE No need. Eventually they give in—

WALTER *All of them?*

MELANIE   Of course, *all of them*, yes. You can delay the inevitable for a time, but that's what it is—inevitable. How many times do you think *you've* given in? I'm sorry, Walter, but you're no Jacob, and I'm no angel…

WALTER   Funny—you said you were—

MELANIE   *You* said that, not me. I don't believe in angels. Well, I can't say it was nice to see you again this time, Walter, but I'll be seeing you again shortly—

[MELANIE *begins to exit.*]

WALTER   Wait, wait, wait—

MELANIE   I do have other appointments, Mr. Mitchell—

WALTER   You're seriously just going to walk away?

MELANIE   I don't see an alternative.

WALTER   What about everything you've told me?

MELANIE   Gone—

WALTER   *Gone?*

MELANIE   Well, mostly gone. There will be a few new associations I'll have to root out—

WALTER   Everything will be gone?

MELANIE   Mostly gone—

WALTER   My wife?—

MELANIE   Melody?

WALTER   Yes, dammit, Melody!

MELANIE   Gone. Mostly. If she were all gone, I wouldn't be here.

WALTER   I lose her either way?

[*A beat.*]

MELANIE   I'm sorry, Walter. I really am. But you already lost her, you know. I'm just here to help clean up.
[WALTER *cries.*]
But that's life! We lose people—sometimes people die, accidents—

WALTER It is *not* the same thing!

MELANIE It is—

WALTER *It is NOT the same thing!*

MELANIE How is it different?

WALTER Because when people die, you *mourn*! You *remember* them!

MELANIE You would rather live with grief? Melody isn't grieving. She doesn't know who you are... Walter, please. Just talk to me. Please.

[*A beat.*]

WALTER I remember... *God*—what am I even supposed to be *remembering*?

MELANIE Please, Walter, just try. What did you see when you heard her name?

WALTER Just a picture, like a photo...

MELANIE Can you still see it?

WALTER Yes, but—

MELANIE Tell me what it was—start there.

WALTER [*Closes his eyes.*] A girl, maybe sixteen...

MELANIE Go on—

WALTER Dark hair, a blue dress... Her face is round, full. She has this little half-smile, like she's keeping something secret. God, she's beautiful... How did I forget her eyes? Her eyes are so dark... Her hair, everything, is just a frame for those eyes... You have eyes like your mother's...

[WALTER *slowly opens his eyes, considers* MELANIE.]

MELANIE I'm sorry?

WALTER You... she looks like you—why?

MELANIE You're clearly mistaken, Mr. Mitchell, how could I—

WALTER *Why?* Why does she—

MELANIE STOP. You don't know what you're saying... Look, Walter—

WALTER Oh God, I remember... How could I—

MELANIE [*Quickly repacking her briefcase.*] I think that's enough for today, Mr. Mitchell—you're forming an association between me and this memory, that's all—

WALTER I forgot you—

MELANIE You forget me all the time, Mr. Mitchell, but whatever you're remembering now—

WALTER My little girl, Melanie—

MELANIE *Is not real*, okay? We've gone too far—you're reaching out, trying to make sense of this memory being reintroduced, and you're placing me in it—

WALTER No—

MELANIE I'm going, Walter—

WALTER *No*, please, Mel—

MELANIE This was a mistake, I was just impatient, trying to close your case—

WALTER Please, don't go. *Mel*—

MELANIE Don't *CALL* me that! No one calls me that!

WALTER I called you that.

[*A beat.*]

MELANIE I'm going, Mr. Mitchell. As soon as I'm gone, your memory will start to reset. You'll feel disoriented at first, but don't worry—it will be over in a few moments—

WALTER Mel, please, *stay*—

MELANIE Good-bye, Walter, I'll see you again soon—

[MELANIE *begins to exit.*]

WALTER You look so much like your mother…

    [MELANIE *stops.*]

    I didn't—couldn't…We were so *young* when we got married…Your mom and I—we weren't even out of high school yet, she had to change the date on her birth certificate so they'd give us the marriage license…Our parents found out, it was annulled, we weren't allowed to see each other after that…

[*A beat.*]

It was probably twenty-five years before I saw your mom again, and Brenda was so *sick*, and then...she died. Brenda died, and it was just me and the baby, Brittany—

MELANIE Mr. Mitchell—

WALTER We didn't mean for it to happen—Brittany was about eight when you were born. For some reason we didn't think we could have children, both of us pushing forty—can you imagine? We felt so old...But then there you were—

MELANIE [*Beginning to cry.*] Walter, *STOP, please...*

WALTER Mel, I don't understand all this, how did this happen? What's going on?

MELANIE I *told* you, when you take the job, your family has to be subtracted, okay?

WALTER *You* did this?

MELANIE *Did this?* You think this is what I *wanted?*

WALTER If you knew this was part of the job, how could you take it?

MELANIE I wanted to *help* people...Do you have *any idea* how many people I've helped? People who have lost husbands, wives, sisters, friends, *children?* Imagine walking past a child's bedroom for a child you don't remember—pictures on the wall, faces you almost recognize—*THAT'S* what we do, *that's* what we protect people from...

[MELANIE *cries,* WALTER *moves to embrace her.*]

DON'T.

[*A beat.* MELANIE *collects herself.*]

Look, Mr. Mitchell—

WALTER [*Quietly.*] Don't call me that—

MELANIE Well, what am I supposed to call you—*Dad?* In a few minutes you won't remember who I am...

WALTER So what do we do? How do we fight this?

MELANIE You don't.

WALTER There *has* to be a way! We find out why this happened, what we're making room for, right—and we, we—

MELANIE [*Quietly.*] You're making room for me...

WALTER What?

MELANIE It's me—I take up too much room now, I'm the one...I know too much. When we start the job, we have to subtract our families— that's the price we pay for remembering, *everything*...God, we get so hung up on the things we forget, but I promise you, it's much, much worse to remember.
[MELANIE *laughs weakly.*]
This was supposed to be your last session, you know? Just one more session and I was supposed to be out of your life...No matter what my clients go through, I leave, and they forget—whatever they're carrying, that burden leaves with me, and this...I have left you here so many times, Walter, but you just keep hanging on...

[WALTER *sits. A beat.*]

WALTER I hated keeping you a secret—from Brittany, from everyone. I loved you, loved your mother *so much*...We were so scared of what people would say—Brenda's family, your mom's husband...I hated that he could be there with you whenever he wanted.

[MELANIE *sits, takes* WALTER'*s hand.*]

MELANIE Do you remember, when I was little, Mom used to take me here, to the park. We used to sit here, this bench—I'd play, or splash in the fountain by the square, and pretty soon, this nice man would show up, and we'd feed the pigeons...You'd hold my hand, and tell me stories, and sometimes I'd play with the other kids, and I'd see you sitting there, with your arm around Mom. You both looked so happy...
[MELANIE *lets go of* WALTER'*s hand.*]
You have to let me go, Dad...

WALTER But I feel like I just found you—

MELANIE I know...Life's not fair sometimes.

WALTER So I won't remember you again? Won't remember your mom?

MELANIE No, you won't. Not much, at least. I'll have to come back for the rest.

[MELANIE *stands and collects her briefcase.*]

WALTER Mel?

MELANIE Yes?

WALTER I'm so *proud* of you, Mel. I love you, so much.

MELANIE I know, Dad. I love you too.

[MELANIE *exits. A few beats pass.* WALTER *slowly resumes feeding the pigeons. A beat.* MELANIE *enters.*]

WALTER Beautiful day.

MELANIE Certainly is. Beautiful. Do you mind if I sit with you?

WALTER No, not at all—grab some bread if you want.

MELANIE Thanks.

[MELANIE *and* WALTER *feed the pigeons for several beats. Lights fade to blackout.*]

• • •

Flare

Edith Freni

Flare by Edith Freni. Copyright © 2014 by Edith Freni. All rights reserved. Reprinted by permission of the author.

CAUTION/ADVICE: Professionals and amateurs are hereby warned that performance of *Flare* is subject to a royalty. It is fully protected under the copyright laws of the United States of America, and of all countries covered by the International Copyright Union (including the Dominion of Canada and the rest of the British Commonwealth), and of all countries covered by the Pan-American Copyright Convention and the Universal Copyright Convention, the Berne Convention, and of all countries with which the United States has reciprocal copyright relations. All rights, including professional and amateur stage performing rights, motion picture, recitation, lecturing, public reading, radio broadcasting, television, video or sound recording, all other forms of mechanical or electronic reproduction, such as CD-ROM, DVD-ROM, information storage and retrieval systems, and photocopying, and the rights of translation into foreign languages, are strictly reserved. Particular emphasis is placed upon the matter of readings, permission for which must be secured from the author's agent in writing.

Inquiries concerning rights should be addressed to Ron Gwiazda, Abrams Artists Agency, 275 Seventh Ave. 26th Floor, New York, NY 10001. 646-461-9325 (tel), 646-486-0100 (fax), ron.gwiazda@abramsartny.com.

Edith Freni

Edith Freni holds both her BFA and MFA from NYU's Department of Dramatic Writing, where she was the recipient of a Goldberg Playwriting Fellowship and the Harry Kondoleon Graduate Playwriting Award. Her work has been produced, developed, and read at numerous professional theatrical institutions, including Steppenwolf Theatre Company, New York Theatre Workshop, LAByrinth Theatre Company, the Public Theatre, the Williamstown Theatre Festival, Ensemble Studio Theater, PS 122, Partial Comfort Productions, the McCarter Theatre, and the Lark, among many others. Edith is a two-time nominee for the prestigious PONY Award, has been a finalist for the Jerome Fellowship and the Heideman Award, and was a semi-finalist for the 2013 O'Neill Playwrights Conference. Her play *Total Power of Exchange* was nominated by New York Theatre Workshop for the New American Plays for Russia Initiative, co-sponsored by the Center for International Theatre Development and the U.S. Embassy in Moscow. *Total Power of Exchange* is a current nominee for the 2014 L. Arnold Weissberger Award for Playwriting. She is a former member of the emerging playwrights group Youngblood and a member of Obie Award–winning Partial Comfort Productions. Edith is currently at work on commissions for Steppenwolf Theatre Company and the University of Miami, where she has been on faculty since 2010. She is a former competitive amateur boxer and a dedicated age-grouper triathlete. She currently lives under a canopy of avocado trees in Coconut Grove, Florida.

···production history···

Flare premiered on May 17, 2013, in the 11th Annual 7th Inning Stretch: 7 10-minute plays about baseball at Mile Square Theatre in Hoboken, New Jersey. Chris O'Connor, artistic director.

PASSENGER Jen Ring

PILOT Elia Ganias

Directed by Joseph Gallo

Lighting by Jeff Carr

Costumes by Victoria DePew

Set by Jen Price Fick

Projections by Amith Chandrashaker

characters

PASSENGER a woman in her thirties. A very bad flier but a semi-decent human being.

PILOT a man in his forties, an airline pilot. A very good flier. Also a semi-decent human.

setting

A two-seater row on a somewhat empty commercial aircraft. Night flight from New York to Miami.

time

None like the present.

[*A row of seats on a jet plane. A* PASSENGER *(thirties) sits next to a* PILOT *(forties). Not the pilot. Just a pilot. Obviously the pilot is flying the plane and this guy is not. He is, however, wearing his pilot's uniform. He's handsome in the way of most pilots. She is pretty in the way of most women. However, she is very obviously nervous and trying desperately to hide it.*]

PASSENGER I just decided, after several years of trying to become someone I am not, that it wasn't worth it anymore.

PILOT Well, yeah, no, that's never a good idea.

PASSENGER   And I'm not a pill popper on like a daily basis or anything but in this regard I just decided the pros outweighed the cons. I take half a pill. It's like .05 milligrams.

PILOT   Does it work?

[*Big bump.*]

PASSENGER   Jesus-H-mother-fucking Christ.

PILOT   Maybe you should think about taking the whole pill.

PASSENGER   Maybe.

PILOT   Or you could just, you know, do a little research.

PASSENGER   Into?

PILOT   The science of things. How things work.

PASSENGER   Oh no, no, no, I couldn't do that. I don't have that kind of mind. And then also, it just becomes too real.

[*Bump. She clutches the seat. Tries to breathe.*]

PILOT   What exactly do you think is going to happen?

PASSENGER   Exactly? I think exactly that the plane will fall out of the sky.

PILOT   It won't.

PASSENGER   They have.

PILOT   Not really.

PASSENGER   A plane has never fallen out of the sky? Why am I saying these words right now?

PILOT   Planes don't just *fall* out of the sky. Is what I'm saying. Certainly there have been plane crashes over the years but it's never about the plane just falling.

PASSENGER   What about flight 800? That flight from New York to France. That plane exploded and fell out of the fucking sky.

PILOT   Is that really necessary? There are kids right behind us.

PASSENGER   Fuck me, planes with kids like always crash!

PILOT   There is no data to support that.

PASSENGER   And what about the Miracle on the Hudson? A bird gets caught in the engine? *Really?*

PILOT   Everyone survived. Including that baby.

[*Bump.*]

PASSENGER   Hey can I hold your hand?

PILOT   You don't need to hold my hand.

PASSENGER   Maybe not but I want to.

PILOT   It's never about the plane just dropping. It's almost always a matter of several small but important mistakes made by several people. And those mistakes add up to one big cataclysmic event.

PASSENGER   Are you really not going to let me hold your hand?

PILOT   It bothers me that you don't understand how this works.

PASSENGER   I hope you know that I have great respect for what you do. I mean, you're responsible for keeping me alive.

PILOT   Not just me. At least a dozen people have been tasked with keeping you alive. That's why this works. That's why flying is amazingly safe. Because each person does his or her job.

PASSENGER   But what if someone messes up?

PILOT   That's the thing, though. If one person doesn't do his job correctly, the plane still doesn't go down. It takes at least eight or nine of the dozen people to screw up on the same day, same flight, same plane, to create even the remotest chance of a crash.

PASSENGER   Like a baseball game.

PILOT   Sort of. Not really.

PASSENGER   I went to see the Yankees play the Sox on Saturday.

PILOT   Oh, well, *that* game, yes.

PASSENGER   Several small but important mistakes made by several people. People who generally, at least this season, have not been making those mistakes. And yet, on Saturday, that one day, they made them. In spades.

PILOT   Nobody died.

PASSENGER You don't know that.

PILOT Nobody died because of the game.

PASSENGER You don't know that.

PILOT Two hundred people did not die because the Yanks lost to the Red Sox on a Saturday afternoon.

PASSENGER They didn't just lose. They were obliterated. Did you watch it?

PILOT Some of it. I turned it off after the bottom sixth.

PASSENGER I never walk away. No matter how bad it looks. I have to watch the whole thing play out.

PILOT I'll be honest I walked away from the season because of Jeter.

PASSENGER I miss him so much.

PILOT But even if he'd played—

PASSENGER Don't say it.

PILOT No, listen, to follow through with your plane analogy. Jeter couldn't have saved that game by himself any more than he could have won it by himself.

PASSENGER Still. It feels like the end of something.

[*Bump with a weird sound.*]

PASSENGER Oh my God oh my God oh my God. What was that sound?

PILOT It was nothing.

PASSENGER It was. It was like a pop. Don't tell me you didn't hear that sound like something…popped. It could be the engine.

PILOT The engine doesn't pop. And even if, let's say this plane lost an engine right now—

PASSENGER Let's not—

PILOT If it lost an engine, the pilot could continue for the rest of the flight.

PASSENGER If it lost both?

PILOT Could continue long enough to land safely.

PASSENGER Seriously?

PILOT It would not be the ideal scenario but a proficient pilot—

PASSENGER What if I have a shitty pilot? Or a pilot who didn't get enough sleep the night before?

PILOT That's why there are two of them.

PASSENGER Or *two* pilots who didn't get enough sleep the night before. Or two pilots who are sleeping together and that causes this insane tension between them and it, like, plays out over the course of the—

PILOT Do you want to die?

PASSENGER NO! I very much do not want to die.

PILOT Well, you're going to.

[*Long pause.*]

PASSENGER I know that. I'm not stupid.

PILOT You have a better chance of being elected president of the United States than you do of dying in a plane crash. That is a true statistic.

PASSENGER Are you married?

PILOT [*Beat.*] Yes.

PASSENGER Why did you pause?

PILOT You caught me off guard with the question.

PASSENGER Do you have kids?

PILOT Are you hitting on me?

PASSENGER I just asked if you...where the hell did you get that?

PILOT This line of questioning / you're getting personal. You wanted to hold my hand.

PASSENGER What? I'm. No. We're just...you're a stranger and we're talking about some deep shit. Maybe something's happening here but it doesn't have to be sexual. Are *you* hitting on *me*?

PILOT No.

[*Pause. She looks a little hurt.*]

PASSENGER Do you have two families? Because I've heard that about pilots.

PILOT I don't have two families. I have one family.

PASSENGER In Miami or—

PILOT New York. Upstate.

PASSENGER But you spend a lot of time in Miami.

PILOT Half and half.

PASSENGER Is it hard for you? To be away from them?

PILOT Of course it is.

PASSENGER Why would you choose this career if you also want to have a family?

PILOT It's my right to have a family.

PASSENGER It's not your right to have kids who grow up never knowing their father.

PILOT My kids know me. They spend ample time with me.

PASSENGER Fifty percent of the time. Do they even recognize you when you come through the door? Do you think they like you?

PILOT They love me; I'm their dad.

PASSENGER You think they love you *because* you're their dad.

PILOT That's not what I said. What are you—I swear to God. Every time. Every *time*. Every damned time I fly off duty, I get seated next to the nervous flyer and they look at me, in my uniform and they expect me to make them feel better. So I listen to what they have to say and I answer some technical questions and I smile a lot, try to make them feel comfortable but you know what, I've learned something. About the people who are bothered by flying.

PASSENGER And what's that?

PILOT They tend to be assholes. And you take the cake, my dear. You are the worst flyer I have ever encountered. *Ever.*

PASSENGER And you're a middle-aged airline pilot who doesn't love his family and won't hold a poor girl's hand.

PILOT I love my family.

PASSENGER And I'm on the plane aren't I? I managed to get myself *on* the plane. I'm not crying or hyperventilating or screaming.

PILOT Why did you fly to New York for a baseball game?

PASSENGER Because I don't think the Marlins should exist.

PILOT Yeah but if this is such torture for you—being up in the air.

PASSENGER I did it for a man. Is that what you want to hear? Back off.

[*She turns towards the window. Pulls down the shade. Fumes.*]

PILOT I was just asking a simple question.

PASSENGER My dad is sick. No, my dad is dying. He will likely be dead in a couple of weeks if not sooner.

PILOT I'm sorry.

PASSENGER Don't be. It's a long time coming and he doesn't even know who I am anymore, so…It's something we used to do together. It's the only thing we did together. Go to baseball games. So I thought…my God this is so fucking stupid.

PILOT Why do you do that? This is a nice thing that you're talking about and then you go ahead and say that it's stupid. Just be sincere. You love your father.

PASSENGER Yeah but maybe I shouldn't.

PILOT Of course you should.

PASSENGER You don't know him. You don't know what kind of man he is.

PILOT It doesn't matter what kind of man he is. He's your father. You're scared that he's going to die; you flew home to take him to a baseball game. There's nothing—

PASSENGER He *is* going to die.

PILOT —stupid about that.

PASSENGER I was just really hoping the Yanks would win.

[*Beat.*]

PILOT I'm sorry I called you an asshole.

PASSENGER You didn't really. And I am one, so...

PILOT I'm sure that's not true.

PASSENGER My father is a Red Sox fan. Die-hard. Born and raised in Boston. The fact that he's gonna die in New York makes him crazy, I can tell. And yet I get this weird satisfaction...Last game he's ever gonna see. I wanted his team to lose.

[*She relaxes a bit. He does as well. They both sit back in their chairs.*]

PILOT I have a Colombian girlfriend. She lives in Kendal and has ass implants. And breast implants, actually. And she had this procedure where they sculpted a six-pack onto her.

[*She looks at him.*]

PASSENGER That's disgusting.

PILOT She looks really good, though. Really good.

[*Beat.*]

PASSENGER Do you pay her bills?

[*He looks at her. Shrugs. She turns away from him again. Somehow disappointed. She rests her head on the seat back. Looks up.*]

PASSENGER I hate Miami.
[*Beat.*]
It's a terrible sports town.

PILOT Not for basketball fans.

PASSENGER Miami sucks for sports specifically because of the Marlins! Because of Jeffrey Loria, who is literally stealing from me. Stealing my money to build this new stadium, stealing from me to fill it with $140 million dollars worth of crap free agents who don't know how to win games and don't need to because as quickly as they come, they go. They're gone. And nobody cares! The fans don't. Loria doesn't. The city of Miami doesn't. Everyone's too busy eating Joe's stone crabs and then drinking raw sea turtle eggs at Nikki beach off the tits of Brazilian volleyball models who balance mangos on their heads while dancing salsa in platform stilettos and triathlon wetsuits. It's absurd.

PILOT [*Beat.*] What?

PASSENGER It's a terrible, terrible place to live. To be a fan. Especially when you grew up somewhere like New York. Where people live and die by this shit. In the '90s. In the late '90s. I graduated from high school during Jeter's rookie year. That does something to a person. People live or die. Do you understand me?

[*Beat.*]

Sometimes it's like, it's like the only thing you have to talk about with a person. You meet a stranger and you don't know them but you can talk about baseball.

[*Beat.*]

I think my pill is kicking in.

PILOT Let it.

[*She looks drowsy. Her eyelids are getting heavy.*]

PASSENGER I'm gonna.

PILOT Just go with it.

PASSENGER I'm going.

PILOT Relax. I'll wake you when we land.

PASSENGER Thank you.

[*She closes her eyes. Her head drops down onto his shoulder. He takes her hand. Blackout.*]

• • •

Blue, Blue Moon

John Patrick Bray

Blue, Blue Moon by John Patrick Bray. Copyright © 2014 by John Patrick Bray. All rights reserved. Reprinted by permission of the author.

CAUTION/ADVICE: Professionals and amateurs are hereby warned that performance of *Blue, Blue Moon* is subject to a royalty. It is fully protected under the copyright laws of the United States of America, and of all countries covered by the International Copyright Union (including the Dominion of Canada and the rest of the British Commonwealth), and of all countries covered by the Pan-American Copyright Convention and the Universal Copyright Convention, the Berne Convention, and of all countries with which the United States has reciprocal copyright relations. All rights, including professional and amateur stage performing rights, motion picture, recitation, lecturing, public reading, radio broadcasting, television, video or sound recording, all other forms of mechanical or electronic reproduction, such as CD-ROM, DVD-ROM, information storage and retrieval systems, and photocopying, and the rights of translation into foreign languages, are strictly reserved. Particular emphasis is placed upon the matter of readings, permission for which must be secured from the author's agent in writing.

Inquiries concerning rights should be addressed to: JohnPatrickBray@yahoo.com

John Patrick Bray

John Patrick Bray (PhD, theater, LSU; MFA, playwriting, the New School for Drama/Actors Studio Drama School) has written plays under grants from the National Endowment for the Arts and the Acadiana Center for the Arts, and he has earned commissions from organizations in Louisiana and Off-Off Broadway. He is a member and moderator of the Athens Playwrights' Workshop, and has previously been resident writer and literary manager for the Rising Sun Performance Company in NYC, a finalist for the 2013 Ingram Play Lab at Tennessee Repertory Theatre, and a finalist for the 2010 Playwriting Residency at the Hangar Theatre. Bray's works have been produced Off-Off Broadway (including productions with the Samuel French Off-Off Broadway Festival and Planet Connections Theatre Festivity, and the Strawberry One-Act Festival), and in venues around the country. Bray's plays have been developed with a number of organizations, including the Actors Studio, the Platform Group, EndTimes Bunker, Epic Rep. Theatre at the Players' Club and the Last Frontier Theatre Conference in Valdez, Alaska. Most recently, his play *Donkey* was read as part of the Dramatists Guild of America, Inc.'s Friday Night Footlights-Atlanta Style. His works are published with Next Stage Press, Indie Theatre Now, the Riant Theatre, JACPublishing, and Heartland Plays, Inc. Additionally, Bray has a one-act play published in *The Best American Short Plays 2010–2011* (Applause Theatre & Cinema Books) and a monologue published in *The 2011 Best Women's Stage Scenes and Monologues* (Smith and Kraus). Originally from upstate New York, John is a lecturer in the Department of Theatre and Film Studies at the University of Georgia. Visit: www.johnpatrickbray.webs.com

···production history···

Blue, Blue Moon was the first-place winner of Rough Magic Shakespeare's 2012 Bag of Tricks! Festival. The play received its world premiere as part of the GOOD Works Theatre Festival at the GOOD Acting Studio in Marietta, Georgia. The production was directed by Emma K. Harr, and featured the following cast:

JANINE   Laura E. Meyers

GREGORY   Ralph Del Rosario

LITTLE GREG   Sean Fife

VOICE OF LITTLE JANINE   Sky Cameron Johnson

Production Stage Manager: Jim Walsh

Costume Design: Emma K. Harr

Lighting Design and Set Design: Robert Drake

Produced by Michael M. Good

characters

JANINE   twenties–thirties, a city gal

GREGORY   twenties–thirties, her brother

LITTLE BOY   about eight–ten

LITTLE JANINE   about eight–ten, an offstage voice

[*Note:* LITTLE JANINE *may appear if the director so chooses.*]

setting

The woods near a campfire. Not too long ago.

synopsis

"Remember when Dad took us to the woods once when we were kids? Where we proved to him once and for all we were destined to be city folk, and…there might have been an alien…and a wolfman…or something worse? It was all part of our imagination, but…wait…wh…what was that sound?"

A brother and sister bring the cremains of their father to the woods, on a dark night with a full moon, only to discover their younger selves playing tricks.

[*Night. A blue moon. A campfire. A couple of sleeping bags. An urn holding someone's cremains.* JANINE *and* GREGORY *are discovered. They are cold, and have been here for a little while. Neither one are used to the "great outdoors," though their flannel shirts suggest they are trying to make a go of it.* JANINE *looks at* GREGORY, *as if waiting for an answer.* GREGORY *looks away.*]

JANINE Oh, come on, Gregory.

[*Pause.*]

You don't think this is a good way to…you know?

GREGORY It's cold. I'm cold.

JANINE Well, sit a little closer. I brought s'mores!

GREGORY You want me to find sticks?

[*She pulls out a box of packaged/industrially made s'mores. She opens one. He reacts.*]

JANINE In the morning, we'll climb to the overlook. Scatter his ashes.

GREGORY Then what?

JANINE You know. Closure.

GREGORY Ah.

[*Pause.*]

JANINE He said he always wanted to come back with us when we were a bit older. When we weren't so scared.

GREGORY There was plenty to be scared of.

JANINE Bugs. And the Wolfman. Remember?

GREGORY [*Beat.*] I remember.

JANINE Kids' stuff. My mind was playing tricks on me.

[*Beat.*]

It was a blue moon like this. I guess awful stuff comes out in a blue moon, doesn't it?

GREGORY Maybe it does.

[*Beat.*]

You didn't come all the way up here to scare me, did you?

JANINE Am I so juvenile?

GREGORY No.

[*Beat.*]

Yes.

JANINE It was a blue moon like this one. You, me, Dad. S'mores. Real s'mores, not, you know.

[*Indicates box.*]

So there I am, looking out at the moon. Walking around. I'm supposed to look for sticks, but that moon. It doesn't seem right. "Blue moon," that's just an expression but...it does look blue to me. And somehow, two-dimensional, like I can just pluck it out of the sky, and it would be like a coin of paper. The world gets funny, it shifts, and there's a rustle...I see its fur...wouldn't have been so...I mean, I've seen bears, wolves, mountain lions...but then I see its shirt, Gregory.

GREGORY Probably a mountain man.

JANINE No...I see its ears. Pointed. It has blue jeans, and big shaggy hands. So I freeze...and wait...it moves away from me. It looks like it's going to attack something...a neighboring camp. That's when I race out and scream—

GREGORY WOLFMAN! WOLFMAN!

JANINE And the creepiest thing—the next day, we go back and...

GREGORY No one's there. Just this urn.

JANINE Can you let me tell the story? I was about to get melodramatic.

GREGORY Okay, sorry.

JANINE Right.

[*Melodramatic.*]

There was no one there. Just the urn, which we now carry, containing Dad's cremains.

GREGORY Right.

JANINE I hate the word "cremains." It's...I don't know. Sounds like there should be cream in there. You know? Like. "Cream of Dad Soup with Mushrooms."

[GREGORY *gives her a look.*]

What? Dad would find it funny. He would.

[*Beat.*]

What did we ever do with the cremains that were in here? Did we dump them out? Eat them?

[*Beat.*]

Not even a smile?

GREGORY I saw something too that night.

JANINE Oh. Your turn, huh?

GREGORY I'm telling the truth, okay? Something I never... this is stupid.

JANINE Don't begin it like that.

[*Imitating.*]

"This is stupid." You have to build it on, I don't know. Something... mysterious. Atmosphere, Gregory. Think *atmosphere*.

GREGORY How do I do that?

JANINE Say, "It was a dark and stormy night."

GREGORY It wasn't. It was a night just like this one.

JANINE Oh, even better! *It was a night just like this night.*

GREGORY Forget it.

JANINE No, go on! I'm gonna eat all the s'mores if you don't!

GREGORY Fine. Okay. So.

JANINE [*Helping.*] *It was a night just like this night.*

GREGORY It was a night just like this night. I'm with you and Dad. And he's... I don't know. It just seems like he's not into it. Like he's being forced to hang out with us. Like he'd rather be with... Buddy or Al or... what was the redheaded guy's name?

JANINE Red.

GREGORY Oh. Well, Red. Drinking beer. Fishing. Telling dirty stories. But Mom sticks him with us, so. I can't blame him for being upset.

JANINE This isn't really... you know.

GREGORY What?

JANINE Doing it for me. It's not scary, it's sad.

GREGORY Oh.

JANINE So can you try, you know. Just a little.

GREGORY Right.

JANINE A little harder.

GREGORY Right. Okay.

[*Beat.*]

Once upon a time, on a night dark as this, my dad took me and my sister to go camping. Now, we had never been camping before. We liked the city. So we go camping near Frost Valley. He builds a fire, tells us to get sticks for marshmallows, and we both wander. You run off in one direction, I run off in another. I have my trusty slingshot with me, thinking I'd take down a bear if I see it. David and Goliath. You know, I practiced with bottles every day, so. I could nail a bear between the eyes.

JANINE You sucked at it.

GREGORY No, I didn't!

JANINE How many bottles did you hit?

GREGORY I don't know—

JANINE Half the stones went into Mrs. Rosalotti's window. That's why you gave up the damn thing, remember?

GREGORY That's not...

[*Beat.*]

I'm walking. I see the glow. An orange glow of another fire. I approach it, and there's this person sitting there. I can't quite make out the face, but...this person has glowing hands.

JANINE Oooh.

GREGORY And I approach this person. They look at me. Close. They hold up their glowing hand and say something about...I can't remember...phoning someone.

JANINE [*In E.T.'s voice.*] E.T. phone home!

[GREGORY *reenacts holding up his slingshot.*]

GREGORY It comes closer with its glowing hand. WOLFMAN!

[*He makes like he releases the shot.*]

It falls. "WOLFMAN, GREGORY!" You scream. I see the glow, and I run off. I nailed whatever it was. Whoever it was. Right between the eyes.

[*Beat.*]

It wasn't till I got back to camp that I realized I dropped my slingshot. I never made another one.

[*Beat.*]

You're screaming "WOLFMAN," and Dad, well. He just looks embarrassed. Like the squirrels are laughing.

JANINE The Wolfman was probably laughing.

GREGORY I don't get a wink of sleep. Especially with Dad playing that jaw harp.

JANINE He really did like the country.

GREGORY And the next morning, we get up. And there's no body...

JANINE No wolfman.

GREGORY Right.

JANINE [*Melodramatic.*] There's no one there. Just this urn.

GREGORY And my slingshot is lost forever.

[*Pause.* GREGORY *picks up a s'more.*]

Here's to you, Dad, and the weirdest night of my life.

JANINE To you. You old bastard.

[JANINE *and* GREGORY *give each other a hug.*]

GREGORY On that note. I gotta drop the kids off at the pool.

JANINE Greg—

GREGORY I was going to say "take a dump," but—

JANINE Good taste prevailed.

GREGORY Right.

JANINE Hey. We're going to be all right.

GREGORY Yeah?

JANINE It's a blue moon.

[*She looks up. Lights change.*]

GREGORY Yeah. Wow. Haven't seen it look like that since...huh. Maybe it's just the way the woods look, you know?

JANINE Mmm.

GREGORY Be back in a sec.

JANINE Don't wipe with poison ivy!

[GREGORY *exits.* JANINE *crouches by the fire. Lights change slightly.* JANINE *notices. There's a rustle.*]

Gregory?

[*Beat. She takes out her cell phone and starts texting.*]

I.Will.Hear.You.Receive.This.Text.You.Can't.Scare.Me.Enter.

[*She looks at her phone.* LITTLE BOY *enters holding a slingshot. She leaps back holding her phone. He raises the slingshot.*]

JANINE It's a phone. Damnit. I just sent you a text!

LITTLE JANINE [*Offstage.*] WOLFMAN!

[*Startled,* LITTLE BOY *releases a stone,* JANINE *is hit and drops.*]

WOLFMAN! GREGORY! WOLFMAN!

[LITTLE BOY *drops his slingshot and races off. Rustling. A Wolfman* (GREGORY)— *furry face, big ears, sharp teeth, furry hands—LEAPS OUT.*]

GREGORY [*As Wolfman.*] RAARRRGH!

[*A moment.*]

Ahem. RAAARGH!

[*Beat.*]

Really? Did you see me?

[*Beat.*]

You can't scare me, Janine. I told...

[*He notices the slingshot. He raises his mask. He walks over and picks it up. He looks at* JANINE. *He races over and holds her up. He looks at the phone in her hand. He holds her close.* JANINE *takes in air, very sharply.*]

Is this a joke? Is this a...? Janine, shit. Janine, are you there? Are you...

JANINE [*Coming to.*] You're a terrible friggin' shot.

GREGORY What?

JANINE You're a terrible friggin' shot.

GREGORY Your scalp is bleeding.

JANINE God.

GREGORY Stay with me. We'll get you to a hospital. Just…can you lean on me? Come on…

JANINE Wasn't even close to my eyes…wait…what about…?

[*She turns, forcing him to turn. They look at the urn. GREGORY gives her a look. He sets her down carefully. He picks up the box of s'mores. JANINE smiles. He gets her back up. They slowly exit, as the fire and moon reflect off the urn.*]

• • •

Kid Gloves

David Rusiecki

For Connie

Kid Gloves by David Rusiecki. Copyright © 2013 by David Rusiecki. All rights reserved. Reprinted by permission of the author.

CAUTION/ADVICE: Professionals and amateurs are hereby warned that performance of *Kid Gloves* is subject to a royalty. It is fully protected under the copyright laws of the United States of America, and of all countries covered by the International Copyright Union (including the Dominion of Canada and the rest of the British Commonwealth), and of all countries covered by the Pan-American Copyright Convention and the Universal Copyright Convention, the Berne Convention, and of all countries with which the United States has reciprocal copyright relations. All rights, including professional and amateur stage performing rights, motion picture, recitation, lecturing, public reading, radio broadcasting, television, video or sound recording, all other forms of mechanical or electronic reproduction, such as CD-ROM, DVD-ROM, information storage and retrieval systems, and photocopying, and the rights of translation into foreign languages, are strictly reserved. Particular emphasis is placed upon the matter of readings, permission for which must be secured from the author's agent in writing.

Inquiries concerning rights should be addressed to David Rusiecki at djrusiecki@gmail.com

David Rusiecki

David Rusiecki is a playwright, director, and actor. He is a member of the New Voices Playwrights Theatre based in Orange County, California, and has served as head of the New Works Festival Literary Committee and board of trustees with the Long Beach Playhouse. His full-length plays and one-acts have been given staged readings and produced in California at STAGES Theatre, Stage Door Repertory Theatre, and Theatre Out. His full-length *Sides* was selected for the Long Beach Playhouse New Works table-read series while in the same year...*Prep*...received honorable mention with Panndora Productions' annual festival of new play readings. As an actor, David is a graduate of South Coast Repertory's (SCR) acting intensive program and has performed at Long Beach Playhouse Studio Theatre and Stella Adler Theater in Hollywood. He is a graduate of Loyola College in Baltimore, Maryland, and holds an MBA. He is a currently working on a full-length play about standup comedy entitled *Bringer*.

···production history···

Kid Gloves (originally entitled *Have a Nice Day*) was first performed as part of Summer Voices 2012: Eight One-Act Plays produced by New Voices Playwrights Theatre from July 28 to August 11 at Stage Door Repertory Theatre in Anaheim, California, featuring Toni Beckman, Paul LeSchofs, and directed by Vanessa Wolf.

characters

> **SYLVIA**   early fifties, female
>
> **CLAUDIO**   late twenties, male

setting

CLAUDIO's desk.

time

The present.

[*We see* CLAUDIO, *in a business outfit, suit and tie, sitting at his desk reviewing papers. A framed photo of a woman and a folder sits on his desk along with a desk calendar, laptop, keyboard, and mouse. An empty chair on the other side of the desk faces him. We then see* SYLVIA, *also in professional attire, matching skirt and jacket, appearing at the entrance.*]

SYLVIA   Claudio, you needed to see me?

CLAUDIO   Thank you, Sylvia. Please, have a seat.

> [SYLVIA *positions herself at the empty chair.*]
>
> Did you log off under meeting?

SYLVIA   Yes.

CLAUDIO   Good. I wanted to go over your performance review.

SYLVIA   Okay.

CLAUDIO   Just a head's up, we're going to do things a bit different this year. Stepping away from the usual processes we've done in the past.

SYLVIA   Oh.

CLAUDIO   First, I'm going to brief you on your rating. Then instead of physically signing it, I'll shoot you an e-mail with the link and you can acknowledge online that you received your scorecard from me. Real simple.

SYLVIA Sure.

CLAUDIO It's merely a new directive we've implemented for the purpose of efficiency.

SYLVIA Of course.

CLAUDIO We also ask that you please don't share your score with other employees. With regards to, you know, any potential animosity.

SYLVIA Animosity?

CLAUDIO To mitigate any ill will. And maintain confidentiality.

SYLVIA I see.

CLAUDIO Any questions for me?

SYLVIA No.

CLAUDIO You sure?

SYLVIA Yes.

CLAUDIO Terrific, let's begin. First of all, how are we doing?

SYLVIA We're... I'm fine, thanks. And you?

CLAUDIO It's Friday, it's payday. I'm good, appreciate you asking. Now, I wanted to start by thanking you for your help this past year. We've seen some significant growth as a department and we're hoping to continue to improve on our system enhancements. We've announced strong results for the fourth quarter and the full year. We improved our performance during the last quarter but we lost some momentum in other areas. Bear in mind, while we are segmented, every area measures their numbers the same way. The process is very similar in the East as it is in the Midwest, to the South region to out here in the West. And, of course, the data we come up with lends itself to things we can update in the future. It all boils down to adaptability. Adapt or die, nothing personal, just business. It's all about change. As you know, change energizes us. You have to embrace change. Not everybody here embraces change. Our employees are naturally stubborn in their ways. I understand, I get it. How's the ancient Chinese proverb go again? "The most consistent thing in life is..."

CLAUDIO/SYLVIA   [*In unison.*] "...change..."

CLAUDIO   Correct, now the key is to follow through with these numbers, continue to improve our processes, find new efficiencies so no details go overlooked, and do our best to try to make us better. My job is to call it out when something isn't working. Why duplicate efforts, you know? Yet at the same time, have employees bring up issues and ideas, provide candid feedback, cut out unnecessary steps, streamline the process, and work together to make sure we're all on the right track. Any questions so far?

SYLVIA   No.

CLAUDIO   You sure?

SYLVIA   Yes.

CLAUDIO   One moment, please.

   [CLAUDIO *pulls open his desk drawer and takes a swig from a bottle of water. He puts the water bottle back in and shuts the drawer.*]

   Okay. Now to synthesize all this, we must tell you...

SYLVIA   Excuse me.

CLAUDIO   Yes.

SYLVIA   What exactly do you mean when you say synthesize?

CLAUDIO   Sort of, you know, putting things in perspective.

SYLVIA   Interesting.

CLAUDIO   We okay?

SYLVIA   Just never heard "synthesize" used in that context before. I'm sorry, please go on.

CLAUDIO   Before we go any further, we need to share...

SYLVIA   How did you find that word?

CLAUDIO   Say that again?

SYLVIA   I mean, where did you come across a word like "synthesize" and incorporate it into your vernacular?

CLAUDIO   It's a word I use often.

SYLVIA   You use "synthesize" every day?

CLAUDIO I'd like to finish with your review if that's okay.

SYLVIA Sure.

CLAUDIO Going back to what I was originally saying, we must first put your mind at ease and tell you the good news.

SYLVIA Yes?

CLAUDIO You still have a job.

SYLVIA Oh…okay.

[CLAUDIO *opens* SYLVIA's *folder on his desk.*]

CLAUDIO Let's break things down and take a closer look at your evaluation. Now our numbers indicate a solid level of productivity. Attendance-wise, you've posted solid numbers as well. If we focus on your addressing issues with urgency and accuracy within service level guidelines, you received a rating of "performing."

[SYLVIA *nods her head.*]

Based on our rating system, if you remember, "leading" is considered above-average, "performing" is average, and "developing" would be below average.

SYLVIA Yes.

CLAUDIO Any questions so far?

SYLVIA No.

CLAUDIO You sure?

SYLVIA Yes, I am.

CLAUDIO So, like I said, you received a "performing" rating when it came to addressing issues with urgency and accuracy within service level guidelines. Like I said, "performing" being average. In terms of interacting and building partnerships with various departments in resolving customer complaints, you again received a "performing." With handling cases in a professional and confidential manner, you did receive a "leading," which is good.

SYLVIA Okay.

CLAUDIO When it came to identifying trends and submitting process improvement suggestions, you also received a "leading," which is very good. Same with identifying and submitting feedback opportunities and handling incoming calls from customers, agencies, and executives, as well as being available during scheduled queue times.

SYLVIA Right.

CLAUDIO In summary, after further evaluation, your final year-end rating is a "developing."

[CLAUDIO *closes her folder.*]

SYLVIA [*Pause.*] I beg your pardon?

CLAUDIO After review and careful consideration, I feel that the "developing" rating best matches your performance based on last year's numbers.

[CLAUDIO *starts searching his desk drawer.*]

SYLVIA But you said "developing."

CLAUDIO Yes.

SYLVIA Which is, in your terms…below-average.

CLAUDIO Correct.

SYLVIA I don't understand.

[CLAUDIO *fishes out a plastic back scratcher and begins scratching his back.*]

CLAUDIO Which part?

SYLVIA You mentioned earlier that my performance was solid.

CLAUDIO In certain categories, yes.

SYLVIA If my numbers, as your data indicates, are solid, how come my overall rating is, in your words, subpar?

CLAUDIO Well, like I said before, this year we've decided to go a different route with incorporating new weights to each bucket we scrutinize based on real-time data.

[CLAUDIO *opens a drawer, puts away the back scratcher, and retrieves a roll of dental floss.*]

SYLVIA Bucket?

CLAUDIO Correct.

SYLVIA Can you explain to me in this scenario what you mean by bucket?

CLAUDIO Certainly. We scrutinize each bucket, or metric, in terms of (1) quality, (2) productivity, and (3) people and teamwork. All of these scales, mind you, are based on our company's guiding principles. As we said before, things around here are evergreen. Work changes, volume changes. They're constantly changing. We're looking for employees who are champions of change, individuals who not only elevate but also display a positive attitude towards new processes and new procedures.

SYLVIA So then, help me "synthesize" what I just heard from you. Which bucket, or metric, did I not perform to our company's satisfaction?

[CLAUDIO *opens* SYLVIA's *folder.*]

CLAUDIO Judging by your scorecard, I found that your people and teamwork was unsatisfactory.

[CLAUDIO *pulls out a string of floss.*]

SYLVIA Unsatisfactory? How so?

CLAUDIO Well, I noted down here…
[*Reads* SYLVIA's *folder.*]
…that "while I am proud to have Sylvia Morrison as a valuable part of our team, I challenge her to focus on demonstrating sound judgment and decision-making on a consistent basis. I also challenge her to adapt better to work changes in a manner that continually improves her level of contribution."

[CLAUDIO *turns to the side and begins flossing his teeth.*]

SYLVIA I'm still baffled. What specific area did I not demonstrate this alleged sound judgment?

[CLAUDIO *stops flossing.*]

CLAUDIO I think I went over this same action item before when you forgot to update your out-of-office notification.

[CLAUDIO *turns his head and resumes flossing.*]

SYLVIA I went out of town, yes. And I forgot to update my notification in Outlook. It slipped my mind. Why is that worth noting?

[CLAUDIO *stops flossing.*]

CLAUDIO That was one of our highly coveted national accounts you were working on when they escalated their request.

SYLVIA I'm aware of this, so?

CLAUDIO They weren't able to get through to you. As a result, their e-mail was held up in your inbox for over an eight-hour period of time. They didn't know you were out of the office since your automated notification...

SYLVIA But they should know better. They should have sent their request to our national box, not to me directly.

CLAUDIO With our new service level and turnaround time, their needs weren't addressed in a timely fashion. In your haste to leave the office, which happens...you're excited to go away, I get it...easily could have resulted in a major financial catastrophe.

[CLAUDIO *turns his head and resumes flossing.*]

SYLVIA First of all, I wasn't in any haste to leave. And secondly, I only offer my personal e-mail address to the sales reps if they were unable to reach anyone. But what about the other thing?

[CLAUDIO *stops flossing, tosses the string away, opens a drawer, and stashes the roll inside.*]

CLAUDIO Which other thing?

[SYLVIA *reaches over, pulls her folder around, and opens it.*]

SYLVIA The one...right here, where it says I need to..."adapt better to work changes"?

CLAUDIO Yes.

SYLVIA Can you expand on this for me?

[CLAUDIO *casually removes one of his shoes.*]

CLAUDIO The reality is, I'm essentially calling out your response to new processes and new procedures. Which, in my opinion, I viewed as negative.

SYLVIA I never once demonstrated a negative attitude to any new processes.

[CLAUDIO *casually rolls down one of his socks.*]

CLAUDIO Again, when we decided to extend our hours of operation last summer and were looking for volunteers to adjust their schedule, we did not hear from you.

[CLAUDIO *casually pulls off the sock, opens a drawer and removes a nail clipper.*]

SYLVIA That's it? Because I didn't volunteer myself to change my work hours, you consider…

CLAUDIO Based on our company's guiding principles, strategic objectives, and office credo, we were hoping for you to be more productive.

SYLVIA Lemme get this straight. Two isolated incidents. That's the basis you deem worthy of a "developing" rating for the entire fiscal year?

CLAUDIO I've also on numerous occasions walked past your PC unlocked with sensitive information on your screen while you were away from your desk. And there was the month you logged out on Break instead of Lunch, which affected your missing minutes. And during our last earthquake drill, you did not fully go underneath your desk as instructed.

SYLVIA So, after all this, you still stand behind your assessment?

[CLAUDIO *slowly and casually reaches for his bare toe with the clipper.*]

CLAUDIO That is my final consideration, yes.

SYLVIA And by my signing off on this review, I'm basically agreeing to what you've said…which is, I'm a "below average" employee.

CLAUDIO You're looking at this all wrong.

SYLVIA Every day for the past six years, I do what I'm told. I'm given nothing but work, work, and more work. I take ownership of all my work. Okay, I may fumble a couple times here and there. But in the grand scheme of things, I do what I'm told to do with no pushback, minimal questions, and zero complaints.
[*Points to his toe.*]
Do you mind?

[CLAUDIO *sits up, opens a drawer, and puts the nail clipper away. He casually puts back his sock and shoe.*]

CLAUDIO I can understand your frustration, Sylvia—I get it. However, if it's any reassurance, all employees are subject to the same scrutiny regardless of tenure.

SYLVIA And exactly how does this affect my job status?

CLAUDIO Like I said at the outset, you still have a job.

SYLVIA What about financially?

CLAUDIO Based on your…"developing" status, you do not receive a base pay increase. Nor do you qualify to receive any profit-sharing compensation based on this year's financial results.

[SYLVIA *tosses her folder on his desk.*]

SYLVIA You're joking.

CLAUDIO But you still have a job.

SYLVIA Are you serious?

CLAUDIO Naturally, it's fair to say you may be bitter. And I completely understand, I get it. While we appreciate your professionalism, we do recommend you stay focused on your work, continue momentum, and put your best food forward. And please, feel free to give me your feedback on this and I'll be happy to go over it with you sometime. Any further questions?

SYLVIA I'm…stunned.

CLAUDIO If you believe there's any confusion on this issue or you wish to voice your complaint…

SYLVIA Voice my complaint? I most certainly would. This is ridiculous. I mean, how can you sit there at your desk and with a straight face tell me how this "developing" or below-average rating is an accurate reflection of my work. Of my contribution to this department, let alone this company. While we're on the subject…may I ask, did you receive a bonus? Or a bump in pay?

CLAUDIO I'm afraid, I'm not at liberty to discuss…

SYLVIA Sounds like a "yes" to me.

CLAUDIO I'm sensing some hostility. I understand, I get it.

SYLVIA I'm sorry, but no—I don't think you get it at all. I think livid is more apropos to describe how I'm…how on earth can you be so…so delusional about what we do around here. I don't think you can manage your way out of a paper bag without having to run to other consultants in our department for verification. Every time you announce a change in process or a change in procedure, which seems like every month now, your credibility goes out the window. Personally, I think you must be on some kind of medicinal substance if you fully believe this developing rating of mine. Or at least up the dosage.

CLAUDIO Sylvia, look... I'll need to parking-lot your concerns and get back to you another time.

SYLVIA You plaster words like "integrity" and "respect" on the office walls. Or catchphrases like "teamwork enables us to do better." But when you boil it down, you stand behind none of them.

CLAUDIO Sylvia...

SYLVIA Now, let's play devil's advocate here and suppose for a moment I were to say, I thought you were incompetent when it comes to being a manager. Unfit and mentally unsound. Never available for guidance or direction, that kind of thing. Hypothetically speaking, what would you say to that?

CLAUDIO Personally, I'd say you're dead wrong.

[CLAUDIO *slowly reaches and pulls open a drawer.*]

SYLVIA You'd take exception to that statement.

CLAUDIO I would.

[SYLVIA *slams her hand down on his desk.* CLAUDIO *closes the drawer.*]

SYLVIA Now we're getting somewhere. This is progress.

[SYLVIA *takes out and unfolds a letter from inside her jacket pocket.*]

CLAUDIO What are you doing?

SYLVIA I'd like to share something. A manifesto, if you will. I keep this with me in the hope that someday my words would be heard.

[SYLVIA *hands* CLAUDIO *the letter.*]

CLAUDIO You wrote this?

SYLVIA I'd love for you to read it aloud.

CLAUDIO Sylvia, I really don't think this is necessary...

SYLVIA [*Interrupting.*] It's still in the rough draft phase. However, I do feel this is an appropriate time to share my thoughts with you. Go on, please.

CLAUDIO [*Begins reading.*] "While I, Sylvia Morrison..."

[SYLVIA *begins to hum a spiritual like* "Nobody Knows the Trouble I've Seen," "We Shall Overcome," *or* "I Never Picked Cotton." CLAUDIO *looks at her, then continues reading.*]

"While I, Sylvia Morrison, find it a distinct honor to labor for this company...a global industry leader, a world-class operation...with sixty-four billion dollars last year in revenue..."

SYLVIA [*Interrupting.*] Correction, sixty-five. Go on.

[SYLVIA *continues humming as* CLAUDIO *looks on.*]

CLAUDIO "...as a global industry leader with innovative products and high standards in customer services, I must beg the question—is it good business to punish those employees who show up to work on a consistent basis..." Sylvia, I'm afraid this is...

SYLVIA No, no...there's more.

[SYLVIA *hums,* CLAUDIO *continues.*]

CLAUDIO "...to punish those employees who show up to work on a consistent basis while reward employees who show up to the office and spend the majority of their time making coffee, organizing potlucks, engaging in gossip and other non-work-related conversations?"

SYLVIA Supposed to be read as a declarative sentence.

CLAUDIO "...Leaving early every Friday afternoon at 3 p.m. to beat traffic, sending various...pornographic text messages during working hours..." Excuse me, Sylvia, but I don't think this is the best time to discuss these issues.

SYLVIA On the contrary, I think it's an ideal time.

CLAUDIO I'm sorry, but who exactly is sending these...as you say, pornographic texts?

SYLVIA If you continue, you'll see.

CLAUDIO "Certain employees sending inappropriate text messages while sitting outside their supervisor's cubicle." Are you alluding to...Ruben?

SYLVIA Now you want me to blow the whistle on my fellow colleagues? Throw them under the bus, that's rich.

CLAUDIO Sylvia...you've obviously spoken your mind. With a number of important thoughts and unique insights we'll take into consideration.

Again, I'm afraid this is really not the appropriate time to venture into these talking points. I think if we can arrange a good time to get together, we can iron out any concerns you may have.

[*Checks his desk calendar.*]

How's next week?

SYLVIA   I'm afraid that simply won't be possible.

CLAUDIO   How come?

[SYLVIA *pulls out another folder letter from inside her jacket.*]

SYLVIA   You see, I no longer plan on staying with this company. Hard as it may sound, I did have a positive and memorable experience during my tenure. I've made a number of friends and forged some close bonds too. But I feel it's time for me to move on, personally and professionally. So, with that in mind, I'm giving you my two weeks' notice.

[SYLVIA *hands the letter to* CLAUDIO.]

CLAUDIO   Wow, I...didn't expect all this.

SYLVIA   Trust me, it's for the best.

CLAUDIO   May I ask, what will you do next?

SYLVIA   Funny you should bring that up. Remember two Christmases ago, when we had our annual white elephant gift exchange?

CLAUDIO   I do.

[SYLVIA *gets up from her chair.*]

SYLVIA   And if memory serves me correct, you contributed instant-scratch lottery tickets?

CLAUDIO   I did.

[SYLVIA *makes her way around* CLAUDIO's *desk and stands behind him.*]

SYLVIA   I wound up with those tickets, thanks to you, and it just so happened I won a considerable chuck of change.

[SYLVIA *begins rubbing* CLAUDIO's *neck.*]

CLAUDIO   You told me three dollars.

SYLVIA   Yes, I did say that.

CLAUDIO   And?

SYLVIA   I lied.

[SYLVIA *begins rubbing* CLAUDIO's *shoulders.*]

CLAUDIO   How much are we talking about?

SYLVIA   In the range of five digits. Talk about dumb luck.

CLAUDIO   You never bothered to mention anything to me before?

SYLVIA   I do apologize, Claudio. I didn't mean to leave you, of all people, out of the loop.

CLAUDIO   So I guess with all your lotto winnings from the tickets I bought, which you chose not to inform me about...you're what, retiring to Maui?

[SYLVIA *stops rubbing and saunters back to her chair.*]

SYLVIA   Not necessarily. I'm doing what any practical person would do when they come across a significant amount of currency.

CLAUDIO   Investments, I get it.

SYLVIA   Something along those lines.

CLAUDIO   Stocks, bond, ETFs.

SYLVIA   Not really.

CLAUDIO   Mutual funds? CDs?

SYLVIA   No.

CLAUDIO   What then?

SYLVIA   I invested in myself.

CLAUDIO   Yourself?

SYLVIA   You see, it's always been a dream of mine to run my own business. In fact, I was able to invest in something I'm truly passionate about.

CLAUDIO   Which is?

SYLVIA   Shoes.

[CLAUDIO *stares at her.*]

CLAUDIO   Sorry, you said shoes?

[SYLVIA *nods.*]

You took the money, once again from the lotto ticket I bought, and invested in...shoes?

SYLVIA Sandals, to be exact. I designed my own brand of stylish wedge sandals. They're seasonal, mostly for summer wear. My husband happens to know a manufacturer in the area. I came up with a simple strap design in our very own basement. We patented our idea and became business partners together. We call our little enterprise Precious Cargo Footwear. In fact, I have something for you.

[SYLVIA *pulls out a card from inside her jacket pocket and hands it to* CLAUDIO.]

CLAUDIO Anything else you keep in there? Snacks? Diet Coke? The Emancipation Proclamation?

SYLVIA I'd like to extend an invitation to you for my opening. It's three weekends from now. I'd love to have you and your wife in attendance. I've never met her in person before, but by the looks of her in your photo, she seems to have a wonderful sense of style.

CLAUDIO We'll, um...try our best.

SYLVIA So any further questions for me?

CLAUDIO I...not at the moment.

SYLVIA Are you sure?

CLAUDIO Positive.

SYLVIA You may keep my manifesto if you like. I have another copy framed on my wall at home. Consider it my gift to you. One last thing, I took the liberty of sending a compilation of all those inappropriate texts in an attachment and forwarded them to HR. I mentioned they were from a member of your staff. This was right before I logged off on our meeting. I meant to cc: you...again, it must have slipped my mind. It should be in their possession by now, so you may be hearing from them shortly. Take care, Claudio, thank you for all your cooperation and I wish you a splendid day.

[SYLVIA *exits, leaving* CLAUDIO *alone at his desk. LIGHTS DOWN.*]

• • •

The Grim Raper

Daniel Guyton

The Grim Raper by Daniel Guyton. Copyright © 2012 by Daniel Guyton. All rights reserved. Reprinted by permission of the author.

CAUTION/ADVICE: Professionals and amateurs are hereby warned that performance of *The Grim Raper* is subject to a royalty. It is fully protected under the copyright laws of the United States of America, and of all countries covered by the International Copyright Union (including the Dominion of Canada and the rest of the British Commonwealth), and of all countries covered by the Pan-American Copyright Convention and the Universal Copyright Convention, the Berne Convention, and of all countries with which the United States has reciprocal copyright relations. All rights, including professional and amateur stage performing rights, motion picture, recitation, lecturing, public reading, radio broadcasting, television, video or sound recording, all other forms of mechanical or electronic reproduction, such as CD-ROM, DVD-ROM, information storage and retrieval systems, and photocopying, and the rights of translation into foreign languages, are strictly reserved. Particular emphasis is placed upon the matter of readings, permission for which must be secured from the author's agent in writing.

Inquiries concerning rights should be addressed to Daniel Guyton at: www.danguyton.com or dguyton21@gmail.com

Daniel Guyton

Daniel Guyton is a playwright and screenwriter from just south of Atlanta, where he lives with his wife, two dogs, and a cat. He has won numerous writing awards, including the Best Horror Screenplay Award from the 2013 Los Angeles Film and Script Festival, two Kennedy Center/ACTF awards for his plays *Attic* and *Where's Julie?*, and more. He received his MFA in dramatic writing from the University of Georgia, and his plays have been produced throughout the world, including Iceland, England, New York, Australia, Los Angeles, and more. Many of Guyton's plays have been published and are available now. For more information, please visit: www.danguyton.com

···production history···

The Grim Raper premiered at the Theater in S@NE in Schenectady, New York, by Mostly Harmless Productions (Rich Sagendorf, Artistic Director) in June 2013 as part of *Hilarious Nightmares a Night of Daniel Guyton One-Acts*. It was directed by Rich Sagendorf. Lighting and set design by Rich Sagendorf and John Schmiederer. The stage manager was Katie Payne. The cast was as follows:

SANDRA Liz Gerry

JILL Shera Dawn

DEATH Jason Stein

characters

SANDRA

JILL

DEATH

JEFF a typical frat boy

[*Two sorority girls sit at a bar. They each have several drinks in front of them.*]

SANDRA Oh my God, can you believe Rebecca wore that outfit to the formal?

JILL O-M-G! It was totally repulsive. And did you see those shoes she wore? Oh my God, like 2007? Who wears those, right?

SANDRA Oh my God, right?

JILL And did you see what Jackie wore in the…
[DEATH *enters in a hooded robe and scythe.*]
Oh, fuck me! It's him!

SANDRA Who?

JILL [*Shielding her face from him.*] It's that guy I was telling you about. The quiet dude from my math class?
[*She looks, then quickly looks away.*]
God, he's so creepy.

[DEATH *turns his head slowly to look at them.*]

SANDRA Do you know him?

JILL Know him?!? He just sits next to me in math class. He never says a word, he just stares at me.

[*She gets a chill.*]

Ugh. He's like a total stalker.

SANDRA What's his name?

JILL I don't know. Stalker McJerkface? Who fucking cares? The teacher never calls on him. I think he's, like, auditing the class, or whatever.

SANDRA Is he cute? I can't tell with that hood on.

JILL How the fuck should I know? That's all he ever wears. It's like get an outfit, you know?

SANDRA And way to rock that... What is that, like farm equipment or something?

JILL I don't know.

SANDRA But I like his hood. He's got kind of a goth thing going, don't you think?

JILL More like a homeless man.

SANDRA Do you like him?

JILL Ew, Sandra! He's totally fucking creepy. He skeezes me out every time I see him. And it's like... *everytime* he looks at me, the hairs on my arm stand up.

[*She holds up her arm. They both stare at it.*]

SANDRA You should totally get that waxed.

[JILL *rolls her eyes.* SANDRA *calls out.*]

Hey, you!

[DEATH *looks at her.*]

Yeah, you, weird guy in the hoodie, come here.

JILL What the fuck are you doing?

[DEATH *points to himself.*]

SANDRA Yes, you!

[*Under her breath.*]

Dumb ass.

[*To him.*]

Come here!

[*He crosses to them.* JILL *turns away, humiliated.*]

JILL   Oh my God, Sandra!

SANDRA   Hey, my friend says you like her, huh?

[DEATH *stares at her.*]

What's your name?

DEATH   [*Unearthly moan from the depths of Hell.*] Deatttttthhhhhhhhh.

SANDRA   Jeff? Okay, listen, Jeff. You're creeping out my friend here, all right? She's not interested. And why do you have that farm equipment, anyway? What are you, like, a farmer? Mr. Farmer John, hoeing the fields? This is a campus party, bro! You're supposed to be getting your drink on! Like this!

[*She downs her glass and makes a stink-face.*]

Ugh. Would you like one? They're really good.

[*No response.*]

Okay, whatever.

[*She picks up her second drink and downs it.*]

JILL   Hey, what the fuck's your problem, dude? How come you always stare at me?

[*He stares at her, then nods towards the back of the room. The girls look at the back of the room. When they do, he slips something into each of their drinks. The drinks fizz up instantly.*]

SANDRA   I don't see anything.

[*She turns back.*]

Weirdo.

[*She chugs her drink.* JILL *is about to drink, then looks at her glass.*]

JILL   Did you put something in my *drink*?

[DEATH *shrugs his shoulders.*]

Oh my God, you totally put something in my drink! What the fuck is wrong with you?!?

SANDRA   Jill?

JILL You know what, fuck this, I'm calling the cops.

[*She pulls out her cell phone.*]

I mean, what kind of sick bastard does someth—

SANDRA [*Tugging* JILL*'s shoulder.*] Jill?

JILL What? I'm calling the cops, Sandra!

[*To* DEATH.]

Now you better have a good lawyer, ass-wipe, because when my daddy finds out, he will kick the shit of you and all your . . .

SANDRA JILL!

[SANDRA *grabs* JILL*'s face with both hands.*]

JILL What?

SANDRA Why are there three of you? Heh-heh-heh-heh.

JILL Did you put something in *her* drink too?

SANDRA Oh my God, I don't feel so good.

[*She climbs on top of the bar and lays down on it.*]

JILL Come on, Sandra. Stay with me! I'm calling the cops now, all right?

[DEATH *reaches out and touches her phone. She pulls away.*]

Hey, get away from me! You creep!

[*She tries to dial again.*]

Oh, what the fuck? No bars? I just had full bars like a minute ago!

DEATH [*Unearthly moan.*] Drinnnnnnnnnnnkkkkk ittttttttt . . .

JILL No, I'm not drinking that shit. *You* drink it!

[*She tries to roll* SANDRA *over.*]

Come on, Sandra, we're getting out of here.

SANDRA [*Inebriated.*] No, it's okay. I'm okay. I'm just gonna sleep right here, okay, Mommy?

JILL No, this guy wants to rape us, Sandra! We need to get out of here ASAP!

SANDRA No, it's okay, Mommy. It's okay. I'm fine. I always liked tall, dark, and handsome anyway. Hahahaha.

[*She looks at* DEATH, *suddenly serious.*]

Wait a minute. Holy shit, wait a minute. Jill. Wait a minute.

JILL What?

SANDRA [*She struggles to look up at* DEATH.] *Is* he handsome? I can't tell under all that clothing. Hahahahaha.

JILL Well, I'm not about to find out! Let's go!

SANDRA [*To* DEATH.] Do you work at the Gap?

[JILL *pulls* SANDRA *off the bar.*]

Ow, girl! You're fucking with my buzz...

JILL Oh my God, Sandra, what did you gain, like the freshman forty?

SANDRA Fuck you, bitch. Hahaha. *You're* forty.

[JILL *holds her up as best as she can.*]

JILL No, I'm not. Let's go.

[JILL *looks around.*]

Wait, where did everyone go? Donny?

[*She looks over the bar.*]

Donny, are you *asleep?*

SANDRA Donny's fucking hot, Jill. You should totally fuck Donny...

JILL Bill? Marcus? Why is everyone sleeping?!?

DEATH Drinnnnnnnnnnkkkkk itttttttt...

JILL Did you put something in *their* drinks also?

[DEATH *nods.*]

SANDRA Oh my God, do you want to get pregnant, Jill? I totally want to get pregnant.

JILL Not right now, I don't!

SANDRA God, you're such a prude.

JILL What is wrong with you?

[*To* DEATH.]

Look, who the fuck are you really?

SANDRA [*Slapping her playfully.*] I'm Sandra, you bitch. You know who I am.

JILL No, not you, Sandra! I'm...

DEATH [*Same unearthly moan.*] Deatttttttttttttthhhhhhhhhhh.

SANDRA Oh my God, ew, did somebody fart? It totally stinks in here.

[SANDRA *passes out on* JILL's *shoulder.* JILL *gulps.*]

JILL You mean like...the real death?

    [DEATH *nods, slowly.*]

    As in...like...the movies?

    [DEATH *nods.*]

    So you're not just some asshole from my math class?

    [DEATH *shakes his head no.*]

    And what did you do with all these people? You...

    [DEATH *rotates his scythe slowly in his fingers, making a wide arc.*]

    What are you doing? Is that...is that like the circle of death or something?

    [DEATH *nods.*]

    And did...and did you kill Sandra too?

    [*She touches* SANDRA's *neck.*]

    Oh my God, Sandra!

    [DEATH *reaches for* SANDRA, *but* JILL *pulls her away and screams.*]

    STAY AWAY FROM HER!

    [DEATH *pulls back reflexively.*]

    What do you want from me?

DEATH Drinnnnnnnnnnkkkkk itttttttt...

SANDRA [*Snapping to for just a moment.*] Oh shit. You totally saved my life, Jill...I fucking love you...

[*She tries to kiss* JILL *on the lips,* JILL *turns her head, and* SANDRA *plants one on her cheek instead, then* SANDRA *passes out again, sliding down* JILL's *body.*]

JILL Why do you want me to drink it? Are...? Are you...?

    [*Pause.*]

    You're not just trying to stalk me, are you? This...this is...

    [DEATH *shakes his head no.*]

    And this isn't just some kind of date-rape drug, is it? This is...like...

DEATH Drinnnnnnnnnnkkkkk ittttttttt...

JILL I'm afraid!

SANDRA [*Head buried in* JILL's *bosom.*] Don't be afraid, bitch. I'm a' take care of you...

JILL Shut up, Sandra.

DEATH [*Still guttural, but louder.*] Drinnnnnnnnnnnkkkkk ittttttttt...

JILL And what if I don't want to, huh?!? What if...

[DEATH *steps closer to her.*]

You can't make me! You can't force me to drink this!

[DEATH *stares at her.*]

And what about my daddy, huh? What about... When he finds out you...

[DEATH *thrusts his hand in the air and grabs something. He crushes the imaginary object in his fist, then slowly runs a finger across his neck.*]

You... you killed my daddy?!?

[*DEATH nods slowly.*]

You... Oh my God, daddy! You...

SANDRA Just drink it, Jill. It feels really good.

[SANDRA *slides to the floor and passes out.*]

JILL You...

[*She touches* SANDRA's *neck.*]

You killed Sandra. You killed my daddy. You...

[*She looks around.*]

You even killed Donny, and he's head of the football team.

[DEATH *steps closer to her.*]

DEATH [*Softer than before.*] Drinnnnnnnnnnkkkkk ittttttttt...

JILL [*Backing up one step.*] But I don't want to, I...I want to get married and...and be a lawyer someday and...and I can't do any of those things if...if I...

[DEATH *steps towards her. She backs up further.*]

Please stop coming towards me, okay? I'm, like, I'm really freaked out right now!

[DEATH *stops. Pause.*]

Okay. Thank you. I mean, seriously, like...You gotta stop doing that, okay? I mean, if you want me to drink this, fine. But like...You gotta stop invading my personal space, okay?

[*Pause.*]

DEATH Okayyyyyyyyyyy ...

JILL Will it hurt?

[DEATH *shakes his head slowly.*]

Will I like, get into heaven, or...?

[*She looks at the ground and gulps.*]

My hair gets really frizzy in the heat, so I don't think hell would be...

DEATH There issssssss no hellllllllll. Onnnnnly deattttthhhhhhh.

JILL Oh. Okay. Um...Is it nice?

[DEATH *steps closer to her.*]

Is it anything like Ft. Lauderdale? Because we're supposed to go there for spring break, and I don't...

DEATH There isssss no springggg breakkk. Onnnnly deatttttthhhhhh.

JILL [*Tearing up.*] I know, I just...I just don't want it to hurt, okay? I...I don't really like pain, and...and...and I mean, I cry when I get a hangnail, so I just...don't...

[*She chokes back a tear.*]

Will I get to see my daddy again, if...? If...

[DEATH *nods.*]

Oh. Okay. I will?

[DEATH *nods.*]

Oh...okay then. I...

[*She picks up the drink.*]

And Sandra too?

[DEATH *nods. She looks around.*]

And...

[*She points to someone behind the bar.*]

And what about Donny?

[DEATH *shrugs. She looks disappointed.*]

Oh. Well, all right, then, I...

[*She takes a deep breath.*]

You know, you really should consider a new outfit. I mean, that's...

[*She stares at the drink.*]

You know what, fuck it.

[*She chugs it and slams the glass on the counter.*]

There. You happy now? Dick.

[DEATH *cocks his head sideways and stares at her. She stares at her hands.*]

So is it supposed to work pretty qui...?

[*She falls to one knee.*]

Oh. Oh my God.

[*She breathes heavily for a minute.*]

Wow. This is better than Jäger bombs.

[*She looks at her hands, then struggles to look up at* DEATH. *She mutters drunkenly.*]

How many angels of death are there?

[*He holds up one finger.*]

Because I can count five of you.

[*He slowly lowers the finger towards her.*]

This won't fuck up my chances of getting an internship, will it?

[DEATH *touches her, and she collapses to the ground. He cocks his head sideways and looks at her. He circles around and looks at her from another angle. He removes his hood and cloak, revealing* JEFF, *a typical frat boy.*]

JEFF Dudes, it totally fucking worked! Donny, Marcus, wake up, bros! These chicks totally fell for it! Look, they'll be out for at least six hours, man! You can do anything you want with them! Yeah, no, no, you take the fat one. I've had my eye on this Jill chick since last semester.

[*He picks her up over his shoulder.*]

Yeah, that's right, pretty lady! You and me's about to party. Heh-heh-heh.

[*He walks offstage with her. Lights out.*]

• • •

Hurt

Saviana Stanescu

Hurt by Saviana Stanescu. Copyright © 2012 by Saviana Stanescu. All rights reserved. Reprinted by permission of the author.

CAUTION/ADVICE: Professionals and amateurs are hereby warned that performance of *Hurt* is subject to a royalty. It is fully protected under the copyright laws of the United States of America, and of all countries covered by the International Copyright Union (including the Dominion of Canada and the rest of the British Commonwealth), and of all countries covered by the Pan-American Copyright Convention and the Universal Copyright Convention, the Berne Convention, and of all countries with which the United States has reciprocal copyright relations. All rights, including professional and amateur stage performing rights, motion picture, recitation, lecturing, public reading, radio broadcasting, television, video or sound recording, all other forms of mechanical or electronic reproduction, such as CD-ROM, DVD-ROM, information storage and retrieval systems, and photocopying, and the rights of translation into foreign languages, are strictly reserved. Particular emphasis is placed upon the matter of readings, permission for which must be secured from the author's agent in writing.

Inquiries concerning rights should be addressed to the author at www.saviana.com

Saviana Stanescu

Saviana Stanescu is a Romanian-born award-winning playwright based in NYC and Ithaca, New York. Recent productions include: *Ants* at NJ Rep, *Aliens with Extraordinary Skills* (Women's Project, Ego Actus, NYC; B Street Theatre, Sacramento, California; Know Theatre, Cincinnati; Teatro La Capilla, Mexico City; published by Samuel French), *Waxing West* (La MaMa Theatre, 2007 NY Innovative Theatre Award), *For a Barbarian Woman* (Fordham/EST), *Polanski Polanski* (HERE, PS 122, Chain Theatre). Her plays have been developed with: NYTW, Lark Play Development Center, EST, NY Stage&Film, Long Wharf, New Group, PS 122, HERE, etc., etc. Saviana founded *Immigrants Artists and Scholars in New York* (IASNY) and curates *playgroundezero* and *New York with an Accent*. She holds an MA in performance studies and an MFA in dramatic writing from NYU, Tisch School of the Arts, and a PhD in theater from National University of Theatre & Film, Bucharest, Romania. Currently she teaches playwriting and theatre studies at Ithaca College.

···production history···

Hurt was produced by Gun Control Theatre Actions 2013, presented together with other writers' plays as part of this civic action project in various cities in the US and internationally—including NYC at New Dramatists with Greg Keller, Jocelyn Kuritsky, Reyna de Courcy.

Also: Manhattan Repertory Theatre, 2012

> Directed by Adrian Roman
>
> **LAURA**   Homa Hynes
> **TANYA**   Leonie Ettinger
> **DARKO**   Ioan Ardelean

cast

> **DARKO**   forties, depressed handsome man speaking with a strong Serbian accent
>
> **LAURA**   early thirties, cute American woman, girlish, insecure, lonely, big-hearted
>
> **TANYA**   eighteen spunky yet vulnerable student living with her single Bosnian mother

[*A one-bedroom apartment in Brooklyn.* DARKO, *in a business suit and slippers, talks to the audience like to a video camera. His briefcase is on the floor. His cell phone rings.*]

DARKO   [*His cell phone rings and rings.*] I'm not gonna answer. I hope you all know that cell phones are bad for your health. Brain cancer is closer than you think. But we don't see that, we don't, because radiation is invisible, electromagnetic waves are invisible…and sometimes even people, people can be invisible too.

LAURA   [*Talking to her cat, Penelope.*] He didn't ask if I had a pet. But I did, I told him I had a cat. I even mentioned your name—Penelope. He wasn't very good at small talk. He went on a rant about the danger of cell phones. Then he took my hand, made a "cell phone" out of it and whispered: "This is not just a date for me, it's a special encounter, a gift from God, a randomly emerged union of two complementary particles called *souls*."

DARKO I'm a good Christian. I believe in goodness, I believe in honesty, I believe in people. But *they* all disappointed me. Deeply. I still believe in the beauty of a mathematical solution. A neat gorgeous proof. Numbers. Facts. *Corpses.* I believe in God. You might say it's a contradiction here. It's not. Science, mathematics, are just forms in which God has organized this world. God's algorithms are not to be revealed so easily to mortals. Except for the moments when they are close to *death*.

TANYA Sit down, Mom, and don't interrupt me, please. I gotta tell you something kinda important. I mean, not important-important, like it's not about our lives or something. No, it's not about money. I didn't get expelled from school. Don't worry. I'm not sick, nothing like that. No, I'm not pregnant!

LAURA Okay, he's not in my league, you'd say. He's a professor. Why would you say that? I'm more well cultured than all the girls I know! I read a lot. I listen to NPR. I'm a walking Wikipedia, but you wouldn't know that, you're a stupid cat!

DARKO For years I had to pretend everything was fine. Why bother complaining? I tried once and *they* didn't even listen to what I had to say, they told me I had an "unhealthy" attitude. What is a "healthy fuckin' attitude"? A robot following their rules? An ass-kisser? A hypocrite? Another expert in the sucking-up game?

LAURA He called me "dangerously beautiful." . . . That doesn't happen every day. It might actually never happen again. I shouldn't have said that stupid thing about not shaving my legs . . . because I actually did. I did shave my legs before our date, or whatever, our "special encounter."

DARKO They found a so-called reason, of course. They said a freshman student complained about my teaching methods. Bullshit. The students love me. Read my evaluations!

[*Cell phone rings and rings.*]

Creditors. They ring and ring and fuckin' ring. I feel like killing this fuckin' cell phone. But I can't. Yet. It's my only gate to the world. I haven't paid it for the last three months but it still rings. Stubborn motherfucker! Con Ed just cut my electricity. Luckily my video camera has damn good batteries!

[*Laughs weirdly.*]
Soon it will be dark. Darko will be in the dark!

TANYA Okay, would you just listen, please, Mom? Please, just listen.
This time, just listen! I did something kinda weird. Okay, maybe even
wrong. And I'm not sure why I did it, but...okay, it's like...this
professor we have...had...Darko Rasnin...yeah, a Serbian guy, but
he lived here like forever, like you, since '93 or something.

DARKO [*The cell phone starts ringing again—he takes a look at the caller ID.*]
The landlord. She's a good woman, from China. Her patience has a
limit too. I don't blame her. I haven't paid the rent in four months.
EVICTION is written in big letters on my forehead. Homelessness—
a new start. Bankruptcy—another great start. Amazing new
beginnings await for me. Fucking bullshit capitalist propaganda.

LAURA Yes, he knows I'm a lab technician, he was okay with that. He's a
scientist! And it's not like I'm doing something shameful! Someone
has to work on those STD tests too. I actually like this job much more
than working at the hospital, we already discussed that. Too many
people over there. We like the quiet time: just you, purring, me,
thinking...a few test tubes around are okay, but people, too many
people are not okay.

DARKO You may ask why don't I take a job, another job, any kind of job.
I did. I worked as a scientific advisor for the Environmental Health
Trust, a public health institution that examines the health impact of
environmental exposures. Did you see that *New York Times* article
about the impact of cell phones? I was quoted in it. I spoke about their
health effects and social implications. Didn't you notice those couples
in a restaurant, on a romantic evening, each of them texting someone
else...People don't connect with each other anymore. You invite a
woman for a romantic dinner and she's freakin' texting between two
bites...Women don't know how to connect with men anymore. And
men don't know how to connect with women. Shall I be polite, shall I
open the door for her or will she hit me on my head with her purse?

LAURA I really dressed well for that date, I did. Classy restaurant. I
could tell from the name: Marseilles. French. He has good taste.

DARKO I don't understand women anymore. You want to make her feel
good, you don't have lots of money but you book a fancy dinner at a

super-fancy restaurant in Chelsea, you bring her roses, you ooze sex appeal and desire and interest in her, you pay the bill, and what does she do? She accuses you of sexual harassment. She's "not ready" to do it yet. She doesn't want to be "pushed." She wants to wait for the "right moment." She didn't shave her legs to make sure she doesn't respond to your erotic advances on the first date. You know what, go fuck yourself, Laura!

LAURA How many days have passed? A week. And he didn't call, he didn't. I only told him he shouldn't sexually harass me, that's all I said. Like a joke, you know. Well, half a joke. I wasn't ready to... I need to first erase all those beautiful Latin names of STDs from my mind before... I mean, he should understand this—you can't work on STD tests all day long and then jump into it. Sex, I mean.

DARKO Yes, you're pretty, and you didn't text messages at the table, but you don't get me. We could have had something beautiful together. Darko and Laura. A family. Kids. A house full of laughter. Like you see in those stupid American romantic comedies. We could have had all that. And more. You fucking spoiled everything!

LAURA He doesn't take rejection well, I could see that in his eyes. His eyelashes were like... biting the air. His mouth was so sad, his lips... Anyway...

DARKO Anyway... that *New York Times* article was dynamite. Mom framed it. The Internet version. She shows it to all our neighbors. She's really proud of me. No, she doesn't understand English, but she can see my name printed in the paper.

LAURA Yes, I know. I'm a loser. I shouldn't let a man like Darko go. Chivalric men are an endangered species. You don't need to hide under the bed to make your point, Penelope. Of course he gave me his number!

[DARKO*'s cell phone rings and rings.*]

DARKO Mom doesn't know. I got fired after that article. I couldn't find any other job in my field. But I still have dignity and prestige! I'm not a human Kleenex. I told them the emperor was naked. *Bio sam u redu* [*"I was fine"* in Serbian].

[*He opens his briefcase and takes a handgun out of it. He loads the semi-automatic pistol.*]

TANYA Okay, so…he's like, in class, and after class, he's like you know talking to me in Serbian, although I told him we don't speak Serbian at home, I told him you're Bosnian…But no, he's like talking to me in Serbian, and that's like so embarrassing, like Julie asked me like why don't you answer him in Yugoslavian, or whatever language you guys speak over there in the Balkans…And I'm like, I'm not from the Balkans, my mom is, I was raised here, and she's like "Whatever." And then Jessica is like "You guys are Muslim?" And I'm like my mom is Muslim but I'm not, I'm an atheist, I don't believe in that religion shit, that's only to control the masses. And she's like "Whatever." And Patrick is like "Serbians are Christian, Bosnians are Muslim, that's why they fought against each other in the Balkan war, isn't that so, Tanya? And I'm like "Whatever."

DARKO 9 x 19 mm Grandpower K100 Slovak semi-automatic pistol. The best.

TANYA Okay, so that kinda discussion, or variations of it, I had like each time we had a class with that freakin' Darko…so I was like, couldn't take it anymore…and one day, when I had the monthly meeting with my academic advisor, I was like telling her: our Intro to IT professor Darko Rasnin, you know…I'm sorry to have to say this…his teaching methods are…I mean, he's a little sexist, he was kinda…you know, I kinda feel like he was like kinda flirting with me…I feel a little sexually harassed, yes…No, he didn't touch me or anything…but the way he looks at me, and he always keeps me after class to talk to me in Serbian…I mean, yes, we both have Balkan roots, but that doesn't make it okay to…I mean, my mom was gang-raped by the fuckin' Serbians and I just can't, I can't have him look at me like that!

DARKO [*Holding the gun in his hands.*] So here's the plan. I have nothing to lose, have I? Actually there's a lot to win: fame. Posterity will know my name. Yes, in connection to a killing spree, but who cares. Fame is fame. Bad publicity is good publicity too. People will know my name. Write books about me. Make movies. Win Oscars. And after my name is known by millions, that's when they will look at my interview and see what I had to say about the danger of cell phones. A controversial discussion will escalate. Globally. The "Darko" effect will be in everyone's mind when they speak on a cell phone. And they speak on cell phones all the time. They speak like they breathe. All of them.

Everybody on this planet will know Darko's name and the ideas he died for.

TANYA   I know you don't want me to talk about that anymore. But that doesn't change the way I feel, Mom. I'm not doing well with anger management when it comes to Serbians. Why did he have to talk with me in Serbian? I mean, when I had that guy Marko in class for a semester in high school, it was kinda okay, he never talked to me in Serbian. Even if we don't talk about this, Mom, it doesn't change the fact that I am a rape-child, I'm the product of that freakin' rape, Mom, I'm the daughter of a gang of motherfuckin' Serbians! And if we don't talk about this, Mom, you're not gonna heal, and I'm not gonna heal, and we can't move on, I can't move on, I wanna deal with this, Mom!

[*A cell phone rings and rings.*]

LAURA   [*Calling* DARKO.] He's not answering. Of course. Why should he? I bet he found another woman. Well. Better like this. What can I tell him? That I changed my mind and now, after a week, I kinda am in the mood for...I can't tell him that. Maybe I can. Why not? I gotta learn to be more direct. When I want something I gotta say it. Yes, I will say it. If he gives me the chance. If he answers the phone. No. He won't.

[*She hangs up.*]

Why am I talking about him "giving me a chance"? Do we still have Dr. Phil's book, *Self Matters*? Okay. Let's work on my self-esteem. I tend to wait for validation from other people. Or cats! That's not good. That's eating me. I must find my authentic self. Create my life from inside out. How does Dr. Phil put it? "I am asking you to call a huge time-out from this scramble you call life, and to focus on the one doing the scrambling: you."

DARKO   In some countries I'd be a hero. Here I'm gonna be called a crazy terrorist. It's okay. It's still worth taking the risk. There's nothing to lose. I will die with a little dignity. Shouting at those hypocrites: "Adjuncts! You're all adjuncts! Adjuncts of human beings!" No, I'm not gonna shout. I'm gonna be very calm. I'm gonna hold the Chair at gunpoint and I'm gonna talk—[*He mimics that talk:*]—slowly, clearly, professorially.

TANYA Yeah, I reported the Serb for sorta sexual-harassment attempt, and he got fired. He never knew what hit him, they told him that, you know, in this economy, blah, blah...they had to make cuts, to cut some adjuncts. Adjuncts are not like real professors. They are hired like on part-time, no-responsibility basis. So he didn't get any more courses. They kicked him out. After like fifteen years of teaching. Part-time teaching.

DARKO Tomorrow is the monthly faculty meeting at 10 a.m. They will all be there...Everybody will be there. The "professors."

TANYA Mom? I kinda feel guilty now. I mean, I fucked him up and he didn't really do anything bad to me. Except for speaking in Serbian. But still. He could be one of the bad guys, couldn't he? One of the guys who raped you. He could be my father. Couldn't he?

DARKO I'm going to enter the building calmly—I still have the university ID. The guard will smile at me and say, "What's up, man," as always. A really cool guy, Jamal. He likes me. I like him. We played soccer together on a Sunday, last year. A good guy. Underdog. Born into no money, bad circumstances. What's up, bro?! It's down, man. I'm freakin' down. Eating the ground.

TANYA So I kinda think I should talk to him. If that doesn't completely freak you out. I should try to explain to him, to see if...I got his address from school. He lives in Brooklyn too. I thought I should let you know. Maybe you see him in the supermarket and it freaks you out. If he's one of them, the bad guys. But maybe he's not. Maybe he didn't even fight in the war. Maybe he was on a fellowship in the US. Maybe he's a good guy...He seemed to know a lot, he seemed to love teaching. I fucked him up, Mom. I gotta talk to him.

LAURA No, we can't afford a therapist this year, but we already know what he will say: work on your self-esteem. Negative internal dialogue has physiological consequences: chronic adrenaline arousal, elevated blood pressure, headaches, depression, low libido...Darko would have helped me. But I didn't let him. Because I'm fucked up and afraid of love. Afraid of people. Who might like me. See the vicious cycle? I gotta break it. I will call him again. And again. Until he answers.

DARKO I'm leaving all my belongings to Jamal. It's not much, but still. I wrote a last note on this Kleenex.

[*He shows it.*]

Jamal is to take all my possessions. No way to have them shipped to Mom back home. No money. No time. Tomorrow is the day. The last day. I'm not a human Kleenex.

[*His cell phone rings and rings and rings.* TANYA *bangs at his door.*]

TANYA   Professor?! Professor?!

• • •

Cell

Cassandra Medley

Cell by Cassandra Medley. Copyright © 2011 by Cassandra Medley. All rights reserved. Reprinted by permission of the author.

CAUTION/ADVICE: Professionals and amateurs are hereby warned that performance of *Cell* is subject to a royalty. It is fully protected under the copyright laws of the United States of America, and of all countries covered by the International Copyright Union (including the Dominion of Canada and the rest of the British Commonwealth), and of all countries covered by the Pan-American Copyright Convention and the Universal Copyright Convention, the Berne Convention, and of all countries with which the United States has reciprocal copyright relations. All rights, including professional and amateur stage performing rights, motion picture, recitation, lecturing, public reading, radio broadcasting, television, video or sound recording, all other forms of mechanical or electronic reproduction, such as CD-ROM, DVD-ROM, information storage and retrieval systems, and photocopying, and the rights of translation into foreign languages, are strictly reserved. Particular emphasis is placed upon the matter of readings, permission for which must be secured from the author's agent in writing.

Inquiries concerning rights should be addressed to Cassandra Medley at cassandramedley @gmail.com

Cassandra Medley

Cassandra Medley's recently produced plays include *American Slavery Project* (2012–2013), *Cell* (Ensemble Studio Theatre Marathon, 2011), *Daughter* (Ensemble Studio Theatre Marathon, 2009), *Noon Day Sun* (Diverse City Theatre Company—Theatre Row, New York City 2008), and *Relativity*, a commission from the Alfred P. Sloan Foundation, Ensemble Studio Theatre (2004). *Relativity* won the 2006 Audelco August Wilson Playwriting Award and was featured on Science Friday, National Public Radio. It was published by Broadway Play Publishing. *Relativity* was featured in an online radio broadcast, Los Angeles Repertory Theatre—February 2008. Ms. Medley has also received the 2004 "Going to the River" Writers' Life Achievement Award, 2002 Ensemble Studio Theatre 25th Anniversary Award for Theatre Excellence, the 2001 Theatrefest Regional Playwriting Award for Best Play, the 1995 New Professional Theatre Award, and the 1995 Marilyn Simpson Award. She was a 1989 finalist for the Susan Smith Blackburn Award in Playwriting, and won the 1990 National Endowment for the Arts Playwright Award.

··· production history ···

Cell received its world premiere on June 9, 2011, in Ensemble Studio Theatre's 33rd Marathon of One-Act Plays.

characters

> **RENÉ**   African American woman of fifty
> **CERISE**   René's sister, African American, forty-five
> **GWENDOLYN**   Cerise's daughter, African American, twenty-three

place

Flint, Michigan.

setting

The living room of RENÉ's mobile home.

time

Summer 2011.

scene 1

[RENÉ's *trailer, early evening. Sound of outside door opening, door chimes,* RENÉ *enters and immediately runs offstage into another room.* CERISE *and* GWEN *enter. All are dressed in the same dull, tan, short-sleeved shirts and uniform green pants.* GWEN *is operating a cell-phone video camera, pointing it at herself and* CERISE.]

GWEN   [*Into the cell-phone camera speaker.*] Here we are back home, after our first day on the job.

CERISE   [*Re: the camera.*] Daughter, honey. Baby, that's enough, now. That's your auntie's, you can't just use it up.

GWEN   Just wanna show us coming home after our first day at work.

[RENÉ *runs on holding a small chocolate cake, with a balloon on a string that reads: "WELCOME."*]

RENÉ   WELCOME HOME, Everybody!

[*They all hug.* GWEN *kisses* RENÉ *on the cheek.*]

GWEN   Ahhhhh! WONDERFUL! Thank you so much!

CERISE [*Delighted.*] Sis! Ain't you so sweet! You didn't have to!

GWEN [*Continues videotaping with the cell phone. Into the cell phone.*] And here's Auntie's cake she got for us!

CERISE My big sis is the very, very best.

[RENÉ *playfully waves this off.*]

RENÉ Girl, get outta here with all that! Family is family.

GWEN [*Continues filming.*] Auntie, your trailer's so nice.

RENÉ It's a roof over my head.

CERISE Don't wanna crowd you—if you ever need y'know complete privacy, Gwen and me can go to the mall for a few hours.

RENÉ Let's get the blankets out 'fore we're too tired.

CERISE Tonight, I'll take the corner. Gwen, you sleep on the love seat.

GWEN Momma, you need the love seat for your back. Corner's fine with me.

CERISE [*To* GWEN.] We not here to freeload off your aunt. I want us serving her every chance we get, understand?

GWEN Of course, I understand.

RENÉ Relax, Cerise, this not no boot camp.

CERISE Sis, I'm making us some meatballs and spaghetti for tonight. You got bath salts? Gwen, go in the bathroom, find bath salts, make a hot tub for your aunt.

[*To* RENÉ.]

All the standing you do on your feet.

[GWEN *suddenly turns and videotapes the badge on her sleeve.* CERISE *turns and "politely" snatches the cell phone away from* GWEN, *handing it to* RENÉ.]

RENÉ [*To* CERISE.] Ah, give her a break, let her 'lone.

[RENÉ *hands* GWEN *back the camera.*]

CERISE [*Exasperated re: the badge.*] All damn badge say is, "Thurston Corporation."

GWEN I now work for Thurston Corporation Immigration Detention Center.

RENÉ It's the first real job she's ever had. Nothing wrong with being proud.

CERISE René, what can I get cha? As I recall, you like great big glasses of ice cold lemonade filled to the brim with ice…

RENÉ You wanna pour me a gin and tonic, that'd be great. Better still, hold the "tonic."

[RENÉ *winks at* CERISE, *who is very surprised. Laughing at* CERISE*'s shock.*]

Baby Sis, if you looking for René of ten years ago, you looking for a mirage.

GWEN [*Turns camera on herself, speaks as if being interviewed.* CERISE *and* RENÉ *exchange amused glances. Into camera lens.*]

How do I feel after my first day at Thurston Corporation? Great. I feel great. I never knew there were so many immigrants from so many places. And Momma's working there too.

RENÉ [*To* GWEN.] Tell on that phone how you was promoted to the front desk right away.

CERISE [*To* GWEN.] Now, that is something to crow about. Promoted to the front desk on the very first day!

[*To* RENÉ.]

Sister, I'm so glad I broke down and—and—

RENÉ Hello? What'd you think, I was gonna let you be sleeping on the streets back in Cleveland and starve to death?

CERISE [*To* GWEN.] You didn't put that on camera?!

[*She puts the cell phone down with an irritated expression.*]

CERISE [*To* RENÉ.] Child, when my unemployment run out, I thought, "Hello, welfare." Then they come talking 'bout I don't meet the regulations. I said to that woman, I said, "So what we supposed to eat, air? Don't tell me God's works ain't wondrous!"

RENÉ Remember now. Always look sharp. Keep in mind that "our kind" is always on the radar with upper management.

CERISE Girl, ain't that the truth! They never wanna give black folks a break.

RENÉ [*To* CERISE.] Why should they? If we gotta work twice as hard as anybody else, I say, so be it. Builds character. Have no time for excuses.

[*To* GWEN.]

I may be a supervisor, but I also got a supervisor, know what I'm saying?

CERISE Leon Banks. We understand. She understands.

[*To* GWEN.]

Auntie's taking a big risk in hiring us.

RENÉ Never mind that.

CERISE [*To* GWEN.] Don't forget it.

RENÉ Why would she forget it?

CERISE [*Cheerfully to* RENÉ.] Least we come cheap for Thurston—don't have to worry 'bout no union workers or—paying benefits...

RENÉ *Shhh!* Never mention that, understand?! Never. To nobody.

CERISE Of course, of course.

[*Trying for a joke.*]

This trailer ain't "bugged" is it?

[*Serious.*]

You don't gotta worry about us, we your family.

GWEN [*To* RENÉ.] All them folks in the waiting room? They trying to get to they families locked up inside. Right?

CERISE Never you mind. Just do your job.

RENÉ [*To* GWEN.] Sister, I'm getting thirsty.

[CERISE *runs off.* RENÉ *places a gentle arm around* GWEN.]

RENÉ What are your front desk responsibilities?

GWEN [*In a studied tone.*] Man the front desk on the shift I'm given. Make all visitors stay in the line, and in order...keep the waiting room calm.

RENÉ Good. Very good.

GWEN Waiting room be so packed.

RENÉ If they keep they seats, like they should, they'll fit. Thing is for you to keep order whenever you're assigned to the front desk.

CERISE [*Yells from offstage.*] That's right!

RENÉ Otherwise, we'd have a mad house.

CERISE [*Enters with a tray—hands* RENÉ *her drink, hands* GWEN *a can of soda.*] A mad house. That's exactly right.

RENÉ Good. Remember, now Leon likes you. Took one look at ya and said, "Front desk."

CERISE [*To* GWEN.] Ain't that something?! And he's the supervisor over your auntie!

RENÉ [*Tosses back her drink.* CERISE *is shocked.*] Trouble is...

CERISE [*Alert.*] Trouble? What trouble?

RENÉ [*Strokes* GWEN*'s cheek.*] Baby, I'm not criticizing, alright?
[GWEN *nods, curious.*]
After all, it was just your first day. I understand that.

CERISE What'd she do? She punched the right buttons on the computer, didn't she?

RENÉ [*Centers on* GWEN.] I'm the visitor coming to the window. "I want to see Maria Concita Elena Gonzalez!" Here's you...
[*A too soft, mousy voice.*]
"Step away from the window, please. Please, step away. From the window..."

CERISE [*To* RENÉ.] Oh, she gotta *booming* voice when she wanna use it. Just wait till you hear her *booming*.
[*To* GWEN.]
Remember, now, you're seated behind plate glass.

RENÉ [*Studies* GWEN.] Twenty-three years old. All grown up.

CERISE And ready to use that *booming* voice.

RENÉ [*To* GWEN.] Okay, I'm the visitor—what's the first thing you do?

GWEN Get the name, then check the computer screen to see if they got clearance to visit the resident.

RENÉ Which, nine times out of ten—they won't have. Or the person they wanna see'll have been moved out.

GWEN Moved to where?

CERISE [*To* RENÉ.] Girl, I'm just so thankful I finally broke down and called you when I did.

GWEN [*Booming voice.*] STEP AWAY FROM THE WINDOW! WAIT YOUR TURN!

[CERISE *and* RENÉ *clap. To* RENÉ.]

The people living behind the locked door. Where they sent to when they moved out?

CERISE Is that our business?! *No, it is not.*

RENÉ [*Admonishing* CERISE.] Don't talk to her like that.

[*Then to* GWEN.]

They flown back into the wide world. Wherever they come from in the first place. That way we get to have our country to ourselves.

GWEN But...

CERISE Lookit you! My daughter doing a service for her country.

GWEN What about all them waiting-room families left behind?

RENÉ [*Pause, then.*] It's complicated.

GWEN [*Whirls on* RENÉ.] I'm not retarded!

CERISE Is that how you speak to your aunt?

[*Claps her hands.*]

Okey-dokey... Who's ready for spaghetti in about a half hour?

GWEN STEP AWAY FROM THE WINDOW! WAIT YOUR TURN!

RENÉ Terrific. And if they don't wanna be patient, and start screaming, and hollering, or threatening, then what?

GWEN Press the button. Let the armed guards handle the situation.

RENÉ Excellent. Remember, you're behind plate glass. You're protected.

GWEN STEP AWAY FROM THE WINDOW. WAIT YOUR TURN. STAND IN LINE!

[RENÉ *and* GWEN *nod, impressed, smiling.* RENÉ *opens her arms wide.*]

RENÉ Welcome to my 'lil hideaway.

CERISE Spaghetti coming up!

scene 2

[RENÉ's trailer, the next night. The "Welcome" balloon dangles, still bouncing in the air. All three sit with dinner trays on their laps and empty plates having finished their meal. They are in their bras, their work pants still on. RENÉ and CERISE soak their bare feet in small basins. RENÉ has a shot glass on the floor next to her feet. RENÉ holds the TV remote and channel-surfs, various program sounds come from the unseen TV on the invisible wall.]

GWEN [Speaking into the cell-phone video camera.] Day 2 at Thurston Corporation. How do I feel? Very good.

[She clicks off the phone, and refers to a stack of brochures in her lap and she slowly turns the pages, reading. Holds up brochure.]

Thurston Corp. Head Office is located way, way off in Houston, Texas. They got Thurston places in ten states!

[She watches RENÉ with admiration. Pause, then.]

Auntie, ten years away from you is too long.

RENÉ Well, we all together now.

CERISE [Clears the plates. To GWEN.] Momma gonna save up enough money, we'll get our own trailer, give her back her privacy.

[CERISE disappears off with the plates. TV plays. GWEN reads.]

RENÉ What about stayin' here with me?

GWEN Thurston's number three in the nation.

[CERISE returns with towels. She hands a towel to GWEN, who wipes her feet dry, still reading the brochures. CERISE stops cold, smiles.]

RENÉ [To CERISE.] Thought you always wanted to go to community college. Use your savings for that.

CERISE Girl, that old pipe dream done gathered ten years worth of dust.

[CERISE kneels down and proceeds to wipe RENÉ's feet dry. RENÉ snatches her feet away.]

RENÉ [Embarrassed.] Cerise! Now, no call for you to be—

[CERISE grabs RENÉ's feet and continues wiping and massaging them.]

CERISE [Playful.] Hush up. You the one been standing on your toe jams for twenty some years, me and Gwen only have had two days...

RENÉ   Sister, you could take a criminal justice course over at er... uh...uh...

[*Snaps her fingers to help her memory.*]

Gilmore Community—

GWEN   [*Holds up brochure.*] Ain't that something, Momma? "Third in the nation."

CERISE   [*To* RENÉ.] Tell ya what I got—and it's thanks to you. A job. A job that'll go on and on and on, that's what I got. Long as there's foreigners getting caught without their papers, me, and you, and Gwen here, won't never be laid off. Now, I call that way more real than taking some chance on some community college.

[*To* GWEN, *playful.*]

What you think about it, baby?

GWEN   [*Holds up brochure.*] The rooms they got pictured here are just rooms. See? There's no jail bar on a window or on the front of the cell.

CERISE   Gwen, Momma said for you to let that go. Rest ya eyes and get some rest!

[CERISE *snatches the brochures from off* GWEN's *lap.*]

RENÉ   [*Playful.*] Who's ready for cake, raise ya hand!

CERISE   Sister, sing pretty like you used to! Let's hear you hit them notes. Gwen, wait till you hear this.

[*To* RENÉ.]

You oughta go back to church and sing in a choir, like when we was coming up.

RENÉ   [*"Playfully" waving this away.*] Oh, stop.

GWEN   I think I *do* remember...Auntie sounding like a songbird.

CERISE   Soprano.

RENÉ   [*Sips from her shot glass, notices* CERISE's *disapproval.*] Ha. Don't be so cross-eyed.

CERISE   Now, you remember my own tribulations with that.

[*Pause, then.*]

Sing to us, like you used to!

[GWEN *and* CERISE *wait on* RENÉ, *her smile drops.*]

RENÉ [*Quite serious.*] I said, drop it!

[*Silence.* CERISE *and* GWEN *stare at* RENÉ. *Motioning to* GWEN.]

Leon Banks is sweet on our girl.

[GWEN *is totally shocked by this news.* RENÉ *nods to* GWEN.]

That's right, that's what he told me.

CERISE [*To* GWEN, *pleased.*] Leon! Your supervisor!

RENÉ He thinks she cute. Specially with that 'lil round behind she carrying around.

GWEN Gross.

CERISE You ain't got to marry the man. Just smile at him once and a while.

RENÉ After all, you're twenty-three.

CERISE 'Bout time somebody started circulating around. That's what happens with normal girls, only natural.

GWEN Pleas-s-s-se . . . He's like thirty-five, or something. *And* with that gut.

CERISE Appearances are only skin keep.

GWEN [*Holds up the brochure.*] How come these pictures don't show the real cells in that place?

CERISE We talking 'bout something important to your whole life. Who the hell cares 'bout some damn photos? Talk sense.

RENÉ [*To* GWEN.] Leon's unmarried. Well. Divorced.

CERISE [*Even more delighted.*] And since you're starting fresh, he wouldn't have to know nothing about where you come from before.

RENÉ He's clean living. Well mannered. Strong in the Lord.

GWEN Well, I ain't.

CERISE Don't say that. Come Sunday, we going straight to some altar, somewheres, getting down on our knees, and thanking Jesus.

RENÉ [*To* GWEN.] Let him take you to the movies.

CERISE   She certainly will.

[*Pause.*]

He won't be trying nothing?

RENÉ   He ain't no dog like some of these running round here.

GWEN   [*Holds up the brochure.*] Reading this, you'd never know that it was a momma-baby jail.

RENÉ   [*Very calm.*] Sweetheart, they not in no jail.

GWEN   But—

RENÉ   They're in a residence until they can be returned to they countries of origin.

GWEN   Baby cribs in the jail cells, what else can you call it?

CERISE   Gwen, are you hired to judge? Is that your job description?

RENÉ   Look's kinda weird, I know. But that's only cause you're not used to it. Wait till you've been around a couple months.

[*Pause.*]

Remember, it's all supervised. We use government guidelines. You see how we have a 'lil play yard for the kids...

GWEN   That itty-bitty cement square is a yard for the kids?

CERISE   [*To* GWEN.] Do you want your own children someday? Well?

GWEN   Yeah, guess so.

CERISE   And a husband with a good job, and a nice, big house to live in? Answer!

GWEN   Well, who don't want that?

CERISE   Okay, then. Focus on that, and leave the Department of Homeland Security in the hands of the Department of Homeland Security.

GWEN   I'm just trying to teach myself what my job is.

RENÉ   Uh-huh, well, one of the most important parts of the job is to let go when you get home at night. Let go of the day, and like your momma says, focus on your own life.

CERISE Hello?!

RENÉ And I certainly hope you won't be asking Leon none of this nonsense. Or anybody else on the job.

GWEN I know better than that.

CERISE She knows better than that!

GWEN I'm not dumb.

RENÉ Course you not. You're like anybody else.

CERISE [*Takes the TV remote.*] Let's see the *Oprah* rerun for today.

GWEN All I'm saying is like wow...I mean...

CERISE *OPRAH, Y'ALL!*

GWEN I mean, like, what would that be like to have to take a shower with no shower curtain every day...

[CERISE *and* RENÉ *concentrate on the TV.*]

CERISE [*To* GWEN.] Shhhh
[*To* RENÉ, *pointing to the screen.*]
Oh, she just got on white women and they diets...

RENÉ [*To* CERISE.] Turn on *Judge Brown*—he usually got our folks fighting over something...

[*Silence.* CERISE *and* RENÉ *watch the TV.*]

CERISE [*Pointing to screen.*] Now, lookit that hair on her head! Ump-ump-ump!

GWEN What it feel like to have lights-out just 'cause we say "lights-out," to have to eat whatever we give you, like it or not? And you can't take ya baby for a stroll...and...you don't talk English, so you don't understand...and...all the clanging all the time...and the howling, plus the babies crying...and the disinfectant smell mixed in with dirty diapers...families visit, but the immigrants be behind glass. They can't touch them, they can't hug them, nothing.
[RENÉ *switches off the TV, turns to* GWEN. CERISE *glares at* GWEN.]
I'll go brush my teeth. Be all ready for tomorrow.

[GWEN *makes to exit.*]

RENÉ Niece.

GWEN [*Whirls around, frightened.*] No more questions! Promise!

[*Silence.* GWEN *and* CERISE *wait in apprehension.*]

RENÉ I got a slinky, short silver, nylon dress. Fit me fifteen years ago. Still in style. You can wear it on your date.

CERISE [*Claps in relief. To* RENÉ.] Like I say, what would we do without you?!

[RENÉ *and* GWEN *lock eyes.*]

RENÉ Sweet dreams.

[RENÉ *exits to her bedroom.*]

scene 3

[*Third Night.* RENÉ *sits.* GWEN *stands over her with an electric hot comb.* GWEN *is pressing, or refreshing* RENÉ's *hair. R&B music from radio.*]

RENÉ Your momma sure 'nough loves that hot shower, don't she?

GWEN [*Instantly yells offstage.*] MOMMA, GET OUT THE SHOWER SO OTHER PEOPLE CAN USE IT!

[GWEN *continues to comb* RENÉ's *hair.*]

RENÉ How come Starbucks and McDonald's didn't work out back in Cleveland?

GWEN Orders come in so fast at them places...customers start yelling.
[*Pause.*]
I really like living here in Flint, Michigan.
[*She continues pressing* RENÉ's *hair.*]
How come, you and Momma let ten years go by without speaking?

RENÉ Child, there's so much blood under the bridge 'tween me and y'momma...you don't wanna dip a toe in it, believe me.

GWEN You was always letting me snuggle on your lap. That's what I'll never forget.
[*Pause.*]
How come I always been slower than other girls my age?

RENÉ [*Stroking* GWEN's *face.*] Nonsense. How could you be slower if you're learning to speak Creole?

GWEN Huh?

RENÉ "Huh?"

[*Strokes* GWEN's *face, then suddenly tightens her hold on* GWEN's *arm.*] I'm hearing that you learning to speak French and Spanish. Guess you'll start up on A-rab talk, next, huh?

[GWEN *attempts to pull away from* RENÉ, *who holds her tight.*] You must think I'm a fool. You think I'm a fool?

GWEN Whatsamatter?

RENÉ [*Sadly.*] What we gonna do with you? You're supposed to be our flesh and blood.

GWEN I...I'm doing everything just like you told me.

RENÉ Naw-naw, you going around speaking French, Spanish, or patois, or whatever the hell it is—that's what you doing!

[CERISE *appears dressed in a bathrobe, smiling, is about to speak, then backs into shadows, watching* GWEN *and* RENÉ.]

GWEN I'm following orders, just like you've told me.

RENÉ You got orders to speak to cell 293? Or cell 156?

CERISE [*Steps forward.*] What is all this?

[*Pulls* GWEN *from* RENÉ's *grip.*] You hurting her.

RENÉ [*Calmly centers on* GWEN.] Don't you realize they got cameras all through that place? Think, Gwendolyn, think!

CERISE Don't be talkin' to her like that...

RENÉ [*To* GWEN.] Everywhere you turn there's a lens watching us *and* them breathe, swallow, piss, and take a shit.

CERISE Hold up! Leon told me Gwen is doing a terrific job...

RENÉ Sure! 'Till he caught sight of her on camera, sneaking a chat with cell 293! That Haitian woman. She's holding her baby up to the bars on her cell, so Gwen here can pat the baby's head!

CERISE What?

RENÉ Yep. Y'know the one we hadda put in isolation? We gotta close-up of Gwen here!

[*To* GWEN.]

Tell her, Gwen!

GWEN Her name's Marie-Louise.

RENÉ It's not your job to know what her name is.

GWEN I was just saying hi.

RENÉ You was stroking that Creole woman's baby's head...! TELL HER. And the Mexican? Gwen here is sharing her curried chicken leftovers with the Mexican. We got it live on camera!

CERISE [*Turns to* GWEN.] You know that's way, way against regulations.

GWEN The Haitian baby may have a fever...

RENÉ Doctor comes second Friday of every month. The momma's been given a cold compress to use. Meanwhile, only reason you gonna get one more chance is 'cause Leon thinks you gotta sweet ass! Otherwise, he would've kicked you out this afternoon. He's got his own supervisor!

CERISE Tell your auntie you ain't gonna never do this again.

GWEN Me and Marie the same age. But she got a baby she gotta keep in jail.

RENÉ [*Pause, then to* GWEN.] When ya new friend is put on the plane back to Haiti, guess you wanna go to the shanties too? Or go with ya Mexican back to the filthy hovels there, see how well you enjoy it!

CERISE Okay, okay...no need to be so rough. She won't do it no more. No need to climb the walls about it...

RENÉ Weren't for me you two wouldn't have no walls!

CERISE What you want? Huh? Me groveling on me knees in gratitude? Would that be enough?

GWEN Momma, don't. She's right. I was wrong. I apologize.

RENÉ Girl, it gets to be where these "apologies" ain't nothing but breath in and breath out.

CERISE [*Dramatically falling to her knees.*] Thank you, Sister, for all your kindness.

RENÉ Well, I'm sorry, but am I to—to—to always be your Red Cross for the rest of my natural life?

CERISE I ain't asked you for nothing in ten years.

RENÉ Right, and when you do call—it's 'cause you ain't got a pot to piss in, or a window to throw it out, or a front, or backyard to soak it up!

CERISE 'Least I don't feed on bitterness 'cause my dreams didn't work out.

RENÉ Cerise! I'm *not* gonna end up on the unemployment line just 'cause your daughter was marinated in moonshine!

[RENÉ*'s hand flies up to her mouth as if wanting to take back this slip.* GWEN *glances from one to the other.*]

CERISE She don't mean nothing by that. Do you, René?

RENÉ Niece, only job security I got is my rep for following orders. This ain't Never-Never Land where life just gives me this trailer to live in 'cause God is good, and Jesus Christ done had a Second Coming.

GWEN I won't do it, no more. I promise.

CERISE She means it, René.

RENÉ [*Focusing on* GWEN.] Sit. We do not speak to them in the cells, and we do not let them speak to us. It's for they own good. DO NOT FRATERNIZE. You do that, you get the boot before you can sneeze. Never get the inmates' hopes up, chaos would break out. The rules are for the good of everybody. You think you helping your Creole and Mexican ladies by befriending them? You are not.

GWEN Yes, m'am.

CERISE [*Attempts to embrace* GWEN, *who backs away from her.*] Momma will help you.

RENÉ We do not find out about them, we do not let them find out about us. We do not answer their questions. We do not ask them questions. We do not get involved!

GWEN We do not get involved.

RENÉ Hidden camera don't lie, and my home don't come free.

GWEN Yes, m'am.

RENÉ And as far as you concerned: don't wanna hear no Creole, no Mexican, no South American, no A-rab, or nothing else coming out of your mouth.

GWEN I'm gonna be so much better tomorrow.

[GWEN *goes to* RENÉ *in supplication, she reaches to embrace* RENÉ. RENÉ *holds back, then returns the hug after a pause.* CERISE *crosses over and embraces them both. Lights cross fade.*]

scene 4

[GWEN *enters, her shirt untucked, and slightly disheveled. She is obviously upset. She lays across the couch, takes out a joint and puffs on it for a few moments. A sustained beat…* RENÉ *and* CERISE *enter, dressed as just coming from work.*]

CERISE and RENÉ What in the world…? Where you been?! We been looking all over for you!

GWEN [*Mocking.*] Hitched a ride with Leon.

[*She holds up the joint, mocking.*]

He give me this to "calm my nerves."

[*Then to* RENÉ.]

That's right, Leon.

RENÉ Now, look here—it was nobody's fault.

GWEN That's Leon over, and over: "It was nobody's fault."

RENÉ He's absolutely right. It probably had a special condition before the momma even came here…

GWEN "It"?

RENÉ Don't you *be* getting all up in my face. Y'know what I'm trying to—

GWEN Patrice! The baby's name was Patrice.

CERISE We all know that.

GWEN Now y'all got a tiny corpse on ya hands. Yesterday, his little head…felt so hot…now his teeny body bundled up like a package…little Patrice…

RENÉ [*Shocked.*] The morgue is off-limits.

GWEN Not if I let Leon cop a feel on my booty, it ain't.

CERISE [*Moves to slap* GWEN. GWEN *ducks.*] Gwendolyn, that's enough.

GWEN Only acting like a normal girl, y'all. Hold up, I don't gotta act normal, I was marinated.

CERISE René, don't let her speak to me like that.

RENÉ [*To* GWEN.] We realize it was hard for you to be put through this…

GWEN Me? Me!? Hard for me? The momma's name is Marie-Louise! And now her Patrice is sealed up in a white sack.

RENÉ Oh, for heaven's sake. I got folks I have to deal with week after week, month after—I been working for Thurston for twenty-seven years!

GWEN Marie-Louise. Now put on a plane…
[*Pause.*]
In her lap, her baby's ashes.

CERISE She'll have the comfort of her family.

GWEN [*Bitter.*] Her flesh and blood, huh, Momma? Huh, Auntie?

RENÉ Don't be giving me no evil eye, girl! Babies get sick sometimes without nobody knowing why. It happens.

GWEN Thought they got cameras trained on everybody night and day?

RENÉ I should *never* have talked myself into putting you on staff.

CERISE [*To* RENÉ.] Now, don't say that.

GWEN I bet wrapped-up dead babies is a regular thing in that place. One doctor once a week—get sick on the wrong day, tough.

RENÉ Only thing "regular" is you not doing what you was told.

GWEN I've done EXACTLY what you—

RENÉ Surely you not raising your voice to me?

CERISE [*To* GWEN.] Back off, girl.

GWEN [*Grabs a brochure off the table, holds it up, starts ripping it to shreds.*] It ain't shit!

RENÉ Alright, it's sad! But they know the risks they take, when they take the risk of trying to come here, and trying to stay without documentation. They know this! They break the law, and want us to feel bad for 'em and take the blame!

GWEN No wonder you got insomnia.

RENÉ Now you can slant ya' snake eyes at me all you want, but this the real world, Gwen. And every time you put a piece of pie to your lips, or curl up in ya warm blanket at night—Thurston Corp is paying for it.

GWEN Or was. I'm fired, right? Right?

RENÉ [*Avoiding* GWEN*'s glance.*] Depends.

GWEN You mean, if I keep my mouth shut, I still gotta job.

RENÉ In all fifty states, the unemployed are overflowing the streets.

CERISE [*To* GWEN.] You're a normal person. Hear me? And like any normal, everyday, ordinary person, you gonna just go, day to day, and do what you gotta do to get by.
[GWEN *runs off. Silence as the two sister's hold a stare.*]
She'll settle down. After awhile.

RENÉ [*Pause.*] I know. I'll tell Leon to really romance her. Gifts, flowers, dinner. Y'all can't stay here without her income.

CERISE I know, I know. We understand.
[GWEN *enters, bringing out her duffle bag piled with random clothes.*]
Uh-uh. Where do you think you're going?

GWEN [*To* RENÉ.] You faked my name on the witness form, didn't you?

RENÉ Think how many piles of job applications Thurston gets day in and day out.

GWEN [*To* RENÉ.] You signed my name…saying that yesterday, I felt no fever coming from off that Haitian baby.

RENÉ DAMN STRAIGHT I SIGNED FOR YOU. And I volunteered to do it too.

GWEN I should've screamed and hollered yesterday, and got some help to come to that cell.

RENÉ When will you finally begin to understand that it's your life or theirs—and no in-between?

CERISE [*Attempting to steer* GWEN.] You turn right around and put that stuff back and get ready for bed.

GWEN Gotta be some joint in this town that'll need floors scrubbed in exchange for a meal. Maybe they'll lemme sleep in the cellar.

RENÉ [*To* GWEN.] Patrice? Lemme tell you about your little Patrice. He was born a bottom feeder just like you.

CERISE René, please...

RENÉ Just like me and ya momma and everybody in this broken-down town, and all the ton of nobodies that crowd up the bottom pit of this world. And there ain't no abracadabra that's gonna change that.

GWEN Even a fucking ghost town like this gotta have a Salvation Army...

[RENÉ *grabs* GWEN *and drags her to the window,* CERISE *panics.*]

CERISE René!

RENÉ [*To* GWEN.] See how dark it is out there? See? Vacant lots, and everybody's locked up inside they place. See them pit bulls chained up over there? Bars on they windows, just like bars on my windows—to keep out the thugs.
[*Points.*]
See that van cruising by? They wolves on the prowl, licking they chops, with they fangs drooling and out for prey. You'd be a sweet tasty morsel.

CERISE [*To* RENÉ.] You her auntie! Talking to her like that!

RENÉ [*To* GWEN.] Go on out there, looking at me with that evil eye like that! Since I offend you so much! See if you make it to the end of that lamppost! Go! Get out!

GWEN Gonna have that dead baby in my dreams from now on.

RENÉ Dreams go up in smoke eventually.
[*Beat.*]
Believe me.

GWEN [*To* RENÉ.] I thought you were my guardian angel.

RENÉ [*To* GWEN.] Girl, you, and ya momma was in the Cleveland Greyhound with benches for a bed, and the stinky winos and crack hos surrounding you! Who'd she call collect? Me! You wanna goddamn happy ending, then take your ass to the movies!

CERISE Now-now-now—everybody, let's just take it easy—

GWEN [*To* RENÉ.] I can't stand to look you in the face.

RENÉ I know my life is less than dust. But do you hear me whining and complaining? No, you do not. Do you hear me blaming anybody, or gnashing my teeth, or wailing at God? "God, how come you made me at the bottom of the heap!?" Nonsense. If I'm to be a grain of sand in this goddamn world, then I'm a grain of sand. This is how I must live, and so I live. I take it, and I take it, and I take it. That's right, and I'm gonna keep on taking it...and taking it...and taking it...and TAKING IT...

[*Starts to break down.*]

Keep on. And on and on and keep...keep...keep—keep!

CERISE [*Reaches out to embrace* RENÉ.] Sister.

RENÉ DON'T YOU MUTHERFUCKING "SISTER" ME, GODDAMNIT! Gwendolyn, you turn on that TV!

[*A long moment as they lock eyes.* GWEN *does not move. Finally,* CERISE *snatches up the TV remote, switches on the TV.* RENÉ *and* CERISE *sit, staring into the TV screen.*]

CERISE *Desperate Housewives*, y'all!

[GWEN *stands in place not moving. She looks towards the door for a moment, turns back, drops her backpack to the floor. Lights fade to black.*]

• • •

Abandoned in Queens

Laura Maria Censabella

Abandoned in Queens by Laura Maria Censabella. Copyright © 2014 by Laura Maria Censabella. All rights reserved. Reprinted by permission of the author.

CAUTION/ADVICE: Professionals and amateurs are hereby warned that performance of *Abandoned in Queens* is subject to a royalty. It is fully protected under the copyright laws of the United States of America, and of all countries covered by the International Copyright Union (including the Dominion of Canada and the rest of the British Commonwealth), and of all countries covered by the Pan-American Copyright Convention and the Universal Copyright Convention, the Berne Convention, and of all countries with which the United States has reciprocal copyright relations. All rights, including professional and amateur stage performing rights, motion picture, recitation, lecturing, public reading, radio broadcasting, television, video or sound recording, all other forms of mechanical or electronic reproduction, such as CD-ROM, DVD-ROM, information storage and retrieval systems, and photocopying, and the rights of translation into foreign languages, are strictly reserved. Particular emphasis is placed upon the matter of readings, permission for which must be secured from the author's agent in writing.

Inquiries concerning rights should be addressed to the author's agent, Elaine Devlin, at Elaine Devlin Literary, Inc., 20 West 23rd Street, 3rd Floor, New York, New York 10010. E-mail: edevlinlit@aol.com. Phone: 212-842-9030.

Laura Maria Censabella

Laura Maria Censabella's plays and musicals have been produced or developed at the O'Neill Theater's National Playwrights Conference, the New Harmony Project, the Philadelphia Festival Theatre for New Plays, the Women's Project and Productions, the Working Theatre, Urban Stages Outreach, m2productions, Interact Theatre in Los Angeles, Greene Arts Foundation, Belmont Italian American Playhouse, the Pacific Resident Theatre, Wide Eyed Productions, and the Festival of Faith and Writing at Calvin College. Her new full-length play, *Paradise*, which was commissioned by Ensemble Studio Theatre and the Alfred P. Sloan Foundation will be workshopped at the Athena Project in Denver in March 2014. She has won three grants from the New York Foundation for the Arts for her plays *Abandoned in Queens* and *Carla Cooks the War* (aka *Three Italian Women*) and her screenplay *Truly Mary*. She is also the winner of two Emmy Awards for Writing in Daytime Television. Her independent short film *Last Call* was an official selection in festivals throughout the world and won the Best Short Drama Award at the Breckenridge Film Festival. Her work is published in *Poems and Plays*, *The St. Petersburg Review*, and *IndependentPlaywrights.com*, and she is the director of Ensemble Studio Theatre's Playwrights Unit. Laura is a member of the Dramatists Guild, the Writers Guild of America East, Ensemble Studio Theatre, and the League of Professional Theatre Women. She graduated from Yale College with a bachelor of arts in philosophy and is part-time assistant professor of playwriting at the New School for Drama.

···production history···

Abandoned in Queens will be presented by Wide Eyed Productions at the Underground Lounge in December 2013 under the direction of Kristin Skye Hoffman. Thomas Kopache will play the role of Nick; and Nic Marrone will play the role of Frankie. It was originally produced by the Philadelphia Festival Theatre for New Plays (Roger Serbagi as Nick, Doug Hutchison as Frankie); the Working Theatre in NYC at Theatre Row Theatre (Roger Serbagi as Nick, Dean Nichols as Frankie); and the Belmont Italian-American Playhouse in the Bronx. *Abandoned in Queens* was first developed at the O'Neill Theater's National Playwrights Conference (Victor Raider-Wexler as Nick, Greg Germann as Frankie) and Ensemble Studio Theatre's New Voices Series.

characters

> **NICK GABRIOLA** a man around fifty
>
> **FRANKIE GABRIOLA** his son, sixteen, an almost-man's body with a child's face

time

The present.

place

A kitchen in Queens, New York, in an apartment on the highway.

[*The Gabriola kitchen at dinnertime on an unusually warm spring day. This is clearly the mother's space. A Formica table and three chairs are off-center—they are feminine and a little too small for the men. There are large posters of far-off places taped to the brightly colored walls, and stacks of Mom's paperback books and folded papers lie precariously on the lopsided shelves among the sugar, napkins, and small appliances draped in flowery dust covers. In many of her little touches, there is something that just misses; for example, she might have hung a crystal by the window, but somehow it doesn't catch the light. The overall effect is that of the tacky mixed with the genuinely beautiful.*]

[*There is an open window through which the sun can be seen setting. Soft pastel colors shade the sky gradually turning brilliantly electric as the action progresses. By the end of the play the sun has just set. There is an unseen expressway outside. The soot that comes in from this highway gives the kitchen a gritty look despite Mom's efforts to keep things clean.*]

[*At opening* FRANKIE *is seated on the windowsill looking at* NICK *with his back slouched against the window frame.* NICK *is setting the table. We hear the sounds of trucks and cars on the highway, which fade out as* NICK *and* FRANKIE *begin to speak.*]

NICK A couple a times the cars come so close I thought they were gonna hit me! Here I am sweating and waving this handkerchief and Sally May's conked out, nothing I can do with her, right in the middle a the speed lane—I finally locked up her doors and just left her there—-

FRANKIE Why were you driving her in the speed lane?

NICK I was trying to get home! 'Course this has to happen on the night we wanna get out a here and 'course you didn't do nothing to start the food—

FRANKIE All right! I thought you said we weren't gonna talk about this no more.

NICK You're right. I did.

[*Silence. He goes to check food on stove.*]

I only wanna say one more thing—

[*Turns toward* FRANKIE.]

THANK YOU.

FRANKIE What's that supposed to mean?

NICK You know.

FRANKIE No, I don't.

NICK Don't pretend, buddy, you know.

[*Silence. They stare each other down.*]

FRANKIE The dentist office called. They wanna know when Mom'll be back to work.

NICK [*Overlapping.*] You think you could slice some bread?

[FRANKIE *stands up as if he might but then impulsively swings himself onto the windowsill so that he is facing out with his legs spread. He presses his face against the glass.*]

NICK What a you doing—you're gonna fall!

[NICK *goes over and grabs* FRANKIE*'s arm.*]

You're gonna get hurt!

FRANKIE [*Shakes the arm* NICK *is holding.*] Let go.

NICK Frankie!

FRANKIE [*Sees that his father will not let go.*] Okay, cool your jets...I'm coming down.

NICK Are you crazy?

FRANKIE You can really see far.

NICK [*Keeping his hands ready to grab* FRANKIE *in case he slips.*] Why? Who you looking for?

[FRANKIE *gives his father a hurt look. Beat.*]

I guess there's one good thing in this mess. At least I left work early—I mean I would a been dead if this happened in rush hour (that's why I suggest you always gotta give yourself time), and least I finally got a lift home. Oh, and thank God Tommy was at the garage when I called—if he wasn't there, I don't know what I would a done. He said he'd send out the tow truck and put Sally May ahead a all the other cars—he likes me, that Tommy, I can tell.

[*Pause.*]

Don't you think he likes me?

[NICK *looks around suddenly, bewildered, as if he's lost something but doesn't quite remember what it is.* FRANKIE *tries to figure out what he's doing.*]

Where's the knife? There's a hell of a lot of clutter round here.

[*He scoops up some books and papers from the counter and haphazardly throws them into the cabinet.* FRANKIE *watches. When his father is done,* FRANKIE *retrieves them and then searches for an empty place to put them. He settles on one of the chairs at the table as the only clear space. He arranges papers neatly.* NICK *watches him.*]

How we gonna sit?

[FRANKIE *sits on one empty chair and then the other to show there is still room for them at the table. Then* FRANKIE *goes back to windowsill.*]

Did you take a look at that salad? I made it this morning while you were still sleeping. I put in the radishes and tomatoes and I cut the carrots long, not short, for you.

FRANKIE Great.

NICK I'm even cooking the french fries the way you like 'em...and I'm making not one but two eggs for you...

FRANKIE Terrific.

NICK [*Running out of steam.*] I want you to have food in you so you can clap real loud when they announce me...imagine...top furniture salesman again after four years a being number two...high man...
[*Suddenly overwhelmed.*]
You know how to call the cab company?

FRANKIE What a you mean? You dial.

NICK But I mean how we gonna know which one?
[FRANKIE *doesn't bother to answer him.*]
Who knocked over Mom's perfumes?

FRANKIE [*Taken by surprise.*] I did—I was dusting.

NICK They're all over the floor. You know soot's coming in that window...

FRANKIE My body's blocking it...

NICK [*Looks as if he's going to say something else but then decides the better of it. He goes back to preparing food.*] I hope you laid out your clothes already like I told you, this way, one-two-three, you jump into them after we eat—and I think your beige pants and white shirt are good—I mean if that's what you picked—you might wanna wear a tie, nah, I'll leave that up to you. Top salesman and I got my son. There'll probably be a little applause when we come through the door, so don't be bashful.
[*Turns to FRANKIE, who has taken out flash cards from his pocket and is looking at them.*]
What a you got there?

[*Goes over to his son who stuffs them quickly back into his pocket.*]

FRANKIE It's nothing.

NICK No, let me see. You're doing a lot a nothing tonight.
[*Beat.*]
I don't see what the hell's so fascinating out there.
[*Leans out the window over FRANKIE.*]
I don't see nothing.

FRANKIE I like to look at the cars.

NICK [*He stays leaning over* FRANKIE.] Why?

FRANKIE I like to think.

NICK About what?

FRANKIE Where everybody's going.

NICK Home.

FRANKIE [*Looking at* NICK.] Not all a them. One a them cars they're not talking to each other 'cause the wife didn't point out the exit. And maybe there's a kid in the back who just got slapped 'cause she was singing and jumping around. And maybe they wonder what kind a lives we got.

NICK Why?

FRANKIE Like when we drive on the BQE and we pass some window where the lady's leaning over the crib, I think, what kind a life she got?

NICK So that's what you're thinking all night...?

FRANKIE Yeah.

NICK What you write down on those cards?

FRANKIE They're just notes for a test.

NICK Mechanics?

FRANKIE No, another class.

NICK Oh.
[*Goes over to stove to check on food.*]
What the hell—oh shit oh my God shit!

FRANKIE [*Jumps off windowsill.*]
You burn yourself?
[*No answer.*]
Dad, you hurt?
[*No answer.*]
Dad?

NICK [*Looks overwhelmed.*] I give up.

FRANKIE What happened?
[*He looks into pot.*]

You're gonna gimme a heart attack—it's no big deal.

[NICK *will not be consoled.* FRANKIE *looks into pot again.*]

So the eggs—[*Searches for word.*]—exploded. Look there's still one okay.

[*Scoops it out with spoon.*]

See? Dad? You can have it.

NICK No I made it for you. It's all ruined.

FRANKIE No, it's not. Huh?

[*Pause.*]

Come on, sit down. I'll bring the stuff. Come on, sit down. That's good.

[*Carrying food to table.*]

Mmm, these fries look nice and crisp. Better than McDonald's. And look at the way you chopped 'em—long, not short—just like the carrots. Nothing like carrots in a salad, right, Dad?

[*He makes more appreciative grunts over food, then sits down at the table with* NICK. *He dishes out salad and french fries onto* NICK's *plate very carefully.*]

NICK [*Eventually.*] I'll just put this egg on your plate.

FRANKIE No, I want you to have it.

NICK How 'bout I just put it in the middle here. Whoever feels like it can have it.

FRANKIE Okay.

[*Sounds of the highway fade in.*]

NICK [*Cautious.*] Can I ask a big favor?

FRANKIE Yeah?

NICK You think we could shut the window a little bit, the trucks're giving me a headache—

FRANKIE [*Gets up.*] Why didn't you say so?

NICK You don't have to close it all the way—

FRANKIE [*Conciliatory.*] How 'bout three-quarters?

NICK Just half. I know you want it open.

[FRANKIE *closes the window halfway but then stands there mesmerized by what's outside.*]

Anything—different—out there?

FRANKIE Teacher says it's 'cause a pollution.

NICK What?

FRANKIE The sunset. Like that cloud. The color a Gatorade on top a the pink.

NICK If there wasn't pollution—what would it look like?

[*Doesn't wait for answer.*]

That's very interesting. I'm glad you told me. Hey, buddy, your potatoes're getting cold.

[FRANKIE *goes back to his seat.*]

Eat some a that salad, it'll open up your appetite.

[*Watches as* FRANKIE *eats some.*]

Good?

FRANKIE [*Surprised.*] Yeah.

NICK [*Happy.*] Don't get your hopes up about the fountains being on. They're not keeping them up.

FRANKIE The fountains?

NICK At the mall. They got garbage in 'em. Nah, it ain't like the old days—you remember that time I saw the frog?

FRANKIE Yeah, I thought you made that up.

NICK [*Shocked.*] You thought I made it up? How could you think that? No, don't you remember I told you—I was sitting there eating a bagel one morning and it was real quiet 'cause the mall wasn't open for shopping yet and I keep hearing this—[*Makes frog sound.*]—but when I turn around—nothing. So finally when I'm about to leave I throw a penny in for good luck and bloop-bloop what do I see?—a little frog swimming through the water and he hops out into the plants. I said holy Jesus am I seeing things or what?—I mean, the plants are plastic! So I spread the leaves and there he is croaking way in the back. Then I called you up from the job. Don't you remember?

FRANKIE And every time I went down there I went looking for it.

NICK   Yeah! I wonder what happened to it.

[*Pause.*]

I never saw it again… Then remember I'd take you to Sweeney's for an ice cream and you told me you looked at all the other little kids and felt sorry for them 'cause their dad didn't belong to the mall. See, this is why I wanna take you to the ceremony tonight! All right so it won't be as grand as it used to be—I'll only get a plaque or something—but they're honoring me.

[*Beat.*]

Let me give you the layout. First we'll have a few cocktails. Then the union guys they make some speeches—which ain't so bad after you had a drink. Then finally the big announcement: Salesman a the Year.

[*Pause.*]

Eat s'more salad.

[*Suddenly very cagey and conspiratorial. Whispering.*]

It's almost six o'clock. If your grandma calls, you tell her the dentist is making your mom work overtime.

FRANKIE   [*Getting up from table.*] I can't eat this.

NICK   What a you mean? You barely touched your fries.

FRANKIE   They're too greasy.

NICK   Well, here, I'll wipe 'em off.

[*Uses napkin.*]

FRANKIE   Never mind.

NICK   But what about the egg?

FRANKIE   I don't want it.

NICK   We'll share it—I'll cut it in half.

FRANKIE   No thank you.

NICK   But I made it for you.

FRANKIE   I hate hardboiled eggs!

[*Silence. NICK is very hurt. He slowly begins collecting remains of food and throwing them into garbage pail. FRANKIE watches.*]

NICK   I think you better go take your shower.

FRANKIE I'll clean up the dishes. You take yours.

NICK Just take your shower.

FRANKIE [*Long pause.*] I don't remember those people.

NICK Who?

FRANKIE At the mall, I don't remember them. I won't know who's who.

NICK I'll be right there. I can introduce you.

FRANKIE Their names won't mean nothing.

NICK What a you mean? What about Rogers—you remember him— he's the one give you those little box a Chiclets all the time.
[FRANKIE *shakes his head no.*]
Sure. He used to let you go up and play on the bunk beds when the manager wasn't looking. I told you he hurt his leg. And then there's Pagnato—the one with all the dandruff—

FRANKIE I got schoolwork to do.

NICK What a you talking about? We been planning this.

FRANKIE I got stuff due tomorrow. They're really overloading us.

NICK You do it after.

FRANKIE I can't. It's too much.

NICK But I came all the way back here for you.

FRANKIE Blame it on that damn school a mine.

NICK Wait a minute. I told the boys you were coming.

FRANKIE I don't wanna talk about it no more.

NICK What the hell're you talking about? I broke my back getting home this afternoon, I didn't have to come back, I could a eaten at Sweeney's. I come back for you.

FRANKIE I'm sorry.

NICK What a you mean you're sorry? I waited two hours on the highway. And did I say anything about how it's your fault the damn thing broke down in the first place? No! I was a saint. I could a reminded you how many weeks I asked you—"Frankie, you think you can take a look at that rattling?" I mean, you're studying mechanics, you think you might do a little free work for your father—

FRANKIE I was busy!

NICK You're always busy. Now it's gonna cost me God knows how much at Tommy's, that's if she wasn't smashed up on the Cross Island when I left her, and that's if she can even be fixed 'cause you let her go so long—

FRANKIE [*Singsong.*] Yeah, yeah, yeah, yeah.

NICK And then I come in two hours late and you're sitting on the windowsill looking at nothing—if you had so much schoolwork to do, why weren't you doing it?

FRANKIE I was.

NICK Looking out the window?

FRANKIE Yeah.

NICK [*Pause.*] I don't understand. Why you doing this to me?

FRANKIE It's a big project and it's due tomorrow.

NICK Why didn't you pace yourself?
[FRANKIE *looks at him in disbelief and then angrily wipes off the table.*]
Okay, I apologize to you, all right? I'm sorry I got on you about making dinner when I got home and I'm sorry I yelled at you now. You satisfied?
[*Pause.*]
All right?
[*Silence.*]
You think your mom's gonna call tonight.

FRANKIE No.

NICK The phone won't ring.

FRANKIE I'll call your cab.

NICK You wanna know how I know?

FRANKIE See you later.

[*Makes move to leave for his bedroom.*]

NICK   Sit down.

[FRANKIE *doesn't.* NICK *blocks his way out the door.*]

Sit down! I wanna tell you some facts.

[FRANKIE *sits.*]

Your mother ain't got no money, no credit cards, and she don't even know how to balance a checkbook. So what's she been living on since Monday? Air? For three and a half days? The most she could be is hiding out at one a her girlfriend's.

FRANKIE   [*Starts to get up.*] I heard this before.

NICK   [*Presses* FRANKIE'*s shoulder down so he sits back in chair.*] You didn't hear this. The reason she won't call tonight is she knows tonight's the ceremony. And she's gotta ruin it for me. She'll call tomorrow when it's over.

FRANKIE   [*Pause.*] When'd you think a this?

NICK   Early this morning. See it's all part a her game.

FRANKIE   I told you I got homework to do. Understand? Homework. Not her.

NICK   No, I think you plan to sit right here and watch the phone and pray that she calls well it won't happen, buddy, 'cause I know—

FRANKIE   [*Overlapping.*] It's a speech.

NICK   What?

FRANKIE   I'm making a speech.

NICK   [*Surprised and pleased.*] You're making a speech?

FRANKIE   [*Dismayed at what he's revealed.*] Yeah.

NICK   For what?

FRANKIE   Class.

NICK   Why didn't you tell me about this?

[*Beat.*]

They ask you special?

FRANKIE   No, everyone gets a turn.

NICK   What's it on?

FRANKIE A bunch a stuff.

NICK This sounds very important. I'm very good at public speaking.

FRANKIE You?

NICK [*Looking at his watch.*] How long is it?

FRANKIE Couple a minutes.

NICK [*Rushing out of room.*] Wait. I'll be right back.

FRANKIE What a you doing?

NICK [*Comes back in with suit.*] I'll just put this on while you do your speech.

FRANKIE I told you, I gotta practice it.

NICK Bounce it off a me.

FRANKIE It's not ready.

NICK You do it one time in front a me, it's worth ten times alone. I'll give you some pointers. What a you say?

FRANKIE No.

NICK How you gonna do it in front a the whole class you can't do it in front a me?

[*Beat.*]

You never give a speech before, did you?

FRANKIE No.

NICK Well, there you are—you gotta get the live experience.

FRANKIE No.

NICK What's the big deal. I'm your father.

[*Silence.*]

You're gonna freeze.

FRANKIE I ain't gonna freeze.

NICK Your mouth'll go dry.

FRANKIE It will not.

NICK I seen it happen. A salesman don't practice his pitch in front a people, he freezes.

[*Pause.*]
You're the type.

FRANKIE I am not.

NICK You're a bit of a introvert. How much a your grade does this count for?

FRANKIE 90 percent. What a you mean I'm a introvert?

NICK I don't wanna see you fall on your face.

FRANKIE I'm not gonna fall on my face. What a you mean I'm a introvert?

NICK [*Beat.*] Just when you talk there's a certain…

FRANKIE What?

NICK I don't know…it's just a feeling…

FRANKIE What?

NICK I watch you when you're with your friends…you hang back.

FRANKIE I do not.

NICK Sort a like you're ashamed.

FRANKIE What the hell a you talking about? You're so full a shit.

NICK Okay, do it tomorrow cold.

FRANKIE I will.

NICK Good.

FRANKIE [*Pause.*] What's wrong with me when I talk?

NICK Nothing.

FRANKIE That's a helluva thing to say.

NICK I'm sorry. Forget the whole thing. Come on, get your coat, you can go like that.

FRANKIE No.

NICK You're not gonna come with me?

FRANKIE No.

NICK Then I gotta go.

FRANKIE Go 'head.

NICK Come on, Frankie.

FRANKIE No.

NICK Then I'm going.

FRANKIE Good.

NICK [*Grabs suit coat.*] All right—good-bye!
   [*Pause.*]
   You got a mirror? I need a mirror.
   [FRANKIE *does not answer.*]
   I'll just look at myself in the toaster.
   [*Pulls dust cover off it.*]
   These covers are such a waste.
   [*He balls it up, throws it to the floor, and smooths his hair looking in the toaster.* FRANKIE *gets dust cover and folds it neatly.* NICK *watches. Pause.*]
   You think I was wrong telling your mom to come to the ceremony.
   [*Pause.*]
   You think I was wrong wanting my wife with me.

FRANKIE [*Reluctantly.*] No.

NICK [Relieved.] I know you stuck up for me, remember? You told her to stop acting like the queen. All she would a had a do is come and smile a little when they hand me the plaque. She's done it before. What's the big deal? It ain't every year I make high man. I mean, what was I asking for, for Christ's sake? She had no right to throw the chop meat at me when I asked her, right?
   [*Pause.*]
   Right?

FRANKIE Yeah.

NICK See, you understand. So the guys at the job they ain't the greatest geniuses, but if you don't have to work with them . . . She should be damn proud I make top salesman—who's buying furniture now? Nobody. And still I make top—if I had two customers all day that's a lot, place was like a tomb.
   [*Pause.*]
   Please. Buddy? How's it gonna look I got no family?

FRANKIE [*Wavering.*] I got that speech to practice...

NICK So you do it after! All right? Remember when you used to come running down the stairs a the store and I'd catch you in my arms and show you to all the customers?

FRANKIE Yeah...

NICK Hey, hey! I got a great idea. When the ceremony's over, why don't I take you to Sweeney's for an ice cream!

FRANKIE [*Suddenly adamant again.*] I don't think so.

NICK Why not?

FRANKIE I don't want ice cream.

NICK Okay, so then you don't have to have any.
[*Beat.*]
But you'll come with me, right?
[*We hear trucks going by outside. FRANKIE doesn't answer.*]
I don't understand—we planned this. I can't go without you.
[*Beat.*]
I don't wanna go.

FRANKIE I'm sorry.

NICK You're ruining this for me—I don't believe it.

FRANKIE I'm not ruining nothing, you go—

NICK How can you say you're not ruining it when you're ruining it—

FRANKIE I told you I got schoolwork to do.

NICK But I told everybody.
[*The traffic quiets down. Pause.*]
All right—do the speech—we can be a little late.
[FRANKIE *shakes his head no.*]
Then I'm not going.
[*Beat.*]
If you're not going, I'm not going.

FRANKIE Bullshit—you know you wouldn't miss it.

NICK Oh yeah?

FRANKIE Yeah.

NICK You think so?

[*Goes over to phone. Punches in numbers.*]

Hello? Amelia? This is Nick Gabriola. Thank you. Listen—
something come up. Yeah, I know I'm supposed to be down there—it's
with Frankie. He's got a problem—nah, he ain't sick. But I gotta help
him. What? Photographers from the papers?

[*Pause.*]

Tell the boys I'm gonna try to get there—but like I said—this thing
with Frankie—there's a possibility I don't make it. Yeah, I'm gonna
try. Thanks. Bye.

[*Hangs up. Beat.*]

You didn't think I'd do it.

FRANKIE Call them back.

NICK I wanna hear your speech.

[FRANKIE *is at a loss for words.*]

I ain't moving.

FRANKIE Dad!

NICK Do the speech.

FRANKIE But—

NICK Do it.

FRANKIE Damnit—Dad—just call them back.

[NICK *remains immovable. Pause.*]

All right—go and I'll do it for you when you get back.

NICK Now.

FRANKIE You won't understand the background.

NICK Try me.

FRANKIE [*Looks around, sees no escape.*] We're not supposed to memorize
it, we're supposed to talk it. And the teacher said to be totally honest
and we couldn't go wrong.

[*He stands there doing nothing.*]

NICK Okay, I got it.

[FRANKIE *reluctantly takes out his flash cards and studies them. Scans his imaginary audience.*]

You gonna take so much time in front a the class?

FRANKIE [*Begins speech in a quavering voice.*] Queens is on an island—

NICK Don't lean, it makes a bad appearance.

FRANKIE I can't do this if you're mad.

NICK I'm not mad.

FRANKIE [*Re-scans his imaginary audience.*] Queens is on an island. Hard to believe, right? I mean—Indians used to hunt and fish right where we're standing and, uh, they made these dirt trails in the woods. You see any woods now? Yeah, maybe Kissena and Alley Pond parks, but on the streets? Uh, it's just the names tell you Queens didn't always look like this. Take Mayfield Avenue. I never even seen a flower on it.

[*His head bobs up and down from the flash cards and turns from side to side scanning his audience. His eyes look glazed. After the last sentence above, he pauses, shuffling his flash cards to find his place.*]

Wait a minute—sorry—

NICK This is a very good beginning.

FRANKIE You think so?

NICK You might wanna say Atlantic Avenue was the old path a the Canarsie Indians. Tell 'em it led from Brooklyn to Jamaica, Queens, and how you and your father used to go fishing and we'd try to imagine there were no towns around and we had to get along just by the woods.

FRANKIE Oh.

NICK Go 'head.

FRANKIE Mayfield Avenue—I never even seen a flower on it. But maybe some of you's remember the lot. Yeah, it had trash and everything, but it was like—the jungle—you know, the way it had grasses over our heads. And when it was gonna rain how they got this funny yellow color and waved around.

[*Self-consciously makes wind sound and moves his arms.*]

Took up half a block. I mean, you just wondered what would happen if you got lost in there or what was living in there. But then when I'm about eight, they clear some of it out and put up a Ferris wheel. You know, a carnival once a year.

[*He half expects* NICK *to interrupt. When* NICK *doesn't, his face becomes more animated.*]

And you could see it from way down the Avenue 'cause they strung up these little pink lights. But then they started clearing more a the field about—yeah—two years ago. And we all thought, maybe a carnival for year-round? We were pretty excited. But you know what they put up? Condos. And they called them Mayfield Townhouses. Every house stuck together.

[FRANKIE *takes a peek at his father to see if he approves. We hear trucks shifting gears outside and* FRANKIE *has to get louder.*]

You see what I mean about not believing you live on an island? When I was a kid, I thought you ever walk on an island, you feel the water underneath it. Like the land would be kind a floaty. And that would be great. And then, third grade, I learn Queens is on Long Island. So what? Until one day I'm walking home by the expressway and oh my God! it hit me—I really live on an island! But what a gyp—it don't feel like nothing and the water's too far to walk to.

[*Pause.*]

But even though it's a gyp, sometimes I feel good. Like at night when I'm in bed before I go to sleep. And this might sound crazy, but the highway—to me it sounds like the ocean. Not the trucks, but the cars, the way they go by, sounds like the way waves hit the shore.

[*Makes car/wave sound.*]

And then maybe somebody honks a horn and's going so fast it sounds like a boat lost in the fog.

[*Makes bending horn sound.*]

You see what I mean? And I wish I could go with them... far out to sea. And I feel this little shiver right before I fall asleep 'cause I remember I live on an island...

[*He trails off. Silence. Eventually sneaks a look at his father.*]

NICK   Is that the end?

FRANKIE   Yeah.

NICK   Hmm.

FRANKIE I was a little nervous.

NICK Hmm.

FRANKIE What'd you think?

NICK [*Pause.*] Let me ask you a question—nothing to do with how I liked your speech.
[*Beat.*]
The guys in your mechanics class, they in this class too?

FRANKIE I don't know—some. Why?

NICK No reason. Just trying to get the layout.
[*Pause.*]
Maybe I didn't hear you correct. You saying there's something wrong with the Townhouses?

FRANKIE You like 'em?

NICK No, I didn't say that, but point is, people need a place to live.

FRANKIE They got lots a other places besides one puny lot on Mayfield Avenue. You're the one always talking about going where there's some space.

NICK True. But the lot was a pigsty. Something had a be done with it. It was an eyesore.

FRANKIE I think it's an eyesore now.

NICK You saying they should a put a park there?

FRANKIE Why'd they have to do anything to it?

NICK 'Cause it was a pigsty.

FRANKIE [*Pause.*] You don't like the speech.

NICK Shouldn't it have more of a point?

FRANKIE What point?

NICK Were you talking about how you feel in bed?

FRANKIE Yeah. What I think about.

NICK You mentioned some kind a word—
[*Searching.*]
"Shiver."

FRANKIE   So.

NICK   Well, I'm a salesman, I'm sensitive to people. You put shiver and bed together and you get people's minds working.

FRANKIE   Like what?

[*Silence.*]

NICK   I don't think you should make this speech.

FRANKIE   What a you know?

NICK   I know about people.

FRANKIE   [*Snorts.*] You don't know nothing about people.

NICK   I know about being a extrovert. I know about making people like you. I was always a extrovert and I never had any problems making friends. Any neighborhood—Irish, Jewish—Nick Gabriola had protection 'cause Nick Gabriola had friends.

FRANKIE   Yeah—where are they now?

NICK   They're all over!
   [FRANKIE *snorts.*]
   You don't think I got friends? I got the boys down the job—

FRANKIE   You hate them—

NICK   Any a my old buddies! If I called them up, said I was in trouble, they'd be down here two seconds flat. You want me to prove it, huh? I'll call 'em right now—

FRANKIE   Forget it.
   [*As* NICK *goes to phone.*]
   Forget it!

NICK   That speech is gonna go over like a rotten fish.

FRANKIE   Mom liked it.

NICK   [*Long pause.*] Oh yeah?

FRANKIE   Yeah.

NICK   What does she know?

FRANKIE   She knows good thoughts.

NICK That's a laugh.

FRANKIE What the hell's that supposed to mean?

[NICK *points around the room derisively at posters and books as if his point is proved.*]

So?

NICK I got news for you, buddy. The rest a the world ain't like your mom.

FRANKIE What a you talking about?

NICK You know damn well.

FRANKIE No, I don't.

NICK She don't know her ass from her elbow.

FRANKIE No, I think it's you.

NICK She's weak. A jellyfish.

FRANKIE You don't know what you're talking about.

NICK Oh, come on—how many times you tell me that yourself?

FRANKIE I never said nothing.

NICK In the car you said it a thousand times—she's got the brain of a jellyfish—

FRANKIE No, it was you, you talk and you think I'm saying things—

NICK Come off it, I heard it with my own ears. That—that time she went to the fortune-teller 'cause she said she had "questions"—huh? But instead a telling your mother's future the broad threatened to curse the whole family 'less she paid her off every week. What'd you say when you caught her stealing $30 out a our fishing kitty to pay her? [*Pause.*]

You told her retards were smarter than her.

FRANKIE That was a long time ago.

NICK One month. I know 'cause I was supposed to bring Sally May in for a tune-up, only I was hoping you'd do it instead—

FRANKIE Okay, that's enough.

NICK I remember these things.

FRANKIE   Yeah, it's interesting how you remember that but you don't remember what happened this morning.

NICK   [*Pause.*] What happened this morning?

FRANKIE   In the car.

NICK   What?

FRANKIE   Yeah, sure, you don't know.

NICK   No, I don't know.

FRANKIE   What you said.

NICK   I don't remember saying nothing.

FRANKIE   Think about it.

NICK   [*Pause.*] I just remember we, uh, swerved for one a them squirrels—

FRANKIE   We?

NICK   Yeah, we was going—"kill 'em, rats with tails!"—like we always do.

FRANKIE   What else did you say?

NICK   I don't know. I probably said something about going over the bumps makes me feel like a rodeo cowboy—something like that.

FRANKIE   What else?

NICK   I don't know—probably that the weather was nice and warm…

FRANKIE   What'd you say about Mom?

NICK   I didn't say nothing.

FRANKIE   No, I think you did.

NICK   What?

FRANKIE   You said, "We can get along just fine without her."

NICK   [*Pause.*] I didn't say that.

FRANKIE   Yeah, you did.

NICK   I wouldn't a said that.

FRANKIE   You did.

NICK   No, I'm positive I didn't say that. I remember everything. I got in the car, adjusted the mirror like I always do, and I asked you to double-check if your door was shut. But you didn't answer. So I look at you but you're staring straight ahead. Then I turn the key in the ignition and pull out a the parking spot nice and easy—that's when I made a little remark about the weather just to break the ice. So we go along not saying nothing and I'm almost at your school, I make a right on Alley Pond and that's when a squirrel runs right out on the road. This is my chance—I press down on the accelerator and say like we always do—"kill 'em—"

FRANKIE   And what were you talking about squirrels for!?

NICK   'Cause that's what we always talk about. I didn't say nothing about we can get along just fine without her.

FRANKIE   Okay, maybe you didn't say it, but you meant to.

NICK   [*Pause.*] This is crazy.

FRANKIE   When did the note say she'd call?

NICK   What's that got to do with this? I told you she'll call tomorrow. After the ceremony.

FRANKIE   No, I'm asking you a question. When did the note say she'd call?

NICK   [*Reluctantly.*] Last night.

FRANKIE   And how did you act last night when she didn't call?

NICK   How did I act? I don't know—

FRANKIE   Like the most important thing you had a worry about was brushing your teeth.

NICK   Hey, wait a minute!

FRANKIE   And what did you do this morning? Squirrels!

NICK   She would a called last night I would a promised her anything.
[*Goes to refrigerator.*]
Look at all the groceries I got her—the Boston salad and the fruit juice with the 10 percent juice she likes and—

FRANKIE   Groceries? You got her groceries?

NICK Hey, you didn't see me last night after dinner—

FRANKIE You went to bed.

NICK I went in the bathroom and I got sick, then I went in the bedroom and sat up all night listening for the phone to ring—

FRANKIE In the dark?

NICK Yeah…sat up and chewed my nails till they was bleeding…

FRANKIE Why didn't you say something this morning?

NICK 'Cause I didn't wanna get you upset.

FRANKIE Get me upset?!

NICK And during the night I figured out her plan.
[*Beat.*]
Is this why you won't go to the ceremony?
[*Beat.*]
Now that we got things straight—

FRANKIE I love how you do this.

NICK What?

FRANKIE [*Pulls out note from his pocket.*] Just forget what you wanna forget. The note said she was gonna call to pick up the rest a her things. Not 'cause she was coming home. Maybe she don't even care to get her stuff.

NICK [*Pause. Measured.*] She ain't got the balls.
[*Pause.*]
Come on, get your coat, we can still make it.

FRANKIE You canceled already.

NICK I only called *Sports Fone.*

FRANKIE You pretended?

NICK It was necessary.

FRANKIE Oh, that's great—you are something else. Damnit!
[*He takes NICK's suit coat and throws it to the floor.*]

NICK Hey-hey! Pick that up!

FRANKIE   You don't even worry if Mom's safe.

NICK   Yes, I do.

FRANKIE   You never said once, I wonder if she's hurt—

NICK   'Cause every time I bring her up you change the subject.

FRANKIE   No, you change the subject.

NICK   Hey, she left me. "I gotta get away from you"—what kind a note is that?

FRANKIE   You haven't done shit.

NICK   What'm I supposed to be doing? Tell me.
   [*Silence.*]
   Oh, you think I should be calling all her friends, right? Asking them—is Rita there? Is that what you want? You don't think I thought a that. She walked out on me, buddy. I never cheated on her, never once missed a day a work.
   [FRANKIE *picks up* NICK*'s suit coat, brushes it off, and holds it out to him.*]
   What a you doing?

FRANKIE   Helping you catch the ceremony. I'm sure they'll still applaud when you walk in.

NICK   Why you looking at me like that?

FRANKIE   I'll call the cab for you.

NICK   Put the coat down.
   [*Pause.*]
   All right, you want me to be making phone calls?

FRANKIE   I don't want you to do nothing.

NICK   Okay, I'll call some a her friends. Put the coat down.
   [FRANKIE *puts it down.*]
   All right—what's that friend a hers always talking about traveling?

FRANKIE   Miko?

NICK   Yeah, let's call her up.

FRANKIE   I don't know her last name.

NICK   Well, what about some a her other friends?

FRANKIE   I don't know any a their last names.

NICK   Then we'll just find her address book and go through it.
[*Begins rummaging.*]
Help me look for it.
[*Pushes things aside.*]
These goddamn books everywhere! Help me look.
[FRANKIE *begins rummaging halfheartedly.*]
Where the hell is it?

FRANKIE   [*Stops.*] It's not here.

NICK   Sure, it's here.

FRANKIE   No, I been looking the past three days. I can't find it.

NICK   It's gotta be up here—it's just all this crap in the way.

[*He drops books and papers roughly to the floor.*]

FRANKIE   Watch what you're doing.

[*He goes to collect them carefully.*]

NICK   No, we can't operate like this. We gotta get this place cleared
out.

[*He continues dropping things to the floor.*]

FRANKIE   Cut it out.

NICK   No, this is the crap. This is the crap.

FRANKIE   Don't touch them!

NICK   The precious books.

[FRANKIE *is trying to collect things neatly.*]

FRANKIE   Stop it!

NICK   Come on—how many times I seen you roll your eyes when she
opens 'em?

[*About to throw another one to floor.*]

FRANKIE   [*Grabs it out of his hands.*] Gimme that.

[FRANKIE *is piling the books to take them out of the room.* NICK *grabs the top one
off the pile.*]

NICK Look at this—*Harness Your Power by Galloping Into Your Dreams.*

[*Beat.*]

I say no more.

FRANKIE Cut it out.

NICK [*Grabbing another one.*] Or this: *Living the Act of Love.* What is it? Porno? Maybe this is why she puts her face so close to the page.

FRANKIE She has trouble with the words.

NICK Amazing—barely finished high school and she reads all these big books. You know what kind a people read these books? 'Course you do. You said it yourself.

[FRANKIE *doesn't look at him.* NICK *thrusts himself in* FRANKIE's *view and makes crazy sign.*]

FRANKIE It wouldn't hurt you to read once in a while.

NICK Why? You been reading them? Come off it. You run as fast as I do any time she starts talking about them.

FRANKIE Get out a my way.

NICK So now you think these books might be good?

[*Pulls another one off* FRANKIE's *stack.*]

Let's see how good they are. *The Body: Our Secret Revealer.* Look she's still got her bookmark in it.

[*Opens it.*]

Looks great.

[*Reads at random.*]

"When the tightly held jaw is released by deep-tissue massage, anger and rage are often felt and expressed. It is interesting to note the relation of the jaw to the pelvis, for the pelvis is a vehicle for deep release of the self. Hence, the jaw may be seen as the pelvis a the face."

[*Gives* FRANKIE *a look.*]

FRANKIE Please stop.

NICK What is this? You see what she's reading?

FRANKIE   Come on, Dad. Put it down.

NICK   You saw—when she threw the chop meat at me—she would a liked to kill me if she didn't miss... the anger in her sometimes... and instead a me getting angry back, I wind up comforting her like a baby 'cause she breaks that vase she made...

[*Pause. Looking at book.*]

What's this underline?

[*Reads.*]

"A major complaint is not having enough energy to get things done. If the shoulder also droops, that person has great difficulty in taking charge of her own destiny. This person should do everything in her power to change her life."

[*Taking it in.*]

What is this?

[*Pause.*]

What kind a stuff is she reading?

[*Beat.*]

What about me? I never felt like changing my life? The year she kept seeing those spots on her arms and knew she had cancer—there weren't no spots, there wasn't no cancer. But who held her when she said she had such crazy thoughts? Who promised her she wouldn't never have to be alone?

[*Pause.*]

Sometimes I reach out for her at night... just to caress her. Maybe I touch her cheek. She's still asleep but she claws my hand.

FRANKIE   Dad...

NICK   I'm gonna call the police.

FRANKIE   [*Trying not to show alarm.*] Why?

NICK   Something ain't right here. You don't just disappear, you got no money.

FRANKIE   No, don't call the police. There's no reason for that.

NICK   I don't know what else to do.

FRANKIE   Isn't there anybody else we can call?

NICK Who? Not her mother. She's not with her. Her mother thinks I'm a piece a bread dipped in milk, the way she likes me. She would a had her back here in two minutes.

[*Pause.*]

Aunt Ida.

FRANKIE Aunt Ida?

NICK What a fool I am. Why didn't I think a this? Of course. You know the way Aunt Ida always babies her 'cause she's her godmother! That's the only place she could be.

FRANKIE So call her.

NICK [*Thinks of number. Punches it in. False heartiness.*] Hello? Aunt Ida. Uh, it's me, Nick, you know, Rita's. Yeah. Oh, not bad. Yourself? Aunt Ida, one reason I may a called—you haven't seen Rita?

[*Pause.*]

Nothing's wrong. Nah, she just went for a drive, I thought maybe she stopped by you. No, I didn't upset her. Jeez, why you always think I upset her? No, I'm sure she'll be back in half an hour. No, don't call her mother, I already called her mother. No, I'm sure she didn't have an accident, she probably just went shopping at Daffy's or something. No, I'm positive she didn't have an accident. There's nothing wrong with that car. I'm gonna hang up now, Aunt Ida. Okay? No, I don't wanna hang up while you're still talking. Shh, shh. That's right. Calm down. Yeah, if she don't come back in a little while, I'll call you. That's right. Take it easy.

[*Hangs up.*]

God, I hate her. Tell you one thing. I'm glad she's not with that woman. I don't care what anyone says, her house smelled from the day she bought it like there's a dead body underneath. I don't care how much paneling she puts up.

[*Runs out of steam.*]

9-1-1.

FRANKIE You don't wanna get them involved.

NICK [*Punches in numbers, but before he can finish FRANKIE goes over and grabs the phone.*]

What a you doing? Take your hand off the phone. You're the one asked me to do something. What's wrong with you?

[*Long silence.*]

You know where she is.

[*Stares. Finally.*]

Where?

FRANKIE I'm not sure.

NICK Tell me where you think.

FRANKIE I—I'm not supposed to say.

NICK She told you?

FRANKIE No.

[*Beat.*]

Not really.

NICK What a you mean not really?

FRANKIE She made me promise.

NICK What a you mean? You mean you knew the past three days?

[FRANKIE *shakes his head no.*]

If she made you promise, then you knew.

FRANKIE No, she said she might be going there.

NICK Tell me.

[*Pause.*]

I won't get mad. I just wanna talk to her.

FRANKIE There's no way to get in touch with her.

NICK [*Beat.*] A man?

FRANKIE No.

NICK She's with a man?

FRANKIE No!

NICK It's a man!

FRANKIE No—no—it's not anything like a man. I swear, it's not a man.

NICK Then who the hell is it? I'm your father and I order you to tell me.

FRANKIE No.

NICK Right now.

FRANKIE No.

NICK Right now!

[*Silence.*]

You been in touch with her?

FRANKIE I told you, I can't reach her.

NICK If you know where she is, you know what she wants.

FRANKIE Get this straight. I don't know.

NICK You gotta know!

FRANKIE I'm getting out a here—

[*Goes to grab his jacket, which is on a wall hook.*]

NICK Oh no, you're not—

[NICK *gets there at the same time as him and they struggle with the jacket. Something falls to the floor and* NICK *picks it up.*]

FRANKIE You idiot! My camera! Did you break my camera?

NICK [*Studying it.*] Where'd you get this?

FRANKIE From school—I just borrowed it. Give it back.

NICK What a you do with it?

FRANKIE Take pictures.

NICK Of what?

FRANKIE Different things.

NICK What things? This got something to do with your mother?

FRANKIE Of course not.

NICK I think it does. Show me the pictures. Are they on this?

FRANKIE [*Trying to take it back.*] No—it's film—gimme back my camera.

NICK What're they—porno?

FRANKIE No.

NICK Then why you ashamed?

FRANKIE I'm not ashamed.

NICK It's all over your eyes—that sick look like your mother gets always folding up papers when I walk in the room—like I caught you playing with yourself. Here.
[*Puts camera on table.*]
Take your damn camera.

FRANKIE They're not sick.

NICK I don't wanna see 'em.

FRANKIE Sit down.

[*He leaves the room for his bedroom, which adjoins the kitchen.*]

NICK I'm not interested—where you going?

FRANKIE [*Comes back in with two 4 x 6 photos in hand.*] You don't wanna sit down?

[NICK *shakes his head no.* FRANKIE *hands him one.*]

NICK [*Studies first one.*] This looks like an empty lot and there's garbage and old tires in it. Is this the lot from your speech?

FRANKIE No. But it could be.

NICK What's this on the sidewalk?

FRANKIE Kotex. [*Silence.*]
You don't like it.

NICK Let me see the other one.
[FRANKIE *hands it to him.* NICK *grows agitated.*]
Where'd you get this?

FRANKIE I took it.

NICK When?

FRANKIE A few weeks ago.

NICK Why?
[*Silence.*]
Why didn't you tell me you were taking it?

FRANKIE That would a ruined it.

NICK Ruined what? Why didn't you tell me?

FRANKIE You were sleeping.

NICK But I'm in my underwear and I got no shirt on.

FRANKIE That's the way you fall asleep in the chair.

NICK My mouth's open. What kind a joke is this?

FRANKIE It's not a joke. It's a picture. It's a good picture.

NICK You snuck up to me?
[*Examines it more closely.*]
My underwear's stained!

FRANKIE That's the way you look.

NICK You didn't show this to anybody—I mean, that's why they're at home, right?

FRANKIE I brought them to school.

NICK You showed this to your class?

FRANKIE We were supposed to show pictures a things as they are.

NICK I'm not a thing! What'd you do—show off how ugly I am?

FRANKIE No!

NICK I look like a disgusting out-a-shape old man who don't wash. This what you want people to see?

FRANKIE It's not what I wanted—

NICK Nobody took control a your hands and made you take it—what everybody think about it, huh? You get a good grade for it?

FRANKIE Teacher thought it was interesting.

NICK Like a bug? What the hell sick kind a teacher is that?

FRANKIE He's not sick—he said they were a little—too sensitive—for school, so I brought them home.

NICK Your mother put you up to this.

FRANKIE She did not.

NICK It was her idea.

FRANKIE No.

NICK You would a never thought a this yourself.

FRANKIE Yes, I did.

NICK You and her must a had a good laugh.

FRANKIE We didn't laugh.

NICK But she saw them. You just admitted it! Did you talk about how disgusting I am?

FRANKIE We didn't talk.

NICK I bet she got a big kick out a this. Well, what about her? How 'bout the times she was sick and she smelled 'cause she was too tired to wash herself and I washed her. Did I think she was disgusting then? Or the times she cried and I let her dribble on me?

FRANKIE I don't wanna hear this.

NICK Did I stop having sex with her?

FRANKIE Just gimme back my pictures.

NICK Yeah, I'll give 'em to you.

[*He rips them up and throws them at* FRANKIE, *who is stunned.*]

FRANKIE [*Silence.*] Okay.
[*Pause.*]
She's with a man.

NICK [*Silence.*] Who?

FRANKIE Someone you don't know.

NICK Who?

FRANKIE He's in a wheelchair.

NICK What? You're making this up—

FRANKIE He's rich—he writes poetry—

NICK Get off it—

FRANKIE No, you get off it! I got something to tell you here. She met this guy on a night you worked late. About a month ago. I didn't know what happened to her. When she finally got in, she couldn't stop smiling—even when she turned away from me I saw. Finally she said she had the most wonderful secret. A man walked in her dentist's office with a toothache and they noticed each other right off.

NICK I thought you said he was in a wheelchair.

FRANKIE He didn't have one then, he was on crutches.

[*Beat.*]

I watched her while she was talking. It was like she was drunk. She said his eyes were the kind that knew suffering. And he told her he could tell she was sensitive just by the way she put the bib around him. Then she said it was like fate 'cause he asked her right out a the blue if she had read this Indian book a philosophy—the—something—It a—I don't know—this book a spiritual peace. Anyway—it happened to be the book she started that week.

NICK The what?

FRANKIE And not only that—he started telling her he wrote poetry and he said she could write it too 'cause she was sensitive enough. So he asked her out to dinner and she went 'cause she was interested in what he said about the poetry. And they drove to the restaurant in his limousine—

NICK [*Overlapping.*] Wait a minute—

FRANKIE This fancy place on Third Avenue and she had the duck. And they were able to talk about everything—reincarnation, the power a love—they talked for hours. And he told her about all these books and he asked if he could send her some a his poetry 'cause she was such a beautiful soul.

NICK This is bullshit—you're making this up—

FRANKIE You want proof, I'll show you proof…

[*Goes to the tea canister, lifts the lid, and pulls out a clear plastic case with two colorful but dead beetles in it.*]

He sent these to her a week after.

[*Holds case out to* NICK.]

NICK [*Recoiling.*] What the hell is that?

FRANKIE Beetles. Dead ones. They're collected for their pretty colors.

NICK Put that away.

[*Beat.*]

He's a weirdo.

FRANKIE She didn't think so.

NICK [*Pause.*] What else happened that night?

FRANKIE He drove her home in his limousine.

NICK He came to this door?

FRANKIE Yeah. Though she almost told him to drop her off by Mayfield 'cause she didn't want him to see the way we face the highway—

NICK What he try?

FRANKIE Nothing.

NICK Don't gimme that—a man don't buy dinner for nothing—send her gifts—

FRANKIE He liked her company.

NICK [*Sarcastically.*] Did she tell him about the pains in her chest?

FRANKIE That's not the only thing she has to talk about—

NICK The pelvis in the face?

FRANKIE They talked about giving away money to charity—

NICK What money?

FRANKIE His money. How he should give most of it away 'cause he don't need it all. And she told him about the time she bought a pair a shoes for a bum she met on her way home—

NICK What bum?

FRANKIE One she met on the bus—

NICK She bought a bum a pair a shoes?

FRANKIE Yeah.

NICK And she's always complaining I don't make enough money?

FRANKIE He needed them.

NICK Okay—cut the crap—what he want from her?

FRANKIE   Nothing.

NICK   When she came in—did she have on her brassiere?

FRANKIE   That's disgusting.

NICK   Pig.

FRANKIE   Don't talk about her like that.

NICK   Pig.

FRANKIE   He had crutches.

NICK   There's ways a having sex without getting up off your ass—you wanna hear them?

FRANKIE   No! It's the poetry—

NICK   Fuck the poetry—it's his money—

FRANKIE   It's not for money—I told you she wants him to give it away to charity—

NICK   As long as there's leftover for her—

FRANKIE   Yeah, a little—

[*He breaks off. They pause.*]

NICK   I could a stopped this. I would a forbid her to go out. 6:30—that's when she'd a had a be home. I would a opened all her mail. I would a spied on her conversations—I should a never let her go back to work—

FRANKIE   It wouldn't a done no good—

NICK   I got ways to make her listen—

FRANKIE   She stopped listening to you a long time ago.

NICK   Oh yeah?

FRANKIE   You should see how she rolls her eyes at me when you talk…

NICK   [*Pause.*] And what a you do?
  [*Beat.*]
  You roll your eyes back?

FRANKIE   [*Slowly.*] No.

NICK   You protected her.

FRANKIE   I thought it was a one-night thing.

NICK You wanted her to get away from me.

FRANKIE Are you crazy?

NICK She won you over. Told you things like your speech and pictures were good so you'd shut up, look the other way while she jerks a cripple off for his money—

FRANKIE SHUT UP!

[*Almost losing it.*]

SHUT UP!

[*Struggles to control himself.*]

You know how I know it ain't for sex—she said if it's sex she wanted, she's had plenty a offers from other guys—but how after living with you she don't think she wants sex again and this guy's safe 'cause he don't want it either.

[*Silence.*]

The next days she started writing him a poem. I was getting scared. She spent every night for a week working on it. She kept asking me how you spell things. I wouldn't say nothing. A couple a times she almost gave up 'cause she said she was too stupid.

NICK What kind a poem?

FRANKIE About the sunset. She took hours copying it over so it'd look pretty.

NICK I wanna see it.

FRANKIE She asked if she could read it to me—

NICK I wanna see this poem.

FRANKIE It's private. It's hers.

NICK Is it in that canister?

[*Heads toward the canister where* FRANKIE *pulled out the case of beetles.*]

FRANKIE Please don't touch it.

[NICK *has gotten to the canister before* FRANKIE *can make a move. He pulls out a folded piece of paper.*]

NICK This it?

[*Unfolds paper.* FRANKIE *carefully takes it out of his hands.*]

FRANKIE   I'll read it.

[*He studies the poem. Highway sounds fade in. He reads.*]

"The Sunset" by Rita Gabriola
From my kitchen window I see
The colors of God's majesty
The sunset that is for me
My window on eternity.

While I cook, the colors change from pink to gold
Then sometimes to blood red.
What am I being told?

Is red the way God cries?
Is pink the way he laughs?
How 'bout yellow?
Is he feeling mellow?

Whatever he is saying, I think this is love.
In olden days he would send a dove.
But for me he sends the sunset
And it helps me not to cry
After all, he had to die.
Why should I think my suffering is more?
And maybe the turquoise sky is the closest I'll get
To seeing the Mediterranean yet.

But I thank the Lord for sunsets and birds and beetles
Yes, beetles, 'cause I did not know how beautiful
they could be.
Especially yellow and purple ones.
All this expresses me.

[*Silence.*]

NICK   [*Quietly.*] She sent this to him?

FRANKIE   Yeah.

NICK   He like it?

FRANKIE   He said it was—a source a strength. He called her up.

NICK   What else he say?

FRANKIE   She said—

[*Pause.*]

She got the most wonderful offer.

NICK What offer?

FRANKIE He said...he invited her...

NICK Where?

FRANKIE Now he was in a wheelchair...he just wanted a do something for her.

NICK What?

FRANKIE She said she couldn't...

NICK What?

FRANKIE [*Very softly.*] Pamper her.

NICK Huh?

FRANKIE He wanted a pamper her.

NICK [*Silence. Softly.*] Take care a her?

FRANKIE [*Can barely say it.*] Treat her nice.

NICK Show her places.

FRANKIE He said he wanted a make her laugh a lot.

NICK [*Pause. Softly.*] Pamper her...then she's not coming back...

FRANKIE [*To himself.*] She never told me she was going.

NICK [*Silence.*] Where's my poetry?

FRANKIE When she read her poem, I laughed at it.

NICK Where's my poetry?

FRANKIE You had your chance, she tried to talk to you.

NICK How could I listen?
[*Beat.*]
Sometimes I come home from work blind, I'm so tired.

FRANKIE I know that.

NICK No, you don't. Not unless you worked in and out for the last seventeen years, six days a week, draggin' yourself to a place where everything in your body says don't go—change your life. But you go. And you don't go complaining to everyone how sick you are.

FRANKIE And you're miserable.

NICK Yeah, I'm miserable.

[*Beat.*]

But sometimes you don't know how good I can feel. Sometimes— when I'm driving back home and I think why I do it. Who I do it for. Sometimes that car can't go fast enough to get me home.

[*Beat.*]

There was a time you used to pant when I come in the door.

FRANKIE I'm not a kid no more. I don't wanna talk about frogs and ice cream.

NICK I don't know how to talk to you.

FRANKIE You don't try.

NICK I'm tryin' every second.

FRANKIE The wrong way.

NICK [*Pause.*] You scare me when I talk to you.

FRANKIE Why?

NICK I don't understand about Kotex and dirty lots and—stained underwear.

FRANKIE You live in it.

NICK No, I don't.

FRANKIE Look around you.

NICK No, it's not ugly. All right, maybe this ain't where I dreamed we'd be living or what I dreamed I'd be doing—but I'm always fighting for us. I'm top salesman, I know all the secrets for being good. Sometimes with the customers around—I pretend you're with me in the store, and I talk to you in my head. We have conversations about them and I show you the tricks. And you should hear how we laugh together 'cause we know I'm getting the better a them. And you don't mind me being like this slave 'cause you know I do everything for you.

FRANKIE All right—not everything's ugly.

NICK Am I?

[*Silence.*]

You took that picture.

FRANKIE That's how you look sometimes.

NICK But not all the time.

FRANKIE All right—not all the time.

NICK You laughed about it...with her?

FRANKIE [*Beat.*] No. She told me to rip it up.

[*Pause.*]

She didn't understand I didn't mean it mean.

NICK She thought it was mean?

FRANKIE Yeah.

[NICK *takes this in.* FRANKIE *goes to collect scraps of his pictures on the floor.* NICK *watches for a while before speaking.*]

NICK How would you take a picture a her?

[*Pause.*]

How did she look?

FRANKIE [*Confused.*] I'm not sure.

NICK Why'd you only take me?

FRANKIE [*Pause.*] I'd take one a her—face pinched up and lips all sour—the way she got when she made fun a the mall...I'd take another when we made her laugh that time we brought her flowers for the vase she made in ceramics—only we brought so many we had a put them in all the glasses and even in your trophy from four years ago...

NICK If she would call tonight, I would promise her anything.

FRANKIE There's another face she got...It's when she only wanted a read me a couple a sentences from one a her books and I got up and walked away into the other room.

[*Pause.*]

You know how I would take a picture a me? Ugly. There wouldn't be underwear dirty enough.

NICK You're not dirty.

FRANKIE That's how I feel. And when you don't understand how I talk it gets worse.

[*They look at each other. NICK makes a slight movement as if he would like to say something or reach out to FRANKIE but he is incapable of starting the gesture. FRANKIE turns away from NICK and goes to window.*]

NICK I'm listening.

[*FRANKIE turns to look at him. They hold each other's eyes for a moment. Again, neither is capable of speaking or reaching out. NICK looks away. FRANKIE hesitates, then goes over to the chair where he had earlier placed his mother's books. He carries a stack of them over to the counter and begins placing them back. NICK watches and a beat later follows behind him with the remaining books from the chair. As NICK reaches the counter, FRANKIE turns away from him toward the phone. Beat. Cautiously, NICK leans his body in toward his son so they are touching slightly at the shoulders and then also looks toward the phone. They stand like that for a moment, aware that they are finally touching. The sound of traffic is heard from the highway. Blackout.*]

• • •

Free Will

Billy Aronson

Free Will by Billy Aronson. Copyright © 2014 by Billy Aronson. All rights reserved. Reprinted by permission of the author.

CAUTION/ADVICE: Professionals and amateurs are hereby warned that performance of *Free Will* is subject to a royalty. It is fully protected under the copyright laws of the United States of America, and of all countries covered by the International Copyright Union (including the Dominion of Canada and the rest of the British Commonwealth), and of all countries covered by the Pan-American Copyright Convention and the Universal Copyright Convention, the Berne Convention, and of all countries with which the United States has reciprocal copyright relations. All rights, including professional and amateur stage performing rights, motion picture, recitation, lecturing, public reading, radio broadcasting, television, video or sound recording, all other forms of mechanical or electronic reproduction, such as CD-ROM, DVD-ROM, information storage and retrieval systems, and photocopying, and the rights of translation into foreign languages, are strictly reserved. Particular emphasis is placed upon the matter of readings, permission for which must be secured from the author's agent in writing.

Inquiries concerning rights should be addressed to Billy@BillyAronson.com

Billy Aronson

Billy Aronson's short plays have been featured in five previous volumes of *Best American Short Plays* and produced in eight Ensemble Studio Theatre marathons. His full-length plays have premiered at Playwrights Horizons, Woolly Mammoth, Wellfleet Harbor Actors Theatre, SF Productions, and 1812 Productions. His writing for the musical theater includes the original concept/additional lyrics for the Broadway musical *Rent*. TV writing credits include Cartoon Network's *Courage the Cowardly Dog*, MTV's *Beavis & Butt-head*, and Nickelodeon's *Wonder Pets* (head writer, Emmy Award). With artist Jennifer Oxley he created the new PBS math show *Peg + Cat*, and their company 9ate7 Productions. With wife Lisa Vogel he created their offspring Jake and Anna. Visit: BillyAronson.com

···production history···

Free Will has not yet been produced.

characters

> VIOLA
> FALSTAFF
> IAGO
> PROSPERO
> HAMLET
> CLEOPATRA
> JULIET
> WITCH
> SEBASTIAN

setting

The play takes place on an island, once upon a time.

NOTE: The character SEBASTIAN is played by the actress who plays VIOLA.

ANOTHER NOTE: A couple bushes or trees on the sides of the stage indicate the edge of a forest. But the main set piece is a single, very large rock.

[*A large rock.* VIOLA *stands there.*]

VIOLA My brother's dead and I'm alive. He was standing right next to me on the ship when the storm hit. The water took him straight down, carried me to this island. Someone's coming. Someone big. This is not a good time to be a woman. From now on, I'm not Viola.

[VIOLA *hides behind the rock.* FALSTAFF *enters.*]

FALSTAFF You back there, are you a woman?

VIOLA I'm Cesario.

FALSTAFF I'm Falstaff. I was asking because the three of us on the island are all men and I need a woman to hold on to. I'm so shaken up, I was hiding in a laundry basket my friends dumped in the river when a wave came from nowhere and—are you going to come out?

VIOLA Not yet. My clothes, got, uh—

FALSTAFF This amazingly kind man is passing out things he's found washed up, he might have some clothes for you, here he comes now. Iago.

[IAGO *enters with a bag of stuff.*]

Do you have clothes for Cesario here?

IAGO Help yourself.

[IAGO *hands bag to* VIOLA, *who changes behind the rock.*]

VIOLA Thanks, Iago.

IAGO You're the first one to need clothes. The storm dropped the rest of us here completely dry.

FALSTAFF It's amazing how delicately the storm went about completely fucking up our lives.

IAGO I'd just been promoted to captain. How many years of eating shit that took. The general chose me to accompany his wife on a ship, the waves dragged me away, it's all shot to hell. Better find us more food so we don't fucking starve.

[VIOLA *comes out dressed as a man.*]

Here's some fruit for you.

[IAGO *hands* VIOLA *a piece of fruit, goes.*]

FALSTAFF It's really tangy.

VIOLA I'm not hungry. You take it.

FALSTAFF Just finished mine. You're sure? Well, why waste.

[*Bites.*]

It's so great to have a tongue. You put something on this one little muscle for a few seconds and all the shit in your life makes no difference.

[*Finishes eating.*]

I'm going to go masturbate. If you want to join me…

[FALSTAFF *exits.* VIOLA *sits there.*]

VIOLA Even when my brother and I were on different continents I knew he was somewhere.

[PROSPERO *enters carrying a staff, waves it.* VIOLA *falls asleep.* PROSPERO *points to* VIOLA *and to places where other characters have exited.*]

PROSPERO One, two, three, four?
[*Calls.*]
Witch.

[PROSPERO *snaps his fingers as he exits and* VIOLA *opens her eyes.* HAMLET *enters with a knife.*]

HAMLET I knew what had to be done, I was the only one who could do it, but I thought and I thought about doing it 'til they sent me away, the storm dumped me here, I'm stuck knowing it's all getting worse, everyone's being lied to, abused by that shithead. Human beings are amazing creatures, we build towers, fill the planet with music, but to me it's all diseased, I can't cure it.

[*Screams.*]

VIOLA Stop beating yourself up.

HAMLET Why?

VIOLA You have a brilliant mind and a heart, big noble goals, to get all that working together takes time.

HAMLET I'm Hamlet.

VIOLA Cesario.

HAMLET We'll never get off this island, will we?

VIOLA Focus on something else.

HAMLET What?

VIOLA Something light, far away.

HAMLET The thing I used to get wrapped up in was women.

VIOLA If only there was a woman here, right?

HAMLET You in love with anyone Cesario?

VIOLA Someone who doesn't even know my name.

HAMLET I'm sorry.

VIOLA Don't be. It's like loving a star. You'll never reach it, but you feel lucky to be able to look up and see it there.

HAMLET Your talking about love makes me wish there was a woman I could hold.

VIOLA   Can I tell you the truth, Hamlet?

HAMLET   You couldn't tell me anything but the truth, Cesario. Everyone's been lying to me. Family, closest friends. It's brought me this close to killing myself. But I feel like I can count on you for total honesty. You were saying?

VIOLA   I was going to say, I hear women.

HAMLET   This way. Quick.

[HAMLET *leads* VIOLA *behind the rock.* CLEOPATRA *and* JULIET *enter,* CLEOPATRA *clinging to* JULIET's *arm, dragging her around.*]

CLEOPATRA   [*Calls.*] Anthony.

JULIET   You're hurting my arm.

CLEOPATRA   Shh. I hear him calling for me, "Cleopatra."

JULIET   At last I get your name. I'm Juliet.

CLEOPATRA   [*Calls.*] Anthony.

JULIET   We're surrounded by so much water, not even my parents could find us here.

CLEOPATRA   What other people can do has nothing to do with Anthony. He's so far beyond anything I can explain, anything you could dream of, now he's gone, there's nothing beautiful or good anywhere.

JULIET   I've never felt like that about anyone. My parents wanted me to meet someone at a party they're having tonight, but when I stopped to rinse my hands in a fountain the water wrapped around me, carried me here.

CLEOPATRA   I was on a ship when the storm hit. There was a war going on, or something. What is that sick force in the universe that fills your life with beautiful things then takes them away one at a time?

JULIET   There is a force out there, but it moves you around for a reason. When the water lifted me up I saw my life for the first time. My parents are insane, always screaming. I have no idea why. And I don't care anymore. I'm free.

CLEOPATRA   I am so fucking happy for you Juliet.
[*Calls.*]
Anthony.

JULIET I'll go with you but let go of my arm.

[CLEOPATRA *and* JULIET *go off.* HAMLET *and* VIOLA *come out from behind the rock.*]

HAMLET You were right, Cesario. A minute ago everything was dark, now there's light pouring in, this incredible person.

VIOLA She still loves Anthony.

HAMLET Not Cleopatra, she's angry, confused.

VIOLA Like you.

HAMLET Like I was. But Juliet is so brave, she can take in this awful situation and find so much hope.

VIOLA Huh.

HAMLET You like Cleopatra? She's beautiful, right?

VIOLA Yes but no.

HAMLET I hope you're not saving yourself for that person who doesn't know your name.

VIOLA I feel what I feel, what can I say.

HAMLET They're coming back.

[*Heading behind the rock.*]

This way.

[HAMLET *and* VIOLA *go back behind the rock.* CLEOPATRA *comes out, collapses, hugs her knees, shuts her eyes, sits in silence.* JULIET *follows.*]

JULIET He's not there, he's not here. Come on, get up. I need to look for food but I don't want to leave you alone.

[HAMLET *comes out, followed by* VIOLA.]

HAMLET I'm Hamlet.

VIOLA Cesario.

CLEOPATRA I'm visualizing someone so much better than either of you. Shhh.

[*She sits there in silence.*]

HAMLET You were saying you wanted food. There's a man giving out fruit. I'll find him or get you something to eat myself.

[HAMLET *goes,* VIOLA *follows,* VIOLA *returns.*]

VIOLA Hamlet wants to know if you'd like to go with him. I'll stay with Cleopatra.

JULIET Your friend Hamlet is weird. He comes this close to me, runs away, sends you to ask for me, and now he's standing behind a tree spying on me. Why?

VIOLA He's shaken up by the storm, like everyone is except you, and he's intimidated by you. Don't act like you don't know what I'm talking about. You're young and confident and beautiful and that gives you power. Listen. Juliet. He's a brilliant, thoughtful person. You have two perfectly fine legs, walk with him.

JULIET [*Calls.*] Hamlet.

[HAMLET *enters. To* HAMLET.]

I'd like to look around the island with Cesario. Would you stay with Cleopatra?

VIOLA I'll stay with Cleopatra.

JULIET [*To* VIOLA.] You and I were having a conversation I wanted to finish.

HAMLET Why don't we all go?

JULIET I shouldn't leave her alone.

[FALSTAFF *moans offstage.*]

HAMLET [*Calls.*] Falstaff.

[FALSTAFF *enters, zipping up.*]

FALSTAFF [*To* VIOLA.] No luck, too tense, I kept tugging and tugging—

[*Sees the women.*]

Oh.

HAMLET Juliet, Cleopatra, Falstaff.

FALSTAFF So now's the part where you get used to my looks. I'll just stand here and sweat.

HAMLET We're going to look for food. Could you stay with Cleopatra?

FALSTAFF Sure.

JULIET We'll be right back.

[HAMLET, VIOLA, *and* JULIET *exit.* FALSTAFF *regards* CLEOPATRA *in silence.* *Then.*]

FALSTAFF Could I run my fingers up and down the air around your legs? I wouldn't touch you, my hands would be three feet away the whole time, I'd just go up and down your legs very fast, you could keep your eyes closed the whole time, sleep right through it. No? Never mind.

CLEOPATRA I'd kill myself but I'm too sad.

FALSTAFF You're in luck. When people spend time with me they end up laughing.

CLEOPATRA Why?

FALSTAFF Because I'm stupid and ugly.

CLEOPATRA You don't have any admirable qualities, do you?

FALSTAFF No and I don't want any. Bravery gets you beat up. Patriotism gets you killed.

CLEOPATRA The idea of a country is ridiculous.

FALSTAFF Wisdom is annoying. Confidence is boring. What I hate most is pride in your accomplishments. Or respect. Being respected. So what.

CLEOPATRA You're still going to drop dead for no reason.

FALSTAFF If everybody thinks you're a piece of shit you can't let that ruin your breakfast.

[*They sit there.*]

CLEOPATRA Do you want to go into the woods and fuck?

FALSTAFF Yes.

CLEOPATRA You can't tell anyone.

[CLEOPATRA *and* FALSTAFF *go into the woods.* PROSPERO *enters, counts.*]

PROSPERO One, two, three, four, five, six. Witch.

[PROSPERO *waves his stick.* WITCH *enters.*]

WITCH You can't keep calling me back, Prospero. My sisters and me are giving a group of soldiers a whole new kind of mental illness. It takes intense concentration.

PROSPERO There are only six.

WITCH   You only asked for six.

PROSPERO   You said if I asked for six there would be seven.

WITCH   I had a feeling that if you picked out six there would be seven, and like all my weird hunches it was right. One of the six disguised herself as a man.

PROSPERO   One of them...

WITCH   Disguised herself.

PROSPERO   Disguised...

WITCH   I can't fucking believe you. I've been watching them from a pit on the other side of the planet, looking into images in the eyeball of an owl, you're sitting on that hill ten feet away and you can't even follow what the hell is going on.

PROSPERO   One of the men...

WITCH   If you're too senile to follow the story, you'll never be entertained and I'll never be free.

PROSPERO   The one who—

WITCH   She's a woman dressed as a man.

PROSPERO   The one with the brother.

WITCH   She lost her brother, she's dressed as a man.

PROSPERO   You said there would be seven.

WITCH   You're old. Go back to your daughter so she can take care of you. I'll drop you off, let's go.

PROSPERO   I don't have a daughter.

WITCH   Yes you do, but she started listening to her husband instead of you and she wouldn't say I love you with the right intonation so you had a fucking fit and stormed off, literally. You came back to this island where you worked your magic all those years ago, so you could get back the old magic, make the greatest drama of all time, something to entertain you and make your senility bearable, but you've thrown away your book of spells and can't remember them, so when you tried to summon a spirit to carry out your project, instead of some cute sprite you got me, a fucking witch.

PROSPERO Those aren't the six I ordered.

WITCH But I don't make charming entertainment, do I? I pluck out people's eyelashes, spit worms up their assholes, crawl into their brains, and go berserk, so this assignment of bringing characters together to entertain you really goes against the grain.

PROSPERO They're not the ones I ordered.

WITCH Like hell they're not.

PROSPERO When I looked into your robe—

WITCH When I opened my robe you looked into the flame in there, saw images of the most dramatic people, picked your six favorites, I ripped them from their lives, dragged them kicking and screaming over the water, and now I'm done, finished, and so sick of your shit.

PROSPERO They don't feel right together.

WITCH Of course they don't feel right together. They come from completely different places and times. What were you thinking?

PROSPERO They were all made by the same creator. They should work together.

WITCH What fairy tale do you live in?

PROSPERO More needs to happen, make them do more together.

WITCH I can chop off a toe, put out an eye, but as far as the overall course, once it's in motion, you just have to let them do what they're going to do.

[PROSPERO *raises his staff. Her body freezes.*]

PROSPERO Get in there.

WITCH Fine. I'll make something happen, that will lead to something, that will change absolutely nothing, for your viewing pleasure.
[*Wraps her cape around herself, gestures for* PROSPERO *to step aside.*]
I'm invisible, you're not.

[*As* IAGO *enters,* PROSPERO *steps aside.*]

IAGO [*To himself.*] Hamlet and Cesario are all over Juliet, but Cleopatra sounds even better.

[WITCH *speaks into* IAGO's *ear, though he can't see her.*]

WITCH Cleopatra's that way. Go.

[IAGO *exits in the direction* CLEOPATRA *went.* PROSPERO *steps out.*]

PROSPERO So he'll find the big one and the woman together.

WITCH It would have happened eventually, or some other idiotic thing would have happened leading to some other pointless outcome. So get back on the hill and watch your inane drama, I'm going back to my sisters.

PROSPERO Stay. I don't want to keep calling you.

WITCH Oh, come on, Prospero. It's bad enough you make me do this shit. Don't make me watch it.

[*She starts off,* PROSPERO *raises the stick. She freezes.*]

PROSPERO You can go when it's done.

[*He lowers the stick.*]

[WITCH *hisses at* PROSPERO.]

[PROSPERO *and* WITCH *go, as* HAMLET, VIOLA, *and* JULIET *enter;* VIOLA *cutting into a coconut with* HAMLET*'s knife.*]

HAMLET Just stick the knife through the shell, Cesario.

JULIET He's doing fine.

HAMLET I didn't mean it as a criticism.

VIOLA No, Hamlet's right, I'm weak.

JULIET Cesario, you're such a great friend to Hamlet. Every word he says you defend. No one's ever done that for me.

HAMLET Your parents were so awful, Juliet, but you came through with amazing strength.

JULIET Why do you keep praising me every ten seconds? It's condescending.

HAMLET I'm being supportive, which is exactly what you were saying you love when Cesario does it.

JULIET Cesario deeply admires you, that's why he's always trying to make you sound great.

VIOLA I'm not trying to do anything, he really does have an incredible mind.

JULIET See?

HAMLET Really, Cesario, stop.
[IAGO *enters, throws his sack, kicks it.*]
Are you all right, Iago?

IAGO I have things I have to do.

[IAGO *picks up his sack, goes.*]

JULIET He really doesn't want to be here.

HAMLET Who does?

JULIET I do, because of the people.

HAMLET Me too.

VIOLA Me too.

HAMLET Doesn't it feel like there's a mind behind it all that brought us together?

JULIET There is a force out there that holds you in its palm.

HAMLET I think it leaves you alone to get the shit kicked out of you 'til you find your way into a current and sort of drift.

JULIET What do you think Cesario?

VIOLA I think the universe shits on me but it gives me great friends. Then it takes them away. But new ones seem to keep coming.

HAMLET Isn't this where we left Cleopatra and Falstaff?

JULIET They must be looking for Anthony on the beach.

VIOLA You two go ahead.

JULIET Why do you keep trying to get away from us, Cesario?

VIOLA This shirt is itching, I'll see if Iago has another one.

HAMLET [*To* JULIET.] He'll catch up with us.

JULIET [*To* VIOLA.] Don't be long.

[HAMLET *and* JULIET *exit.*]

VIOLA The two of them together. I can't take it.

[HAMLET *comes out.*]

HAMLET I know why you're staying away.

VIOLA You do.

HAMLET You want me to finally tell Juliet how I feel about her.

VIOLA That's it.

HAMLET I love you, my friend.

[HAMLET *hugs* VIOLA, *goes.*]

VIOLA I could stay here and wait for the details of their love making, or I could walk and walk, all the way to the other side of the island, where there are different people, or none.

[VIOLA *goes.* JULIET *comes out, followed by* HAMLET.]

JULIET You need to stop putting your hands on me and breathing on me, Hamlet.

HAMLET Oh, Juliet, since I landed here I've been this bizarre version of who I actually am, I'm trying to squirm back into myself but it keeps slipping away so I have to touch you or scream to give you some fucking idea who I am.

JULIET I see who you are and it's just not for me.

HAMLET Juliet.

[*He grabs her and kisses her.*]

JULIET Get off me.

  [*He steps back from her.*]

  Find Cleopatra. Give her this fruit. Now.

  [HAMLET *takes the coconut, goes.*]

  When Hamlet grabbed me just now I felt a rush of love. For Cesario. He's so aware, of what's inside me. I'm naked before him. I have to tell him I love him this second.

[JULIET *goes off to one side. On from the other side comes* SEBASTIAN—*played by the actress who plays* VIOLA, *wearing a different shirt.*]

SEBASTIAN My sister was standing right next to me on the ship, the water took her straight up like a toy. I'm so alone.

[JULIET *comes out.*]

JULIET   Shh. Listen. Ugh. Anyway, I love you, I love you so much. You're this dear tender thing I want to hold in my hand and keep close to me every second, I'm scaring you, I should act shy, I'll act shy, I can't act shy I'm burning up but the flames soft and cool are washing my entire body these words pouring straight from my soul I've never felt this before I'm sorry I'm spitting it's just that though I've known you for a minute it feels like every second of my life you've been watching me I'm scared to death to stop talking because I have no idea what you'll do, don't go, don't move, let's be together, our hands our bodies, let's not even use words no names just our breathing our pulse I want to be totally with you in the forest right now.

SEBASTIAN   All right.

JULIET   I like the new shirt.

[JULIET *and* SEBASTIAN *go off.* HAMLET *comes out from behind a tree on the left side of the stage, watches them go, puts down the coconut.* IAGO *peeks out from behind a bush on the right side of the stage, watches* HAMLET.]

HAMLET   Saving yourself for someone you'll never have, are you, Cesario? There's no one on this planet I can trust.

[IAGO *enters.*]

IAGO   The nicer somebody is to you, the worse they're about to abuse you.

HAMLET   Oh, Iago. I'm so disgusted with the human race.

IAGO   So you've heard about Falstaff.

HAMLET   Heard what?

IAGO   He's been slipping people these drugs he makes from plants.

HAMLET   [*Laughs.*] Falstaff?

IAGO   You haven't noticed anybody acting weird all of a sudden?

HAMLET   Cesario turned into a lying shit, but—

IAGO   Hmmm.

HAMLET   Hmm what?

IAGO   You're already upset. This isn't the time.

HAMLET For what?

IAGO For you to see the effect of Falstaff's drugs on Cleopatra.

HAMLET What effects? Iago?

IAGO Walk that way. Quietly. Go.

[HAMLET *exits.* IAGO *waits.* HAMLET *enters, stands there.*]

HAMLET Wow.

IAGO He hasn't offered you anything, has he?

HAMLET No.

IAGO Then I guess it was some stupid joke I didn't get.

HAMLET What joke?

IAGO When I was giving Falstaff some fruit before he pointed to you and said tomorrow morning we can kick you, poke your eyes, but you'll never get up, ever.

HAMLET You're fucking with me.

[HAMLET *shoves* IAGO *to the ground.*]

IAGO Forget trying to help, I've got work to do.

[IAGO *starts off.*]

HAMLET Iago. I'm sorry. It's just, I've had this voice telling me something deadly is out there, do something about it, but whenever I do the consequences are so awful I can't think about them without wanting to kill myself.

IAGO You're right to be careful, Hamlet. You shouldn't do anything about Falstaff unless you're sure.

HAMLET Right.

IAGO Luckily there's a way to be sure. The tree over by the clearing? At the base there are a few little green plants with shiny leaves. That's snake root. It's poisonous. That's what Falstaff said he was going to give you.

HAMLET So I can just check around the tree.

IAGO If the little plants are still there, you have nothing to worry about.
[HAMLET *goes.*]

I'm fairly sure the plants aren't there, because they're here.

[IAGO *takes out plants. He opens the coconut, adds water and leaves from the plants, stirs.*]

I was going to use them to make Falstaff throw up, but this new idea is so much bigger and better.

[*Dashes into the woods, calls.*]

Falstaff.

[IAGO *comes back out as* FALSTAFF *comes running out.*]

FALSTAFF   What, Iago, what?

IAGO   Hamlet's having these terrible fits of depression.

FALSTAFF   I'm so sorry.

IAGO   I was going to give him this fruit drink to cheer him up, then I thought it should come from you because you're his favorite person here.

FALSTAFF   I guess Hamlet likes me more than I thought. Usually people like me less than I thought.

IAGO   He'll be here in a minute. Don't tell anybody else about his problem, he's very private.

FALSTAFF   Okay.

IAGO   And remember, the drink is from you.

[IAGO *goes.*]

FALSTAFF   Iago thinks of everything.

[CLEOPATRA *comes out.*]

CLEOPATRA   Come on back into the woods.

FALSTAFF   I need to do something for somebody first.

CLEOPATRA   What?

FALSTAFF   I promised I wouldn't tell.

CLEOPATRA   What's this drink?

FALSTAFF   I'll just be a minute.

CLEOPATRA   Who besides Iago does this have to do with?

[FALSTAFF *is silent.*]

Do you realize that where I come from people would organize their entire month around a chance to be anywhere near me just to say something stupid in passing, and if I'd happen to stop and exchange a few words with somebody he'd start stuttering and perspire and go tell everyone he'd ever met and write about it and I don't mean just letters or diary entrees I mean epic poems and plays or he'd devote his life to making massive sculptures or paintings or stadiums.

FALSTAFF Keeping my word to my friends is the one pretentious virtue in which I indulge.

CLEOPATRA [*Covers her eyes.*] Shit. I'm completely in love with you. Nothing from before seems real.

FALSTAFF Me too, but—

CLEOPATRA It's okay. I trust you. I'll be waiting.

[CLEOPATRA *embraces* FALSTAFF, *goes.*]

FALSTAFF [*To himself.*] Don't you dare get your hopes up, you fat idiot. Any second she'll come back to reality and devote the rest of her life to ignoring you. I'm so tired of scraping you off the floor.

[HAMLET *enters, stares at* FALSTAFF.]

Hamlet.

HAMLET Who are you?

FALSTAFF Your friend, Falstaff. You all right?

HAMLET Funny.

FALSTAFF What?

HAMLET It seems like you really do give a shit about me.

FALSTAFF After knowing you for three seconds I wanted to be you. There's something about you I root for.

HAMLET Falstaff, I believe you.

FALSTAFF Oh, good. So here's this fruit drink I made you. Drink.

HAMLET You drink.

FALSTAFF It's for you.

[HAMLET*'s entire body trembles, he hunches over.*]

HAMLET I'll drink it if you leave me alone.

FALSTAFF Okay.

[FALSTAFF *leaves.* HAMLET *hugs himself, rocks.* IAGO *enters.*]

HAMLET He tried to get me to drink this. It has the leaves in it.

IAGO So from now on be careful what you drink.

HAMLET There's nothing else I can do?

IAGO This conversation is making me nervous.

[IAGO *starts off.*]

HAMLET Wait. Iago.

[HAMLET *follows* IAGO *off, as* JULIET *and* SEBASTIAN *enter.*]

JULIET When I said your name why did you start up with some joke?

SEBASTIAN I wasn't making a joke, you didn't say my name.

[HAMLET *comes back, sees* JULIET *and* SEBASTIAN, *hides.*]

JULIET I said Cesario.

SEBASTIAN And I said I'm Sebastian.

JULIET Were we getting too close so you had to start acting strange?

SEBASTIAN I'm not acting strange, you are.

JULIET I suddenly feel like we don't know each other, it's scaring me.

SEBASTIAN You feel like we don't know each other because this is our first conversation.

JULIET The things we said before meant so much to me.

SEBASTIAN We didn't say anything before because you never let me speak.

JULIET I never let you speak?

SEBASTIAN Not two words.

JULIET What about when you said I was confident and beautiful?

SEBASTIAN When did I say you were confident and beautiful?

JULIET So since the second you got your body on top of me none of the things you said count.

SEBASTIAN I don't know what you want from me, tell me what you want.

JULIET I want you to talk to me like before so there's some trace of continuity, it's not like we're animals.

SEBASTIAN I get it, it's because I'm not big.

JULIET What does your size have to do with anything?

SEBASTIAN I'm not really tall so you think you can drag me off to have sex then get me to say yes to whatever insanity comes out of your mouth, this always happens.

JULIET Drag you off to have sex?

SEBASTIAN I may not have hair all over my chest but I know when I'm being pushed around.

JULIET I don't want to push you around, I don't want to look at you. Where are you going?

SEBASTIAN You said you don't want to look at me.

JULIET That you remember.
[SEBASTIAN *goes.*]
You think you know someone.

[HAMLET *comes out.*]

HAMLET It's not his fault that he's not himself, Juliet.

JULIET You're spying on me again, get out.

[SEBASTIAN *comes out, pulls* HAMLET *away from* JULIET.]

HAMLET Cesario.

SEBASTIAN I'm Sebastian.

HAMLET Sebastian, okay, I was telling Juliet about this thing we need to do something about, we'll need your help, to stop this person—

JULIET I can't deal with your shit right now, Hamlet.

HAMLET Now is all we have, we have to work fast, for all our sakes, listen.

[*As* HAMLET *leads* JULIET *and* SEBASTIAN *off to the side,* PROSPERO *and* WITCH *enter.*]

PROSPERO So now they'll take that stupid lie seriously?

WITCH From the way their eyebrows are twitching I'd say yes.

PROSPERO It's too crazy.

WITCH What do you expect? It was conceived by a senile lunatic on a particularly delusional day.

PROSPERO Make it less crazy.

WITCH I can't.

PROSPERO Then I will.

WITCH You'll step in and tell them everything, send us all home early?

PROSPERO If they keep going wrong, I'll reveal things, tell them I'm a wise, friar or...

[*Thinks.* WITCH *snores.* HAMLET *returns with* SEBASTIAN *and* JULIET. WITCH *leads* PROSPERO *off.*]

SEBASTIAN What you're saying does make sense of things.

JULIET and SEBASTIAN [*To* HAMLET.] The way he's acting.
[*To* HAMLET.]
The way she's acting.

JULIET But why would Falstaff want to hurt us?

SEBASTIAN You can't figure out insanity. You have to just do something about it.

HAMLET [*To* JULIET.] So you're convinced?

JULIET [*Starts off.*] I should see what he's done to Cleopatra.

SEBASTIAN I would think you'd feel safer going in there with me.

JULIET I'm just going to look, I won't get close, I didn't say you couldn't come. Is this about your height again?

SEBASTIAN If you're going, then go.
[JULIET *goes.*]
You look at me like you know me.

HAMLET You remind me of a friend I'm worried about.

SEBASTIAN I'm missing someone I lost who really knew me.

HAMLET I wonder if I'll ever see my friend again the way he was.

SEBASTIAN I wonder if you can ever appreciate someone you love when they're standing right there.

HAMLET You talk ideas, feelings, like the conversation will go on forever.

SEBASTIAN But it doesn't.

HAMLET And those things you could say to that one person become a poetry that's gone from the world.

SEBASTIAN You're saying random phrases to yourself that no one understands.

[HAMLET *kisses* SEBASTIAN. SEBASTIAN *backs off.*]

HAMLET I don't know why I did that, I'm sorry.

SEBASTIAN It happens.

[JULIET *comes out, embraces* SEBASTIAN.]

JULIET Her body's moving like she's not in control of it.

SEBASTIAN We'll go in there and confront Falstaff, and see how he reacts.

[IAGO *appears behind the rock, speaks only to* HAMLET.]

IAGO [*Offers rope.*] This could go around Falstaff's throat, drag him into the water 'til he tells you the truth.

[HAMLET *takes the long piece.*]

HAMLET Thanks, Iago.

IAGO And there's always your knife.

HAMLET My knife.

IAGO [*To* HAMLET.] Let me get Cleopatra out of your way first. Hold on.

[IAGO *exits.* HAMLET *regards* JULIET *and* SEBASTIAN *embracing, regards the knife, waits. Offstage sounds.*]

HAMLET Let's go around this way.

[HAMLET, JULIET, *and* SEBASTIAN *exit, as* IAGO *enters, followed by* CLEOPATRA.]

IAGO   It looked like you were with somebody. Were you with somebody?

CLEOPATRA   What do you want?

IAGO   To introduce myself, give you some fruit.

CLEOPATRA   I'm not hungry.

IAGO   You look like you could use some energy.

CLEOPATRA   What?

IAGO   You seem depleted. Like you need more energy.

CLEOPATRA   What the fuck are you saying?
[IAGO *shrugs.*]
Actually, give me a couple of those.

IAGO   You weren't hungry. Now you're eating for two.

CLEOPATRA   You going to give me the fruit?
[IAGO *doesn't move.*]
So…

IAGO   What will you give me?

CLEOPATRA   What will I give you?
[IAGO *stands there.* CLEOPATRA *laughs at* IAGO. IAGO *grabs* CLEOPA-TRA.]
Get the fuck off me.

[PROSPERO *comes forward.*]

PROSPERO   [*Announces.*] I saw. Everything.
[IAGO *flees.*]
I'll tell everyone everything. The big one is good. The one who said he's bad is a liar.

CLEOPATRA   Who are you?

PROSPERO   I, we…

[HAMLET, SEBASTIAN, *and* JULIET *enter, covered in blood.* HAMLET *holds out his bloody knife.*]

JULIET   So much blood, it kept coming.

SEBASTIAN   I was holding his arm, he wouldn't stop moving.

HAMLET I killed him.

[IAGO *appears behind the rock, watches.*]

IAGO [*Aside.*] To have an idea brought to life, more completely than you ever imagined, is so gratifying.

CLEOPATRA Who did you kill?

JULIET To save you.

SEBASTIAN And all of us.

HAMLET Falstaff.

CLEOPATRA Where is he?

SEBASTIAN In there.

[CLEOPATRA *runs off.*]

HAMLET What we did was right. Remember.

[CLEOPATRA *screams offstage.*]

IAGO [*To* HAMLET.] I'll get a drink that will calm her down.

[IAGO *goes as* CLEOPATRA *returns.*]

CLEOPATRA You cut him up.

SEBASTIAN We had to do something.

HAMLET Iago will explain.

CLEOPATRA Iago?

HAMLET He told me how Falstaff was trying to kill me.

JULIET We saw what Falstaff was doing to you.

SEBASTIAN We know how he drugged you.

CLEOPATRA [*Rages.*] What's going on in your heads has nothing to do with reality.

HAMLET She'll hurt herself, where's the rope?

SEBASTIAN I've got her.

JULIET Hold still.

[SEBASTIAN *and* JULIET *help* HAMLET *restrain* CLEOPATRA. PROSPERO *steps forward with staff raised. All freeze.* WITCH *observes.*]

PROSPERO I, Prospero, had this witch bring you here to make a story so great that my life would feel better.

[IAGO *appears with drink.*]

IAGO [*Aside.*] Every now and then I allow myself the delusion that I have some control over things but I don't I have no control.

[IAGO *exits.*]

PROSPERO But the order of who met who and what they said led you to trust someone bad and kill someone good, it all went wrong, I'm sorry.

[PROSPERO *lets down his arms. The others unfreeze and scream at* PROSPERO *all at once.*]

CLEOPATRA [*Scream at once.*] How could you let it happen, you just stood there!

SEBASTIAN [*Scream at once.*] How could you take me from my sister in that storm?

HAMLET [*Scream at once.*] Why didn't you do anything once you could see what we were doing?

JULIET [*Scream at once.*] That awful storm, the water dragging us all here just because!

[PROSPERO *brings the stick back up, they freeze.*]

WITCH I'll take them back where they came from, it's on my way.

PROSPERO Or we could help them work together to punish the liar.

[IAGO *comes out with rope, puts it around* PROSPERO'*s throat, the others remain frozen.*]

IAGO I have a better idea for an ending. Keep the staff raised and you can see it.

[PROSPERO *gasps for air.*]

WITCH [*To* IAGO.] I was heading out, let me drop you off.

IAGO First take the knife from Hamlet's hand, bring Cleopatra to that low rock.

[WITCH *takes knife from* HAMLET'*s hand, brings* CLEOPATRA *off.*]

WITCH   [*To herself.*] I've been enslaved by another shithead with a vision.

IAGO   Press her back against the rock so the jagged part's digging into her head.

WITCH   [*Offstage.*] Done.

IAGO   Cut out her tongue.

[CLEOPATRA *softly gasps offstage. Tongue flies onstage.* WITCH *enters.*]

WITCH   All right then?

IAGO   Take Cesario over to that patch of dirt by the tree.

WITCH   He's not Ces—never mind.

[WITCH *leads* SEBASTIAN *off.*]

IAGO   Press his face in the dirt.

WITCH   [*Offstage.*] Your choices are weird without being the least bit interesting.

[SEBASTIAN*'s labored breathing is heard offstage.*]

IAGO   Leave him lying there breathing in dirt.

[VIOLA *appears off to the side.*]

VIOLA   [*Aside.*] The world can get so much worse, so quickly.

[VIOLA *hides.* WITCH *returns.*]

WITCH   Any more quirky inspirations?

IAGO   Put out Hamlet's eyes with your thumbs.

WITCH   I'll scoop them out with the knife.

IAGO   No. Drop the knife.
   [WITCH *drops the knife.* VIOLA *steps out, unseen, picks up the knife.*]
   Use your hands. Put your thumbs on his eyes and push.
   [VIOLA *stabs* IAGO, *who falls.* PROSPERO *lowers his arms, the others come unfrozen.*]
   I'm fine.

[IAGO *crawls behind a bush, dies.*]

WITCH   I'll sew Cleopatra's tongue back on.

PROSPERO   Do it. Fast.

WITCH   I was just following his orders like I follow yours.

[WITCH *picks up tongue, exits.*]

HAMLET   [*To* VIOLA.] How did you do that, Cesario? I mean, Sebastian.

VIOLA   Something came over me. Was it right? Did you call me Sebastian?

JULIET   Of course it was right. Iago lied to get us to kill Falstaff.

HAMLET   You don't remember wanting to be called Sebastian?

VIOLA   You killed who?

JULIET   You don't remember what we did to Falstaff?

VIOLA   Who said I wanted to be called Sebastian?

CLEOPATRA   [*Offstage.*] Get your fingers off my tongue.

WITCH   I should have sewn it to your ass.

[CLEOPATRA *enters, followed by* WITCH.]

CLEOPATRA   [*To* VIOLA.] How'd you get there so fast? You were just wiping dirt off your face over there.

[JULIET *and* HAMLET *look offstage.*]

JULIET   He's still wiping dirt off his face over there.

HAMLET   Cesario. There are two of you.

[VIOLA *looks off.*]

VIOLA   It's you. You think you're staring at yourself. I'm not you. I'm someone who hid because everything was out of control, everything is out of control, but if the insanity brings me back to you I'll put up with all the ridiculous shit the universe can throw at me.
[*Reveals herself.*]
I'm Viola. Hug me, my brother.

[VIOLA *hurries off.*]

PROSPERO   So the six did become seven.

WITCH   Fuck if I'm not always right.

JULIET   [*To offstage.*] Which of you did I go into the forest with?

[SEBASTIAN *comes out.*]

SEBASTIAN That was me.

JULIET So all those things you said that made no sense—

SEBASTIAN Made perfect sense. And when you got mad at me for no reason—

JULIET I had a reason.

SEBASTIAN But when you went into the forest with me, you thought I was someone else.

JULIET Someone who said I'm beautiful and confident, which you never did.

SEBASTIAN My sister and I have similar tastes. She's always expressing things I feel very deeply.

JULIET Well then, since it was your feelings your sister was expressing, when I went into the forest thinking I was with your sister, it really was you I was thinking I was with.

SEBASTIAN So we really did love each other from the moment we met.

JULIET And even before.

[SEBASTIAN *and* JULIET *embrace, exit together.* JULIET, *offstage, sighs, gasps, kissing.* VIOLA *backs on, watching the offstage lovers.*]

HAMLET Viola.

VIOLA Hamlet. You look sad. Because it's not you with Juliet?

HAMLET No, because you're the most incredible friend I've ever had, but you're standing there alone, watching your brother with Juliet, thinking about that person who doesn't know your name.

VIOLA He does know my name now. But he'll never love me, unless you love me.

HAMLET [*Sad.*] Oh. [*Happy.*] Oh. Well then, for a friend.

[*He kisses her, they embrace.*]

WITCH The lovers are fucking. We're done.

CLEOPATRA It's not a happy ending for Falstaff.

HAMLET Or for me. I close my eyes and see Falstaff reaching towards me like this.

[JULIET *enters.*]

JULIET I washed off his blood but I still feel it all over me. Sebastian's pacing, he won't talk to me.

VIOLA Maybe after so much bad there can't be a happy ending.

PROSPERO If there's … any way I can make one—

CLEOPATRA Bring back Falstaff.

JULIET That would make up for everything you've done to us.

HAMLET Everything we've done to each other.

PROSPERO When someone's dead there's nothing I can do.

VIOLA [*To* WITCH.] What about you?

WITCH Nothing can be done for the dead—
    [*Suddenly writhes, moans, has a vision.*]
    —except a play.

CLEOPATRA A play?

HAMLET A play can help us see more deeply.

VIOLA Give us hope.

CLEOPATRA Doing a play can make you feel nice but it can't move a fingernail or a hair or actually do anything.

WITCH It can and will.

PROSPERO Her visions are always right.

JULIET Let's at least try.

CLEOPATRA After what's happened, doing a play would feel ridiculous.

VIOLA That we're here is ridiculous, that we found each other is ridiculous.

HAMLET To think you can know the limits of what's possible anywhere ever is ridiculous.

CLEOPATRA Fine. We'll do a play.

JULIET What should it be about?

WITCH Don't ask don't think go go.

[*They sing, dance, as necessary.* WITCH *waves her arms to make music.*]

[JULIET *wails.*]

[CLEOPATRA *moans.*]

[HAMLET *screams.*]

[VIOLA *sighs.*]

[PROSPERO *whines.*]

[WITCH *waves her arms so their crying out reverberates and becomes louder.* FALSTAFF *appears behind the rock. The others see* FALSTAFF *and become silent.* WITCH *stops the music and lights.*]

HAMLET   Is that who I think it is?

CLEOPATRA   If it is there's nothing but nonsense beneath the sky, thank God.

FALSTAFF   What a dream I was having. These ghosts of my friends all colliding in one point. I heard them, followed the sounds.

HAMLET   Iago told us terrible things about you. But Prospero who had us all brought here by this witch told us Iago was lying.

JULIET   Now Iago's dead.

CLEOPATRA   Like we thought you were.

FALSTAFF   Oh no, I just tripped or bumped into somebody, smacked my head on something, got some sleep.

CLEOPATRA   You're covered in blood.

FALSTAFF   That's berries. I stuffed them in my shirt to give Cleopatra.

HAMLET   I felt the knife going through your skin.

JULIET   I saw blood, I thought. It happened so fast.

CLEOPATRA   Your body was all over. A piece of you here. A piece there.

FALSTAFF   That's how I always look when I'm lying down.

HAMLET   Falstaff. When I confronted you in the forest it was like my actions were these wild dogs going in all directions, I could see them but I had no control.

JULIET   We had a fever. We were burning up.

HAMLET I'm sorry.

JULIET I'm sorry, Falstaff.

FALSTAFF It's all right. People get mad at me all the time. Though the stabbing is new.

JULIET Let me get someone else who could really use your forgiveness.

VIOLA I can't wait to see his face.

[JULIET *exits.*]

CLEOPATRA Falstaff. I'm sorry for making you keep our being together secret. What's wrong?

FALSTAFF You're about to tell me to get the fuck out of here.

CLEOPATRA No, I'm not.

FALSTAFF Yes, you are. You just realized I'm shit.

CLEOPATRA No.

FALSTAFF Then realize it already, I can't stand the suspense.

CLEOPATRA What I'm saying is I was wrong to keep our love private like it was a separate story all to itself. On this island we're all part of the same story, we can't be confused or disgusted by each other. We need to help them understand us. I need to come out and say Falstaff I love you and I don't care who knows.

[CLEOPATRA *embraces* FALSTAFF.]

VIOLA You got a woman to hold on to after all.

FALSTAFF Cesario?

VIOLA I'm Viola. It's a long story. But a story we were able to keep groping through 'til we got ourselves a happy ending.

HAMLET It wasn't us controlling the story, it was something beyond even what we think is out there controlling things.

FALSTAFF It was berries that saved my life, the force that can work any miracle is food and I worship it daily.

CLEOPATRA You put those berries in your shirt so you could give them to me. It was love that saved you, the most powerful force, driving everything.

FALSTAFF Love is a fruit so amazing that after you eat it you want to spend the rest of your life with a tree.

CLEOPATRA Love is all there is. The end.

JULIET [*Offstage, screams.* JULIET *comes out.*] I was hugging Sebastian, he flew out of my arms and over the sea.

WITCH He bounced back to his other life. Time's up.

VIOLA Sebastian's gone?

WITCH You will be too any minute.

PROSPERO Things my magic does don't last.

VIOLA Being separated from people you love, it never stops.

JULIET Can I go where Sebastian is?

PROSPERO You each go right back to the time and place we borrowed you from.

JULIET So you meet someone, feel this rush, run off together, suddenly feel like you're strangers, struggle to get back where you started, think you made it, come up against a wall, bang your heads against it, finally figure everything out, hug as hard as you can, go flying apart, and that's love?

CLEOPATRA When you're older you skip some of the steps.

HAMLET I can't go back to what I left, not yet.

CLEOPATRA Not ever.

FALSTAFF [*To* CLEOPATRA.] I'll always remember this feeling of you holding me.

WITCH You won't remember any of this.

PROSPERO Maybe in a dream.

JULIET If Sebastian's not there I'll never love anybody.

WITCH Yes, you will.

JULIET Never like that.

WITCH Exactly like that.

CLEOPATRA So I'll go back to that pathetic love I thought was the greatest ever?

WITCH   And swear it's the greatest ever.

VIOLA   Will I find my brother again?

WITCH   And lose him again.

HAMLET   Will I make the world any better?

WITCH   A little for a time.

[IAGO *drifts on.*]

IAGO   Will I make a real difference?

WITCH   A little for a time.

[IAGO *drifts off.*]

FALSTAFF   I don't want to know what'll happen to me.

WITCH   Wise choice. It's not pretty.

JULIET   [*To* VIOLA.] Can I hold on to you and think of your brother?

[JULIET, VIOLA, HAMLET, FALSTAFF, *and* CLEOPATRA *cling together.*]

HAMLET   [*To* VIOLA.] I wish I realized how I felt about you sooner.

VIOLA   I wish I didn't hide who I was for so long.

JULIET   I wish we didn't waste so much time with those arguments.

FALSTAFF   I wish we could do everything we did again and again exactly
the same.

CLEOPATRA   So do I.

[*All drift apart and offstage, only the* WITCH *and* PROSPERO *remain.*]

PROSPERO   It was you, right? You saved the story?

WITCH   They said it was love or fate. It was masochism.

[*Opens her robe, reveals cuts in her skin.*]

I got in between Hamlet and Falstaff, took the cuts in my skin to save
his. Anything to get you your happy ending, so I can finally get back
to my sisters.

PROSPERO   Stay. Talk to me.

WITCH   I gave you your play, I don't have to talk to you.

PROSPERO   You do.

[WITCH *starts off*, PROSPERO *raises the stick. It doesn't stop her.*]

WITCH   Your stick is out of power.

> [*Laughs.*]
> You don't even have a way of getting home now. Want a ride?

PROSPERO   No.

WITCH   You think you have no reason to go back, but look.

> [*Opens her robe.*]
> Your daughter has a daughter. Want a ride now?

PROSPERO   I want to see the baby.

WITCH   The baby doesn't want to see you.

PROSPERO   I want to see the baby.

WITCH   Your daughter's going to keep right on ignoring you, you'll keep getting weaker and dumber 'til you die.

PROSPERO   I want to see the baby.

WITCH   After all the pain humanity has caused you, you still need to see its latest offering.

PROSPERO   Yes. But you won't take me, will you?

WITCH   No.

[*Laughs at him. Goes.*]

PROSPERO   [*To audience.*] I was wrong to storm off. Drag all the others away from their lives. Maybe everything I've ever done was wrong. But I'm still living. I can keep trying to forgive, and be forgiven by, those I love. I want to see the baby. Don't leave me alone on this island. Send me home. Please clap.

• • •

Dark King Kills Unicorn

Reina Hardy

Dark King Kills Unicorn by Reina Hardy. Copyright © 2014 by Reina Hardy. All rights reserved. Reprinted by permission of the author.

CAUTION/ADVICE: Professionals and amateurs are hereby warned that performance of *Dark King Kills Unicorn* is subject to a royalty. It is fully protected under the copyright laws of the United States of America, and of all countries covered by the International Copyright Union (including the Dominion of Canada and the rest of the British Commonwealth), and of all countries covered by the Pan-American Copyright Convention and the Universal Copyright Convention, the Berne Convention, and of all countries with which the United States has reciprocal copyright relations. All rights, including professional and amateur stage performing rights, motion picture, recitation, lecturing, public reading, radio broadcasting, television, video or sound recording, all other forms of mechanical or electronic reproduction, such as CD-ROM, DVD-ROM, information storage and retrieval systems, and photocopying, and the rights of translation into foreign languages, are strictly reserved. Particular emphasis is placed upon the matter of readings, permission for which must be secured from the author's agent in writing.

Inquiries concerning rights should be addressed to reinahardy@yahoo.com

Reina Hardy

Reina Hardy is a playwright from Chicago who recently moved to Texas. She's a Michener Fellow, a 2013 Terrence McNally Prize finalist, the 2012 Interact 20/20 Commissionee, and a National New Play Network Playwright. Her plays, which usually contain magic and sometimes contain science, have been seen at Capital Stage, Orlando Shakespeare, and the Great Plains Theatre Conference (2011 Holland New Voices Award). In 2013, two of her plays premiered in Austin: *Glassheart* with the Shrewds at Salvage Vanguard, and *Stars and Barmen* at the Vortex. She spent part of 2013 at the Kennedy Center workshopping *The Claire Play*, which was seen at the 2013 National New Play Showcase. Her TYA play, *Annie Jump and the Library of Heaven*, was produced at UT Austin in 2014. Hardy will return to the Vortex in 2015 for *Changelings*, a spectacle about family, fairies, and theft.

···production history···

Dark King Kills Unicorn premiered at Frontera Fringe in spring 2013 at Hyde Park Theatre, Austin, with the support of the Scriptworks Fringe Commission

Director P. Tyson Midkiff

Costumes Kelly Ruiz

Violence Design Joseph Garlock

The **DRAEGERMAN** Andrew Rosas

The **UNICORN** Stephen Jack

The **OTHER UNICORN** Rachel Wiese

synopsis

In this epic fantasy, two legendary warriors meet for battle and mostly talk about girls. Contains a man-on-unicorn fight.

set

A secluded mountain pass, probably best represented by a blank stage. Maybe a rock to sit on.

characters

The **UNICORN** male, youngish but also immortal. Should be an excellent stage combatant and a decent singer.

The **DRAEGERMAN** male, not yet thirty. Should be an excellent stage combatant.

The **OTHER UNICORN** female, youngish but also immortal. Should know how to handle a sword.

[*The* UNICORN *waits in the Schism. The Schism is a secluded and very narrow pass in the eastern Glendabagian mountains on the border between Draegermandia and Sylveness, two countries which do not exist, but are at war. The* UNICORN, *for our purposes, is a good-looking young man, dressed in white, carrying a bright, sharp sword. No costume or mask is necessary, and in fact should be avoided, as the* UNICORN *waits, lying on his back, he sings.*]

UNICORN AND HE TOLD HER, WHEN HE CAME
"THEY WILL NOT SING MY NAME

ONLY YOU, ONLY YOU
ARE THE PRIZE."

"MEN LIKE ME SHOULD BE FORGOTTEN
THIS GOOD DEED IS A BLOT IN
A WICKEDNESS
THAT KNEW NO COMPROMISE"

HAVING NO OTHER SAVIOR, SHE ASSENTED
AND SHE FOLLOWED HIM, NOT KNOWING WHO TO
BLAME
AND FROM THAT PLACE OF TERRORS THEY DESCENDED
THE ROSE OF SUNDOWN, AND THE MAN WITHOUT A
NAME—
THE ROSE OF SUNDOWN, AND THE MAN WITHOUT A
NAME.

[*During the above, The* DRAEGERMAN *enters. He is youngish, roughly dressed, and simply armed. He carries no special marker or emblem of any kind. He listens. When the song seems to be over, he claps, and the* UNICORN *looks at him.*]

DRAEGERMAN   The Rose of Sundown—

UNICORN   And the man without a name. Do you know it?

DRAEGERMAN   It's an old song.

UNICORN   It's my favorite.

[*The* UNICORN *lies down again.*]

AND SHE SAID, "WHOM SHOULD I THANK
FOR A WOMAN OF MY—

DRAEGERMAN   That will be all, however. Get up.

[*The* UNICORN *sits, but does not stand.*]

I've come to kill you, you know.

UNICORN   Ah. I thought you might have. That's what everyone seems to come here for. But look, the small grass is slick with their blood, and I, as always, am stainless. If you want to hear how the song ends, you can stay and listen, but if you want to kill me—

DRAEGERMAN   I don't want to kill you. I don't *want* to. Will you let me pass?

UNICORN   Are you a Draegerman?

DRAEGERMAN I am.

UNICORN Then no. I'm sorry. You don't seem like much of a threat, but if I make an exception for you, all of those dead men will complain. [*The* UNICORN *squints.*] You seem familiar somehow. Who are you?

DRAEGERMAN A man without a name.

UNICORN [*Snorts.*] Who sent you?

DRAEGERMAN I sent myself.

UNICORN Listen, my two-footed friend. I appreciate what you're trying to do here, and I'm all for suicidal valor in a noble cause, but this? Don't you have a family somewhere? Don't you have a girl?

DRAEGERMAN No. I don't.

UNICORN All the more reason to take a piece of advice from someone much older and wiser than you'll ever be. Life is precious, and life is short, and I killed sixty just like you this morning. Turn back, and tell your would-be emperor he may stop sending orphans to die on my horn. The Schism is closed. He'll have to get his army through the mountains the hard way.

DRAEGERMAN It would be wise, on your part, to take me a little more seriously.

UNICORN You? A solitary man, not yet thirty, lightly armed, and, did I mention, completely alone? Why should I take you seriously?

DRAEGERMAN Because you did not kill sixty just like me.

[*Long pause.*]

UNICORN Ohhhh. I *do* know who you are. I thought you'd be bigger.

DRAEGERMAN Most people do. I apologize for my unprepossessing looks. I've seen the paintings, and I know there's a certain expectation of...coal-black chargers and skulls. But the truth is I don't get along well with horses. No offense.

UNICORN None taken.

DRAEGERMAN You killed 340 of my men, beast. I am not interested in vengeance, but I must move at least five phalanx and two units of cavalry through the mountains before moonrise tonight and I am *running out of time.*

UNICORN Not *a* Draegerman. *The* Draegerman. What do you want me to do?

DRAEGERMAN I was hoping you'd run away.

UNICORN [*Snorts.*] Why would I do that?

DRAEGERMAN You know who I am.

UNICORN I know what you are. Vile son of an evil king, raised in exile and underground, a dirt-poor, hard-fisted child of the mines. Proletariat revolutionary. Palace scourge. Fratricide. Regicide. Legendary general. Killed his own twin sister in cold blood. Slaughtered his whole family to win his own rightful throne. A filthy and unscrupulous and unstoppable fighter, once blooded, never sated. They say your sword is hungry to eat hearts. They say you have no equal among men.

DRAEGERMAN And none of this worries you, not even a little?

UNICORN Do you know what I am? I am swift, I am true, I am death's white grace. I am the killing stroke of lightning.

DRAEGERMAN You can stop an army.

UNICORN Well, in a narrow mountain pass...where there's room to march more than six abreast I find that some get by me.

DRAEGERMAN The killing stroke of lightning. Is that what they'll call you, when they sing songs of your great deeds?

UNICORN They call me the Unicorn of Sylveness, actually, and the songs are already being written.

DRAEGERMAN You killed my men.

UNICORN I *blessed* your men. There are kings who have spent ransoms, abbesses who have dedicated a century of virtue to one touch from my horn. I gave your men the honor of their lives.

DRAEGERMAN I am sure they thanked you for it.

UNICORN You are called the blighted king. Do you too seek my blessing?

DRAEGERMAN They say to look into a unicorn's eyes is to see infinity, and know that it is kind. What has Sylveness done for you that you would stain yourself with so much blood? What could move your kind to meddle in our affairs?

UNICORN Love. I'm not pledged to the country. I'm pledged to the queen. Queen Emma Stormswatchdaughter, the Righteous Flame, it is she who holds my fealty and my heart, and has, from the moment I laid eyes on her. No, earlier. From the moment I heard them speak her name. You've met her, I believe, in the course of persecuting an unjust war against her country.

DRAEGERMAN Yes, Emma and I are acquainted, yes.

UNICORN She was your prisoner, wasn't she—

DRAEGERMAN [*Overlapping.*] Guest, she was my guest—

UNICORN [*Overlapping.*] For just over a year, and when after months of penury and coercion she refused to ally herself with you as your bride—

DRAEGERMAN [*Overlapping.*] The princess, at the time, attempted to assassinate me, and I was well within my rights—

UNICORN [*Overlapping.*] You marched on Sylveness, murdering her father and her brothers, just as you murdered your own family—

DRAEGERMAN [*Overlapping.*] That is a mischaracterization, there were a number of complex economic factors in play—

UNICORN [*Overlapping.*] Assuming, as men like you always assume that brute force can win anything, whether a country or a woman—

DRAEGERMAN [*Overlapping.*] *I never hurt her!* I never—this is war! This is war, understand, this is serious business, and to attribute it to some sort of romantic entanglement is morally repellent. On your part.

UNICORN Then what did start the war?

DRAEGERMAN Economics. And how are you in love with a queen, anyway? You're essentially a horse.

UNICORN You'll take that back, before long.

[*The* UNICORN *levels his blade at the* DRAEGERMAN. *He draws.*]

And no, it is not such disgusting stuff as you believe love to be. But it is strong, and it is real. I defend her borders, I defeat her enemies, I carried her bethrothed in his triumphal procession—

DRAEGERMAN Wait. She's getting married?

UNICORN You didn't hear? I thought everyone had heard. I've been involved in the festival planning for months. We are at war, but surely someone must have remembered to send an envoy—

DRAEGERMAN She's getting married to a *virgin*?

UNICORN Of course. She can only have the best and purest knight. Attendant Prince Mammillian defeated a field of one hundred noblemen, all virgins, all in the flower of their manhood, all competing to be Queen's consort. You've never seen such chivalry.

DRAEGERMAN One hundred virgins. Really.

UNICORN If they knew what was good for them. I carried the victor from the field to her feet. Had the prince attempted to mount me in anything less than a state of sublime innocence, he would have instantly died by my horn.

DRAEGERMAN My gods.

UNICORN It's tradition. Well, it's tradition for the woman. But as everyone knew the queen couldn't pass the Unicorn's Trial, and no one held it against her—

DRAEGERMAN What do you mean?

UNICORN That year she spent as your prisoner. No one could blame her for what happened then.

DRAEGERMAN I did not make the princess do anything she didn't want to do.

UNICORN If I believe that, I believe you'll leave this place alive.
[*The two go on their guards.*]
Come on then.

DRAEGERMAN I don't like to draw first blood.

UNICORN Don't worry. You won't.

[*They fight. The* DRAEGERMAN *is hurt.*]

DRAEGERMAN Ah, there it is.

UNICORN Is it true what they say? That the Draegerman fights best wounded? That only the taste of his own blood wakes his killer's heart?

DRAEGERMAN It has some small effect.

UNICORN Oh, good. An interesting afternoon.

[*The* DRAEGERMAN *attacks, with more ferocity and abandon.*]

DRAEGERMAN Everything they say is true. It is true that I fight best bloodied. It is true that I eat guts and livers. It is true that I kill children, women, relatives, household pets, small songbirds, songs, illusions, light itself. It is true that I like swords better than arrows, and knives better than swords, and best of all, my own bare hands...

[*The* DRAEGERMAN *tosses away his sword.*]

You are hurt now. You are badly hurt. You are beautiful and I have never killed anything like you. It is not too late to stop me. Let me pass.

UNICORN No.

[*The* DRAEGERMAN *aiming to strangle, leaps on the* UNICORN's *back. A pause. A realization.*]

Oh, my stars. You're—

[He leaps away.]

You—you're a—

DRAEGERMAN What? What of it?

UNICORN But—you're an emperor. You're nearly thirty.

DRAEGERMAN Nearly.

UNICORN This is not what I expected. There was that...whole year...with the queen—

DRAEGERMAN I told you, Princess Emma didn't do anything she didn't want to do.

UNICORN Then who was it?

DRAEGERMAN You mean she's not—

UNICORN Of course she's not—

DRAEGERMAN But how do you know?

UNICORN Because I always know. Because knowing is my being. Because otherwise I would have run to her, I would have laid my head in her lap, and if she sang to me I would have welcomed death. Stars above, it could have been anybody.

DRAEGERMAN Anybodies. She's an adventurous girl.

UNICORN Woman.

DRAEGERMAN Queen.

[*A pause. The* UNICORN *begins to laugh.*]

UNICORN The Draegerman. The Blighted King. You should hear the stories mothers tell their daughters about you.

DRAEGERMAN I've heard them. I hear them all the time.

UNICORN You could have won that tournament. You could have won it with two broken legs.

DRAEGERMAN I know.

UNICORN The best and purest knight.

DRAEGERMAN There are other ways, Sylveness, of becoming not pure. Anyways, I'm not a knight.

UNICORN No?

DRAEGERMAN I am completely without honor. And I can't stand horses.

UNICORN Truth be told, neither can I. They are extremely limited conversationalists. You are both more and less than I expected, Draegerman. Why are you here?

DRAEGERMAN I need to move five phalanx and two units of calvary through the mountains before moonrise.

UNICORN Yes, I know. I'm supposed to know everything. I don't think I do. Love is peculiar, is it not?

DRAEGERMAN I wouldn't know. But I imagine it is at least as peculiar as loneliness.

[*The* DRAEGERMAN *is sitting. The* UNICORN, *very gently, extends his weapon, and rests it on the man's shoulder. The* DRAEGERMAN *grabs the blade, pulls the unicorn down, and strikes it brutally in the face.*]

It would be wise, on your part, to take me a little more seriously.

[*He attacks, methodically and expertly.*]

I am untouched. I am pure. You cannot bless me, you cannot transfigure me. I am completely what I am. Shall you rest your head in my lap? Shall I sing songs for you?

[*The* UNICORN *is dead. The* DRAEGERMAN *looks at him for a moment.*]

It's true. His blood is silver. He looks smaller. He moved like light on the water, but now he's warm, and cooling. He's meat. Love did this. Love makes meat of us all.

[*He gets up, takes out a pistol, loads it with a flare.*]

This is war, friend. Nothing less. It doesn't matter what started it. It can't be stopped, or forgiven. I have to win.

[*There is a sobbing, tearing cry, and The* OTHER UNICORN *runs out and flings herself on the corpse. She is also dressed in white. She also carries a sword. The* DRAEGERMAN *lowers his pistol.*]

Oh, gods, another one?

[*The* OTHER UNICORN *looks at him.*]

DRAEGERMAN   Oh, it's a girl one. Please leave. Please. You're a very lovely…female…or whatever it is I should say, and I don't want any trouble with you. Once I fire this flare, my army is going to march in from the southern ridge, and I don't feel that they're safe if you are here, but my business was with—your colleague there—your friend, and it is concluded. Please, say something. Tell me your intentions. Communicate.

[*He draws his sword and gestures with it.*]

Come on.

[*She stares at him.*]

Oh, come on!

[*He sheathes his sword.*]

I don't understand what you're doing here. And I'm worried that you're upset. It is getting dark, five phalanxes and two units of cavalry are waiting, and I am sitting here with one dead unicorn and one unicorn who won't even talk to me. I hate this war.

OTHER UNICORN   We were young together. When the world was green. We used to run like the thoughts of the wind. There were hundreds of us then. There are not so many now.

DRAEGERMAN Oh. You *are* upset.

OTHER UNICORN We were all as beautiful as starlight, but even in that he was different. There was something in him of fire, of the hot secret in a star's heart. I worried about him. You were right.

DRAEGERMAN I was?

OTHER UNICORN Love makes meat of us. He was like a star's heart, and he is like nothing now. He is not even like the dirt. You are uncomfortable around women.

DRAEGERMAN Extremely.

OTHER UNICORN You should remember that I'm not a woman. We are not as you are. Our sorrows are older, and . . . less specific.

DRAEGERMAN If my men come, will you kill them?

OTHER UNICORN I have lived a thousand years, and in that time I have not killed even a blade of grass. My steps are too light, and our lives are too long.

DRAEGERMAN You're immortal.

OTHER UNICORN Unless we fall in love.

DRAEGERMAN You're worse off than we are. It only makes us stupid.
[*He laughs.*]
This is a very flimsy kind of immortality. Do you disintegrate? Combust? Pop like a soap bubble? How do you die from love?

OTHER UNICORN Like this.
[*She is standing, leveling his weapon at the* DRAEGERMAN.]
We die like this.

DRAEGERMAN Oh.

OTHER UNICORN He cared for your queen, and he cared for your war, and now he is *nothing* and I—I am not as I once was.

DRAEGERMAN You're not going to let me pass.

OTHER UNICORN I care nothing for your queen or your wars, but I am feeling something really rather specific.

DRAEGERMAN You would have me kill you? You would have me kill you too. And behind you, another, willing to die for your love, and

behind him another, willing to die for his love, and another, and
another. Is that it, Emma? Shall I come to you through an infinity of
dying unicorns?

OTHER UNICORN Turn back.

DRAEGERMAN I will not. I cannot turn my course. That ruin on the
ground shows you what I am. I did not come to kill him. I was hoping
for something else.

OTHER UNICORN What?

DRAEGERMAN His blessing.

[*He drops his sword and walks forward, until the tip of her weapon rests lightly on
his chest.*]

This is your chance.

OTHER UNICORN You're unarmed.

DRAEGERMAN See? It's not so easy to change who you are.

[*He turns and picks up his sword.*]

We could fight, but you can't defeat me.

OTHER UNICORN I'm sorry.

DRAEGERMAN It's all right. No one can. Will you let my men through
the Schism?

OTHER UNICORN I don't want him to have died in vain.

DRAEGERMAN Would you rather I killed him in vain?

OTHER UNICORN I will not trouble you.

[*He sheathes his sword.*]

What will your men do, when they come through the mountains?

DRAEGERMAN Oh, undoubtedly a lot of terrible things. Murder, rape,
pillage. They're disciplined, but once they get started they can be
hard to control.

OTHER UNICORN How do you live with yourself?

DRAEGERMAN I don't, mostly. I often imagine that, if I had done one
or two things differently, or if I had been a little bit luckier in my
past—that this might be a very altered world. I think of one or two
moments, long gone now, where if I had turned my hand another way,

I would have had a life of choices, instead of inevitabilities, and in my mind there opens up a wide world, an elaborate world, where the king of Draegermandia is not expected to ride a coal-black anything. I spend most of my time there, in that other kingdom, watching that other king.

He's a good king, getting fat, for his interesting days are long behind him. He is almost thirty. He is working on a progressive energy policy. He has a sister, whom he loves, who has made an advantageous marriage, and has provided him with an extraordinarily ugly baby nephew. Looks just like a little monkey.

At this very moment, he is taking the child to Sylveness, to be presented at their high court and cooed at by their dowager queen. He is bringing a carriage load of presents for the elder princess, and he is going mad with the notion that they are none of them quite what is called for, but he looks well. He has slipped away from the caravan, taking the boy, telling him stories and showing him birds' nests, and through the trees they have both glimpsed something quite extraordinary.

[*He stares at the* OTHER UNICORN *for a long moment. Then he looks at the* UNICORN *on the ground.*]

You should run, and tell her that I'm coming.

[*The* OTHER UNICORN *exits. The* DRAEGERMAN *takes his pistol, points it upward, shoots. Fireworks explode overhead. He watches them fall, then goes to the dead unicorn. He looks. He sits. He pulls the* UNICORN's *head into his lap, and begins to sing.*]

AND HE SAID, WHEN HE CAME
"THEY WILL NOT SING MY NAME…"

Lights out.

• • •

Deer Haunting: A Far Side Cartoon

Andréa J. Onstad

For Nancy, Peggy, and Joyce

Deer Haunting: A Far Side Cartoon by Andréa J. Onstad. Copyright © 2013 by Andréa J. Onstad. All rights reserved. Reprinted by permission of the author.

CAUTION/ADVICE: Professionals and amateurs are hereby warned that performance of *Deer Haunting: A Far Side Cartoon* is subject to a royalty. It is fully protected under the copyright laws of the United States of America, and of all countries covered by the International Copyright Union (including the Dominion of Canada and the rest of the British Commonwealth), and of all countries covered by the Pan-American Copyright Convention and the Universal Copyright Convention, the Berne Convention, and of all countries with which the United States has reciprocal copyright relations. All rights, including professional and amateur stage performing rights, motion picture, recitation, lecturing, public reading, radio broadcasting, television, video or sound recording, all other forms of mechanical or electronic reproduction, such as CD-ROM, DVD-ROM, information storage and retrieval systems, and photocopying, and the rights of translation into foreign languages, are strictly reserved. Particular emphasis is placed upon the matter of readings, permission for which must be secured from the author's agent in writing.

Inquiries concerning rights should be addressed to Andréa Onstad, P.O. Box 297, Willits, California 95490. E-mail: ajonstad@gmail.com. Telephone: 707-456-1067.

Andréa J. Onstad

Andréa J. Onstad's plays have been read and performed in theaters throughout the United States and Germany and published in collections by Heinemann. She has held artist residencies at MacDowell, Yaddo, Vermont Studio Center, Ucross, Djerassi, and Fundación Valparaíso; she has received several Marin Arts Council Grants; she has been interviewed on radio; and she's taught playwriting at the University of San Francisco, the College of Marin, and the University of Missouri. Onstad holds an MFA from the Iowa Playwrights Workshop and a PhD in Theatre-Writing for Performance from the University of Missouri. She currently resides off the grid in Northern California.

···production history···

Deer Haunting: A Far Side Cartoon was presented by FirstStage at the Missing Piece Theatre, Burbank, California, May 19, 2013, directed by Dan Roth with the following cast:

THREE NEWLY INCARNATED DEER MEN Steve Alba, Dan Roth, Arnie Weiss

THREE WIDOWED SISTERS Anita Borcia, Helen Duffy, Cherie Mann

COP Dennis Safren

characters

THREE WIDOWED SISTERS:

NURSEY late sixties, wife of **LESTER**

PANSY mid-sixties, wife of **JOCKO**

BONES late fifties, wife of **ED**

THREE NEWLY INCARNATED DEER MEN dead husbands of the above:

LESTER late sixties/early seventies, husband of **NURSEY**

JOCKO mid-sixties, husband of **PANSY**

ED early sixties, husband of **BONES**

COP male, possibly female, could be voice-over

time

Scenes 1–7: A starlit, moonless night, the present

Scenes 8–9: Months later

place

Scenes 1–6: A lonely country road, rural Wisconsin

Scenes 7–9: Bones's living room and kitchen

synopsis

What happens after death? Three hunters newly incarnated as deer men find out twice when they meet their second untimely death—as road kill.

parados

[LESTER, JOCKO, *and* ED, *three newly incarnated deer men in hunting garb and antlers, stand center singing.*]

LESTER, JOCKO, and ED   [*Harmonizing, a capella, à la Big Mouth Billy Bass.*]
We're the deer fish men
We're the venison fish stew
We're gonna sing and sing and sing
'Til we turn you blue

Our antlers will wiggle
And our deer fins flop
And we'll sing and sing and sing
Until you turn us off

Oh yes, we will...

[*Blackout.*]

1.

[*Starlit, moonless night. The woods alongside a rural back road. Cricket and animal sounds.* LESTER, JOCKO, *and* ED *prance upright on tiny hooves, using flashlights to play Deer-Caught-in-the-Headlights.*]

ED   [*Shining flashlight into* JOCKO'*s eyes.*] Gotcha!

JOCKO   Nyuh-uh.

LESTER   [*Shining flashlight into* ED *and* JOCKO'*s eyes.*] Both of yous.

ED   Did not.   **JOCKO**   No way.

LESTER   Yep. Both of yous. Deader than venison stew.

ED   No way.   **JOCKO**   Nyuh-uh.

[*A car sounds in the distance.*]

LESTER   [*Listening.*] Shhh.

JOCKO   [*Not listening; to* LESTER.] I said no way, man.
[*Shines flashlight into* ED'*s eyes; to* ED.]
You're a dead deer now. Venison steak smothered in onions. Burnt. So die.

ED Nyhu-uh-uh-uh-uh.

LESTER Cram it, you two.

[*Listening; car is closer, louder; LESTER is the only deer man who hears it.*]
Hey, who wants to play roadkill?

ED Me!   **JOCKO** Me!

[*Car is closer, louder; now all hear it.*]

LESTER Sounds like a '59—

JOCKO Rambler.

ED Bones's car!

LESTER Bingo! You're up!

[LESTER *rears back, ready to boot* ED *into the path of the oncoming car.*]
Next stop—Kingdom Come!

[LESTER *kicks* ED. ED *goes flying. Blackout.*]

2.

[*Same moment. Different perspective. The three deer men, LESTER, JOCKO, and ED, are shadows in the woods alongside the road. Car sounds very loud. Approaching. The car. The sillier and simpler the better. BONES drives. NURSEY rides shotgun. PANSY sleeps center. NURSEY wears a fright wig. PANSY wears a contraption resembling an old-fashioned bonnet-type hair dryer with a hose she breathes into. BONES wears big false Halloweeny buck teeth.*]

NURSEY [NURSEY *has been talking nonstop.*] ... And we'll pick out the best rose-colored granite and have it engraved with trees and mountain streams and fish and deer and along the top it'll say: "In memory of Lester, Jocko, and Ed" in big letters and below that, "Beloved husbands of Nursey, Pansy, and Bones," then below that it'll say, "Tragically disappeared on a hunting trip...

BONES Stop. You're making me cry.

NURSEY ...R.I.P. wherever you are."

BONES [*Sniffling.*] Aw. Beautiful.

NURSEY You miss him, don't you, Bones.

BONES Well. No. Not really.

NURSEY Then step on it! Our appointment's at seven!

BONES I'm driving. I'm driving.

[*A moment. Then:*]

NURSEY How much farther?

BONES 'Bout 350.

NURSEY Jesus Mary Mother of God—we'll never make it.
[NURSEY *pokes* PANSY.]
Wake up, Pansy. Pansy, wake up.

PANSY [*Groans still asleep.*]

BONES Leave her lay where Jesus flung her.

NURSEY Watch your mouth, little sister.

BONES La-la. Sticks and stones…

NURSEY What did you say?

BONES I said, "Sticks and stones will break…

NURSEY That's it, Bones.   **BONES** …my bones…"

NURSEY I'll show you what will break your bones.

[NURSEY *reaches across* PANSY, *hitting* BONES.]

BONES [*Hitting back, tussling.*] Jesus Mary Mother of God / Call on us
and you'll get the job.

NURSEY Watch those teeth, Bucky—

PANSY [*Groans over the tussling but does not awaken.*]

BONES Watch that freak wig, Big Fat Sissy-Poo—

NURSEY 'Cause I'm knocking 'em   **BONES** 'Cause I'm knocking it
out right now!   off right now!

[*Full-on tussle.*]

PANSY [*Waking, sitting bolt upright.*] LOOK OUT!

[*Big crash, instant blackout. Silence.*]

3.

[*Five minutes later. Animal sounds, crickets. After a moment, groans.*]

[*Steam rises from the crashed car illumined by broken, cockeyed headlights.* NURSEY *sans wig,* BONES *sans teeth, and* PANSY *sans hair dryer lay sprawled amidst wreckage with* ED *on* BONES'*s lap—the* pietà. LESTER *and* JOCKO *step gingerly, shining flashlights.*]

LESTER That's Bones's car all right.

JOCKO Was.

LESTER That the same one Ed bought her brand-new?

JOCKO Yep. Wedding present.

LESTER Aw. And here he is. Look kind of religious, don't they. Ed. Ed!

[*Wiggles* ED'*s antler.*]

JOCKO Pitiful way to get attention.

LESTER Here's her dentures.

  [*Picks up* BONES'*s teeth, several fall out.*]
  I always thought she shoulda sued.

JOCKO [*Finding* PANSY.] Here's my Pansy! Oh, Pansy, Pansy. Oh, I've got to find your hose—you need your hose—do you see her hose?
  [*Looking around.*]
  Here it is!

LESTER [*Calling.*] Nursey!

JOCKO [*Finding* NURSEY'*s wig.*] Here's her wig!

[*Tosses it to* LESTER. PANSY, NURSEY, *and* BONES *shift and groan.*]

LESTER Uh-oh. They're coming to. Can't let them see us.

JOCKO But what about Ed?

LESTER Leave him lay where Jesus flung him.

[LESTER *and* JOCKO *retreat to the shadows.* NURSEY *bolts upright.*]

NURSEY What did you say?

[BONES, *dazed, is trying to sit up.* NURSEY *bops her back down. Blackout.*]

4.

[*A few minutes later. More groans as* NURSEY, PANSY, *and* BONES *come to.*]

BONES [*Seeing* ED *on her lap.*] Oh my God! It's a deer man. And it looks like—Ed!

[*Examines him.*]

It *is* Ed. And—

[*Shakes his antlers.*]

he's dead!

NURSEY Not again. I suppose now we'll have to change the memorial stone, cremate him, and conduct a real burial—probably mess up your insurance bucks.

BONES Bucks? Awwww.

[*Starts bawling.*]

NURSEY Okay, okay. That's enough. Sorry I said "bucks."

[BONES *bawls again.*]

But he *is* a twelve-pointer. Quite a trophy. Better trophy dead than alive.

BONES Hey!

NURSEY Hey yourself.

BONES Quit it.

NURSEY Quit it yourself.

PANSY Quit it, both of you. Look. You could have him stuffed and mounted. Put a music box in him like those stuffed fish…

NURSEY You are the brains here, Pansy.

PANSY [*Out of breath.*] I need my hose. Give me my hose!

BONES [*To* ED.] You'd look great above the TV.

NURSEY Let's fix this contraption and get back on the road.

[NURSEY, PANSY, *and* BONES *put the car back together and in the process find their missing accoutrements dangerously close to* LESTER *and* JOCKO, *who like wild animals stand very still and invisible.*]

PANSY [*Finding* NURSEY's *wig at* LESTER's *feet.*] Wig—with leaves and twigs.

BONES [*Finding* PANSY's *hose at* JOCKO's *feet.*] Hose—only slightly clogged.

NURSEY [*Finding* BONES's *teeth between* LESTER *and* JOCKO.] Teeth—some missing but better than none.

BONES Car's not too wrecked. Hop in. I'll start it up.

PANSY What about him?

[*Points to* ED.]

NURSEY Backseat. Come on. Help.

[*They drag* ED *into the backseat. Get in car, same seating arrangement as before—* BONES *driving,* PANSY *center,* NURSEY *shotgun.*]

BONES [*Starting the car.*] Come on, girl. Come on, come on, come on.

[*It fires up, missing, spitting, but running.*]

BONES, PANSY, and NURSEY YAY!

[BONES, PANSY, *and* NURSEY *drive off, car sounds fading.*]

5.

[LESTER *and* JOCKO *emerge from shadows as car sounds fade.*]

JOCKO Oh *no*! They're leaving! And taking Ed!

LESTER [*Running, chasing car.*] Nursey! Nursey! Nursey!

JOCKO [*Joining* LESTER, *running.*] Pansy!

[*Car sounds grow louder as* LESTER *and* JOCKO *gain on* PANSY, BONES, *and* NURSEY.]

LESTER Nursey!

JOCKO Pansy!

[*Car sounds very loud; car in sight;* LESTER *and* JOCKO *pass the car, waving at* PANSY, NURSEY, *and* BONES.]

LESTER Nursey!

JOCKO Pansy!

JOCKO Bones!   **LESTER** Hiya!

[LESTER *and* JOCKO *dance nimbly in front of the oncoming car on dainty pointy hooves before flinging themselves onto the car's oncoming path. Screeching. Blackout. Thuds in the dark. Silence.*]

6.

[*Seconds later.* NURSEY, PANSY, *and* BONES *examining* LESTER *and* JOCKO, *dead deer men.*]

NURSEY Sure looks like Lester to me.

PANSY And I'd know my Jocko anywhere.

BONES Load them up.

[NURSEY, PANSY, *and* BONES *drag* JOCKO *and* LESTER *to the car and shove them into the backseat next to* ED.]

PANSY [*To* NURSEY, *dragging* JOCKO.] Give me a hand here. Jocko still has his big gut.

NURSEY [*Helping drag* JOCKO.] Lots of venison on this boy.

PANSY Deer beer, more likely.

BONES Here, let me sit Ed up.

[BONES *props* ED *up.*]

NURSEY Heave—

PANSY Ho!

[NURSEY *and* PANSY *toss* JOCKO *into the car.*]

NURSEY Now Lester.

[BONES *helps* NURSEY *pick up* LESTER.]

BONES Easy. Now. Heave—

NURSEY Ho!

[NURSEY *and* PANSY *toss* LESTER *into car next to* JOCKO *and step back admiring their work.*]

PANSY Looking good.

NURSEY Three boys in a church pew.

BONES Might as well forget the quarry and head right for the—

NURSEY Taxidermist!

PANSY Let's go, girls!

[PANSY, BONES, *and* NURSEY *jump in the car and drive off, car sounds fading as lights fade.*]

7.

[BONES *drives,* NURSEY *and* PANSY *ride—same configuration. Suddenly, a siren followed by red lights.*]

NURSEY Step on it, Bones.

PANSY Give it some gas.

BONES I'm trying. I'm trying. But it *is* a Rambler.

NURSEY Yeah. The one Ed gave you.

PANSY When you got married.

NURSEY About a hundred years ago.

COP [*Voice on bullhorn.*] Pull over or I'll shoot.

[BONES *stops the car abruptly. Wig, teeth, hose go flying. Car door opens, radio sounds, door slams, silence, footsteps.*]

BONES Smile pretty now, girls.

NURSEY Put your teeth in.

PANSY Straighten your wig.

BONES Take a big breath, Pans, and then take that *thing* out of your mouth. It looks stupid.

NURSEY But what about them?

[*Points to backseat. Bright flashlight on* BONES.]

COP [*Visible entity or omniscient voice-over.*] License.
   [BONES *hands over license.*]
   Registration.
   [BONES *hands over registration.*]
   So. Where's the fire?

[*Shines flashlight around car.*]

NURSEY We're just going to a taxi—

COP Shut up. I'm asking her.

[*Shines flashlight on* BONES; *then on* NURSEY'*s wig askew*, PANSY'*s hair-dryer hose*, BONES'*s big buck teeth; then on* ED, JOCKO, *and* LESTER *in backseat*.]

You all going to a costume party or something?

PANSY Yeah! A costume party. That's right! We're going to a costume party!

COP Shut up. I'm talking to her.

[*Shines flashlight on* BONES.]

BONES Uh. Yessireema'am.

COP [*Chuckling at own jokes throughout.*] Well. You seem like a nice bunch of girls. I think I'll just give you a warning. This time. But you slow on down now, hear? Lots of deer out tonight. Just before huntin' season they all take to the road for one last nibble of grease grass. Some say they're committin' suicide—rather take the bash than the bullet. Some stupid city sissy came up with that one. You know, them touchy-feely organic grain–eatin' types. I'd like to skewer one of them at the end of my fork. Betcha they'd be mighty tasty. Anyways. Don't want you and your dates to hit any. Saw evidence of a hit a ways back. Didn't see no carcass. Don't know what people do with 'em. Can't eat the meat all mashed up like that. Suppose you can get 'em stuffed. It's illegal, you know. To take 'em.

[*Shines flashlight into backseat again.*]

You guys are kind of quiet back there. Everything all right?

BONES They're just—

COP Drunk?

[*Nearly inaudible gasps from* PANSY *and* NURSEY.]

BONES Um—

COP No problem. Long as they're not driving. I wouldn't mind a little nip myself. Chilly out here. Okay then. Drive safe.

[COP *exits. Footsteps, car door opening, radio sounds, car door closing, engine starting, headlights, driving off, taillights, silence.*]

BONES [*Catatonic.*] Jesus Mary Mother of God. He flung us. I wanna lay right here. Where he flung us.

NURSEY Shut up and drive, Bones.

PANSY Come on, Bones. Pull off. Nice and easy.
[BONES, *shaking, starts car, drives off.*]
That's right. Good girl.

[*Lights fade.*]

8.

[*Months later.* BONES's *living room.* LESTER, JOCKO, *and* ED's *deer-men mounted heads "hang" from wall (i.e., heads stuck through holes in wall).* BONES *dusts antlers. Tickling. Heads struggle not to react. Doorbell rings.*]

BONES Come on in. It's open.
[NURSEY *and* PANSY *enter.*]
[BONES *pointing to heads.*]
So. What do you think?

NURSEY They look so nice up there!

PANSY I sure wish I had room on my walls.

NURSEY Yeah but with that puny life insurance Jocko left you I'm surprised you didn't have to sell the house and move into a trailer.

PANSY Shut up. I say let's talk about Lester and the debt he left you—

NURSEY Hey, don't you say nothing bad about my man—

PANSY You started it.

NURSEY And I'll finish it, little sister.

PANSY And you know what I'll do.

[PANSY *reaches into purse, takes out a flask, nips from it.*]

BONES Hey, hey, hey. Come on in the kitchen. I fixed up a little stew.

[BONES *exits.*]

NURSEY Now Bones here. She's got that brand-new peach-colored Cadillac in the garage and a new carpet and—

[NURSEY *and* PANSY *exit, following* BONES.]

PANSY [*Exiting.*] Ooh. I can smell that venison.

NURSEY [*Exiting.*] Nothing like venison stew—little onion, garlic, carrots, dash of red wine—

[LESTER, JOCKO, *and* ED *deer-men heads look at each other.*]

JOCKO Hang the guy who invented reincarnation. I'd a never believed—

LESTER Well, I'd a made it if Nursey'd given me my insulin shot that day. Instead I shot you.

[*To* JOCKO.]

I swear you looked like a buck. Guess my eyes were blurry.

JOCKO And I'd a made it if Pansy hadn't driven me to drink. I'd never have loaded my shotgun then sat on it like a barstool that day.

ED And I'd a made it if I hadn't eaten the buckshot venison pie Bones packed for lunch that day.

ED, JOCKO, and LESTER [*Singing, barbershop trio, harmonizing.*] Ooooh that day—

JOCKO You might have made it if you hadn't eaten the whole dang thing.

ED Well, I was nervous. Looking at you two all shot up like that. Didn't know what to do.

LESTER So you keeled right on over and joined us. What a friend.

[ED *and* JOCKO *begin singing to the tune of "What a Friend We Have in Jesus."*]

ED and JOCKO [*Singing.*] What a friend we have in Lester / All our sins and griefs to share.

[*Lights shift. Split stage*—BONES's *kitchen.* BONES, PANSY, *and* NURSEY *are listening to the deer men's singing. Lights fade on living room.*]

NURSEY Do you hear that?

BONES I had them all outfitted with music—like that fish. Pansy's idea. With remote.

[BONES *holds up a remote control. Clicks it off.* ED *and* JOCKO *immediately stop singing.*]

PANSY I'll drink to that.

[*She does.*]

BONES   I always wanted one of them fish—

BONES   But Ed never let me.   **PANSY**   But Ed never let you.

NURSEY   Used to have mine up in the bedroom 'cause Lester'd get all inspired them singin' all at once and start—

PANSY   You tell that story, Nursey, and I'm gonna drink this whole damn thing.

NURSEY   You watch your mouth, sissy. Anyways. I got 'em up in the attic now. You want 'em, they're yours.

PANSY   And I got a few you can have. I need to make room for the grandkids' photos.

BONES   That'd be great! I'll put one over the clock, one next to the kitchen witch, one by the toaster, and—and—I'll turn them and the deer all on at once and I'll have a—a—

NURSEY   A hump fest! Whooee!   **PANSY**   A woodland symphony!

[NURSEY, PANSY, *and* BONES *dance around the kitchen. Lights shift to living room.*]

LESTER   Oh, Ed. You mean you never let Bones have one of them fish?

[ED *hangs his head as best he can.*]

JOCKO   I gave my Pansy three of them. Three!

LESTER   Nursey had what—five? I can't remember. All in the bedroom. Had them going all at once and—

ED   I couldn't *stand* them things—that song—over and over—

LESTER   But you coulda given her just one, Ed—

JOCKO   You coulda pulled the batteries—

ED   I gave her that car.

LESTER   Oh, right. The car.

JOCKO   Yeah. That was a nice car.

ED   Yeah. Was gonna modify the engine, put in some overhead cams in, paint her up—

ED   One of these days...   **LESTER**   One of these days...
                                                        Yeah.

JOCKO Yeah.

[ED, JOCKO, *and* LESTER *hang their heads in prayer for a moment of silence for the dead Rambler.*]

ED Ah, well. Still. I'd never have believed I'd come back as a deer.

LESTER A buck.

JOCKO A twelve-pointer.

LESTER If I had a gun I'd shoot you right now!

JOCKO I'll drink to that.

LESTER High five!

[*A moment. They realize they can't drink or high-five anymore.*]

Yep. If we hadn't been messing around hunting and fishing and drinking beer, we'd be back in our wives' kitchens eating venison stew right now.

ED Instead they're eating—

JOCKO Us!

[*Blackout.*]

9.

[*Lights rise on* BONES's *kitchen.* BONES, PANSY, *and* NURSEY *sit at venison-loaded table. A toast.*]

NURSEY Here's to one helluva venison stew recipe.

BONES Too bad Ed's not here to have some. He sure loved this dish.

PANSY [*Drinking.*] Down the hatch!

NURSEY Well, I'm not waiting. Good gravy, good meat—good God, let's eat.

PANSY I'll drink to that. Again.

[PANSY *drinks,* BONES *and* NURSEY *eat. All three gobble and slurp for a while.*]

BONES Say, do you think I should hang the boys in the kitchen?

NURSEY Yeah, one right over the sink, one over the stove, and one over the fridge,

PANSY Triple trophy—with the fish hanging in between—

BONES Beautiful. Listen.

[BONES *presses the remote "on" button. Lights rise dim on the deer men in the living room.* JOCKO, LESTER, *and* ED *begin singing again, replacing* LESTER's *name with* JOCKO's.]

LESTER and ED [*Singing.*] What a friend we have in Jocko.

BONES Better than a gravestone.

PANSY I'll drink to that.

NURSEY High five!

LESTER and ED [*Singing.*] All our sins and griefs to share.

[BONES, PANSY, *and* NURSEY *high-five. Lights fade on kitchen, rise on living room.*]

LESTER and ED [*Singing.*] What a privilege to hang our [*Swelling.*] severed heads with his midair.

[*They finish. No applause.*]

LESTER Man.

JOCKO Oh, man.

ED Torture.

LESTER Yeah. Sheer.

JOCKO Eternal.

ED It's karma, boys. Fish karma. Okay. My turn. Hit it, boys.

[LESTER *and* JOCKO *begin singing.*]

LESTER and JOCKO What a friend we have in Ed-die / All our sins and...

[*A click. Silence. Blackout. A moment. Faux ending.*]

komos

[*Deer men* LESTER, ED, *and* JOCKO *center, singing.*]

LESTER, ED, and JOCKO [*Singing, repeating if necessary, through blackout.*]

We're the deer fish men
The dear deer men
We're gonna sing to you
Again and again

The deer fish men
The dear deer men
Singing singing singing

We'll wiggle and we'll flop
We'll jiggle and we'll hop
Right off the wall
Having a ball
The deer fish men
The dear deer men

NURSEY and PANSY [*Overlapping, offstage, screaming, continuing.*] STOP! STOP! STOP! Turn 'em off!

BONES [*Clicking.*] I'm trying! I'm trying! This thing doesn't work! Weird!

[*Pause.*]

I'm kind of liking it.

[*Blackout.*]

• • •

2nd Anniversary Near Taurus Major

Gene Kato

2nd Anniversary Near Taurus Major by Gene Kato. Copyright © 2013 by Gene Kato. All rights reserved. Reprinted by permission of the author.

CAUTION/ADVICE: Professionals and amateurs are hereby warned that performance of *2nd Anniversary Near Taurus Major* is subject to a royalty. It is fully protected under the copyright laws of the United States of America, and of all countries covered by the International Copyright Union (including the Dominion of Canada and the rest of the British Commonwealth), and of all countries covered by the Pan-American Copyright Convention and the Universal Copyright Convention, the Berne Convention, and of all countries with which the United States has reciprocal copyright relations. All rights, including professional and amateur stage performing rights, motion picture, recitation, lecturing, public reading, radio broadcasting, television, video or sound recording, all other forms of mechanical or electronic reproduction, such as CD-ROM, DVD-ROM, information storage and retrieval systems, and photocopying, and the rights of translation into foreign languages, are strictly reserved. Particular emphasis is placed upon the matter of readings, permission for which must be secured from the author's agent in writing.

Inquiries concerning rights should be addressed to Next Stage Press, 11174 Josephine Way, Northglenn, CO 80233, licensing@nextstagepress.net.

Gene Kato

Gene Kato has been scripting plays for over twenty years and is the author of over twenty-five full-lengths, one-acts, and short plays. His play *18 Holes* won the Best Play Award at the Rocky Mountain Festivention, which was sponsored by playwright Steven Dietz. His play *Viral Infection* was nominated by the *Houston Post* for Best New Play in 2013. All of his works are represented by Next Stage Press (www.nextstagepress .net). He holds a BFA in theater from Sam Houston State University as well as an MA in theater from the University of Colorado, Boulder. He currently lives in Northglenn, Colorado, with his wife, Jessica, and their three pets Remy, Dodger, and Jasmine.

···production history···

2nd Anniversary Near Taurus Major was originally produced in Houston, Texas, by Cone Man Running Productions as part of the Spontaneous Smattering Short Play Festival (Christine Weems, producer) on March 30, 2013. The play was directed by Sam Martinez and the original cast was as follows:

CAPT. NEWMAN   Rachel Wesley

SGT. NEWMAN   Louis Crespo

IC-PP   Margaret Lewis

C-ME-69   Taylor Biltoft

setting

CAPT. NEWMAN's spaceship, currently orbiting Taurus Major.

time

The future.

[*Intense space-themed music plays in the darkness. The lights come up to reveal a large unknown control room of a spaceship. Two robots standing lifeless near the back portion of the stage. One male, one female. As the music fades, we hear the voice of a woman speaking.*]

CAPT. NEWMAN   [*Offstage.*] Captain's log, star date 03302013. We have just made our second orbit of Taurus Major and the environmental study is complete. Our orders to pick up Sgt. Newman, my husband, from the Space Station Weems [*Pronounced "hweems."*] have been received and we are in route. It's been two months since I have seen him—and tonight marks our second anniversary. It's my hope that I can give him something special this evening. A night he will never forget.

[CAPT. NEWMAN *enters carrying two jackets, she surveys the room for a moment, then walks over and puts a jacket on backwards and moves her right hand up. Immediately, the arm of the female robot,* INTELLIGENCE COLLECTION— POLLUTED PLANETS, IC-PP, *raises to exactly the same height. She lowers her arm, the robot lowers her arm.*]

You are scientific wonders, my dears. Both of you. I can't thank the two of you enough. All of the work you've done for us in collecting samples from the surface has sped our work up by years. The two of you have earned much needed power downtime.

[She takes off the jacket, and as she does, IC-PP mimics her movements. Then she reaches behind her neck and "turns her off." She walks over to the male, COLLECTION-MOLTEN ENVIRONMENTS 69, C-ME-69, and turns him off. Both robots slump. She walks over and hangs one jacket on one side of the stage and the other on the opposite. Almost immediately, there in the sound of a man's voice. When he speaks, he sounds like a cross between Dudley Do-right and the penguins from Madagascar.]

SGT. NEWMAN   Permission to penetrate your air lock!

CAPT. NEWMAN   Permission granted, Sir!

[The sound of the ship "sealing into the air lock."]

SGT. NEWMAN   Ooooh, tight!

[Sound of a swishing door, and SGT. NEWMAN enters. Immediately, the Newmans run to each other, stop, salute, and then immediately begin groping one another.]

CAPT. NEWMAN   Oh, God! I can't believe after two months, you're finally back.

SGT. NEWMAN   I can't believe it either—and I've been with me the whole time.

CAPT. NEWMAN   It's been so long!

SGT. NEWMAN   It still is. Especially right now, and I'm gonna need some help to get me all jiggly again.

[She pulls back.]

CAPT. NEWMAN   Wait. There's something I need to show you first.

SGT. NEWMAN   No, there's something I need to show you. It's bigger than a bread box and just as fresh. It consumes me and makes me chant like I'm a rapper. Here goes one.

[He begins to rap.]

I NEED SOME LOVIN' IN YO OVEN OR THERE'S GONNA BE SOME SHOVIN' 'CUZ MY PENIS IS BETWEEN US AND IT'S GONNA BE THE MEANEST TIME THAT YOU HAVE EVER SEE US WHEN I'M HUMPIN' AND I'M PUMPIN' AND YO LADY PARTS IS JUMPIN' FROM YO PANTS…FROM YO PANTS…WHEN WE DO THE PRIVATE PARTS DANCE… WORD.

[*He collects himself. She stares at him for a moment. He walks up to her.*]

The time for waiting is over, my darling. It's time for me to swoop you into my arms and spirit you to your celestial bedchamber in the stars and lay you down...like Conway Twitty said I should.

CAPT. NEWMAN We will, my darling. I just want you to see what I've been working with the past few months. Come see.

[*He allows himself to reluctantly be lead over to the robots.*]

These are the most important advancement we've made in artificial life-forms.

SGT. NEWMAN Ah, yes. The robots. They look so real. The woman looks like some Irish goddess with her flowing red hair, crystalline complexion, and supple features that make you expect her to look at you and say, "Hi. My name is Rowena." And the man. He looks like Ringo Starr.

CAPT. NEWMAN It gets better. Stay here.

[*She goes and grabs the two jackets, she hands him one.*]

Here. Put this on. Backwards.

SGT. NEWMAN Are we cold?

CAPT. NEWMAN Just trust me.

[*She fires up the two robots. After a second or two, they pop open their eyes. IC-PP calmly walks around the room. SGT. NEWMAN struggles to get his jacket on correctly and C-ME-69 follows his movements, looking mostly like a stuck zombie reaching for its prey. SGT. NEWMAN jumps back, and C-ME-69 pops back into place as well.*]

SGT. NEWMAN Good sweet Jesus Christ Almighty! Why did he do that?! He was lunging at me like some artificial person with artificial bloodlust in his artificial eyes! Did you see him?!

[*He points at the robot, who in turn points back.*]

CAPT. NEWMAN That wasn't him, darling. That was you.

[*He looks at her, confused.*]

It's the jacket. It works like an amazing remote control, and the best part is you can feel everything that the robot feels through the jacket. It's how we test samples for consistency.

SGT. NEWMAN How do you control them?

CAPT. NEWMAN   Basic controls. Lean forward, they walk forward.

[*She demonstrates.*]

Lean left, they turn left, right, they turn right, etc., etc.

SGT. NEWMAN   That's quite amazing. Can they talk? I have their intelligence module turned off. They can only say their name.

[*She walks IC-PP up to the Sgt. She looks blankly at him and says…*]

IC-PP   IC-PP.

CAPT. NEWMAN   Intelligence Collections—Polluted Planets.

SGT. NEWMAN   And Ringo?

CAPT. NEWMAN   You're not far off—he was modeled after a late-'60s human. He is Collection—Molten Environments—69 or…

[*She makes an adjustment on his jacket.*]

C-ME-69   C-ME-69.

SGT. NEWMAN   Amazing. Let me try to drive him to me.

[*The Sgt. uses the jacket to maneuver C-ME-69 to next to him. C-ME-69 turns to him.*]

Yes, my friend. Let me get a look at you. Amazing. Look me in the eye.

[*C-ME-69 turns to him.*]

You have a rugged sense about you that one only sees in storybooks about inchworms or Vikings or the North. I give a slight twist of my shoulder and you hunch forth seeking what? Enlightenment? Instructions? Day-old bacon? What, my friend? What do you seek?

CAPT. NEWMAN   Honey, He's just…

SGT. NEWMAN   Hold on, my love. I look deep into these artificial eyes, and they tell a different story. Not one of love or lust or even woebegone days, but they tell a story. A story of man. Who was a machine. I'll run my fingers through your hair because your hair, it is right there.

[*He does. C-ME-69 also runs his fingers through the Sgt.'s hair.*]

He likes me. He really likes me.

CAPT. NEWMAN   They really are amazing. Tomorrow I need to download the latest entry from IC-PP's memory banks.

SGT. NEWMAN   What sort of information?

CAPT. NEWMAN   Well, they record all of the sensory information from the planet's surface and it's then translated by the ship's computers. Here. I'll show you.

[*She makes a few adjustments on the jacket and suddenly* IC-PP *springs to life.*]

IC-PP   The planet's temperature seems to be able to support life. However, this side of the planet seems to be prone to...

[*The Capt. stops her speech.*]

SGT. NEWMAN   You cut her off at the cliff-hanger!

CAPT. NEWMAN   Probably just weather info. Solar storms, high wind...things like that. Not that important. Let's make them hug one another.

[*They direct the robots to slowly walk to one another and embrace.*]

SGT. NEWMAN   Holy beaver! It feels like...it feels just like...

[*He looks at his wife, who smiles and nods.*]

CAPT. NEWMAN   Feel this.

    [*She drives* IC-PP*'s hands to run down* C-ME-69*'s chest. The Sgt. reacts.*]

    Amazingly real, isn't it?

SGT. NEWMAN   Very, let me try.

    [*He does the reverse and causes* C-ME-69 *to run his hands down* IC-PP*. The Capt. reacts. Both humans laugh.*]

    Amazing workmanship, but not a substitute for the real thing. Shall we put these toys away and retire for the evening?

CAPT. NEWMAN   There is nothing I would love more.

    [*They kiss. The robots kiss. When they break, they take the robots back to their spots. The Capt. turns to the Sgt., pointing to the opposite side of the stage.*]

    Just hang C-ME's jacket up over there.

[*He walks over to hang up the jacket, when suddenly there is a massive crash and a jolt. A siren wails as a voice chants, "AIR LOCK BREACHED! AIR LOCK BREACHED!" A hissing sound signifies that the Capt. and the Sgt. are separated by air locks.*]

SGT. NEWMAN   What happened? What was that?

CAPT. NEWMAN Hold on.

[*She puts the jacket back on and speaks into the sleeve.*]

IC-PP, report please. What hit us?

IC-PP As reported, this side of the planet is prone to meteor showers. It appears the hull of the ship has been breached. This room now has an oxygen content of 4%...3%...2%...1%...the oxygen content of this room is 0%. This room is no longer capable of sustaining organic life-forms. In laymen's term...you are...fucked. It gets worse...

CAPT. NEWMAN How can it get worse?

IC-PP The hull is breeched and we are falling from orbit.

SGT. NEWMAN We have to get off this ship. We can get out on my shuttle.

CAPT. NEWMAN It's not going to work. The airlock is sealed. I'm trapped.

SGT. NEWMAN That's impossible! It's...it's...utterly impossible! And if it's not impossible...then it's...at the very least...highly unlikely.

CAPT. NEWMAN These doors are meant to stay sealed until air pressure and oxygen levels are safe. They won't open. There's no override.

SGT. NEWMAN [*Throwing on the jacket.*] Then, 69 will rescue you!

[C-ME-69 *walks down next to* IC-PP.]

Do something!

[C-ME-69 *lunges out as the Sgt. struggles and knocks* IC-PP *over.*]

C-ME-69 I can see her lyin' back in her satin dress

In a room where you do what you don't confess.

Sundown, you better take care

If I find you bin creepin' round my back stairs.

Sundown, you better take care

If I find you bin creepin' round my back stairs.

SGT. NEWMAN What in God's name?

CAPT. NEWMAN He's of no use. Other than collecting molten lava samples—all he's programmed to do is sing Gordon Lightfoot songs and the signal fucks with IC-PP, sometimes she joins along.

C-ME-69/IC-PP   She's bin lookin' like a queen in a sailor's dream
And she don't always say what she really means.
Sometimes I think it's a shame
When I get feelin' better when I'm feelin' no pain.
Sometimes I think it's a shame
When I get feelin' better when I'm feelin' no pain.

SGT. NEWMAN   How do I shut them off?

CAPT. NEWMAN   Blue button.
[*He pushes the button and both go silent.*]
Well, what to do now, sugar? I just don't know.

SGT. NEWMAN   I'm not leaving you. I don't care if this whole thing
goes up in a fiery twisted ball of flame...

CAPT. NEWMAN   It is, darling. It is.
[*Silence.*]
It's okay. I'm the Captain. I go down with the ship. I knew that when I
took this job.

SGT. NEWMAN   What can I do?

CAPT. NEWMAN   Get C-ME-69 to embrace IC-PP and just hold me.
[*They direct the robots to embrace again.*]
Oh, that feels nice. Now sing me the song. Our song. You know the
one.

SGT. NEWMAN   [*He sings, upbeat.*] Who is the one that locks my latch?
Who is the pumpkin in my patch?
Who is the sweetest one to catch?
It's my little candy snatch.

CAPT. NEWMAN   What the hell was that song? You've never sung that
song to me before.
[*She slaps at him. IC-PP slaps C-ME-69.*]
This is exactly what my mother said would happen to me. She called
it. She said this was like dingle berries in Düsseldorf—and she was
right.

SGT. NEWMAN   What does that mean?

IC-PP Dingle berry—noun. 1. A piece of dried feces caught in the hair around the anus in Düsseldorf , Germany. 2. An incompetent, foolish, or stupid person in Düsseldorf, Germany.

CAPT. NEWMAN We get it, PP.

SGT. NEWMAN We don't have a lot of time.

CAPT. NEWMAN No.

SGT. NEWMAN [*Through the following the couple reacts to one another through the robots.*] I meant what I said. I'm not leaving you. You and I haven't had the benefit of being together. True, I've traveled the universe doing important work while you stayed here with non-people picking up rocks—but you've also had your share of success. You've been a captain of a ship. You've tasted flan. You've married me. Now, we both know the universe can be a fickle bitch. An ugly fickle bitch with a terrible temper. She sometimes rears her ugly head like a club-footed monkey flinging shit at a wall anointed with crotched doilies—but it doesn't mean she's mad. It means she's afraid. Just like we are. But there's no need to be afraid, my love. I'm not going to leave you. I promise you. I will not be your dingle berry. I'm the man you love. [*They kiss air. The robots kiss. Suddenly, they break apart.*]

Hey—since we're running out of time…

CAPT. NEWMAN Yes?

SGT. NEWMAN And we do have the jackets.

CAPT. NEWMAN Yes.

SGT. NEWMAN Shall we go out with a bang?

[*There is another crash and the ship shifts and everyone falls.* IC-PP *and* C-ME-69 *stumble over one another and are on the ground in the 69 position. They immediately keep repeating their names.*]

Jesus! Hang on!

[*He tries to pull himself up by climbing up the "wall"—as he lifts his hands,* C-ME-69 *ends up putting his hands on* IC-PP's *rear end and lifting her back in straight up, the crown of her head rests on his crotch—they are still repeating their names. The Sgt. slides back down, unable to stand.* C-ME-69 *lowers* IC-PP.]

We're tilting.

CAPT. NEWMAN   You have to go, my love. No sense in both of us dying.

SGT. NEWMAN   I'm not going anywhere.

CAPT. NEWMAN   I can feel you against me.

SGT. NEWMAN   Me too. Feels like your legs are on my shoulders and your tits are on my belly. Reminds me of the days when our love was young.

[*They stop the robots from talking. The robots slump.*]

How long do we have?

CAPT. NEWMAN   Not long. Let's try to turn the robots around.

[*They make a few maneuvers and manage to get the robots turned around. Now IC-PP lies with her head on C-ME-69's chest.*]

Good. This is good. This is how I want to go.

[*Silence.*]

SGT. NEWMAN   Me too.

[*Pause.*]

I love you, Captain.

CAPT. NEWMAN   I love you, Sergeant.

[*They both smile. The Sgt. hits a button on his jacket. C-ME-69 begins singing.*]

C-ME-69   I can see her lyin' back in her satin dress
In a room where you do what you don't confess.

[*The others join.*]

Sundown, you better take care
If I find you bin creepin' round my back stairs.
Sundown, you better take care
If I find you bin creepin' round my back stairs.

• • •

The New Models

Rory Leahy

The New Models by Rory Leahy. Copyright © 2014 by Rory Leahy. All rights reserved. Reprinted by permission of the author.

CAUTION/ADVICE: Professionals and amateurs are hereby warned that performance of *The New Models* is subject to a royalty. It is fully protected under the copyright laws of the United States of America, and of all countries covered by the International Copyright Union (including the Dominion of Canada and the rest of the British Commonwealth), and of all countries covered by the Pan-American Copyright Convention and the Universal Copyright Convention, the Berne Convention, and of all countries with which the United States has reciprocal copyright relations. All rights, including professional and amateur stage performing rights, motion picture, recitation, lecturing, public reading, radio broadcasting, television, video or sound recording, all other forms of mechanical or electronic reproduction, such as CD-ROM, DVD-ROM, information storage and retrieval systems, and photocopying, and the rights of translation into foreign languages, are strictly reserved. Particular emphasis is placed upon the matter of readings, permission for which must be secured from the author's agent in writing.

Inquiries concerning rights should be addressed to rory.leahy@gmail.com.

Rory Leahy

Rory Leahy is the founder and artistic director of the American Demigods theater company. He's been an actor and playwright in Chicago for several years and is the author of such works as *The Irrelevant Adventures of Jarvis McFadden* and *The Factory That Makes Devils*. He has recently ventured into screenwriting in collaboration with director David Holcombe, with the short film *Death of a Cybersalesman* and the feature film *Yellow*. The latter is distributed through Maxim Media. His short play *He's Really a Great Guy* will be published in the forthcoming *Best Ten Minute Plays of 2013* from Smith and Krauss. His plays have been performed in Chicago and Champaign-Urbana, Illinois, St. Louis, Missouri, Miami, Florida, and New York City.

···production history···

The New Models was performed by EndTimes Productions in September 2012 at the 133rd St. Arts Center, 308 W. 133rd St, New York, NY, directed by Russell Dobular.

> **ZAURIEL**   Jada Saunders
>
> **AZRAEL**   Ratnesh Dubey
>
> **MALE SUBJECT**   Michael Tyler
>
> **GABRIEL**   Matt Decoster
>
> **FEMALE SUBJECT**   Hannah Abney

It was performed again in March 2013 by Between Us Productions at Roy Arias Studios, 300 W. 43rd, New York, NY, directed by Art Brown.

> **ZAURIEL**   Art Brown
>
> **AZRAEL**   Matt Hammond
>
> **MALE SUBJECT**   Ra Consiglere
>
> **GABRIEL**   Pat Zaudke
>
> **FEMALE SUBJECT**   Heidi Jaye

characters

> **ZAURIEL**
>
> **AZRAEL**
>
> **MALE SUBJECT**
>
> **GABRIEL**
>
> **FEMALE SUBJECT**

staging note

The set consists of a table, behind which the three angel characters can sit. The angels can be of either gender.

[ZAURIEL *stands alone.*]

ZAURIEL I'm not asking for credit. Or perhaps I am. They talk endlessly of your endless love without ever noticing how vague they're being. Do they know that love is a machine, requiring a thousand gears to operate? Do they know that it is a painting composed of a million different colors? Do they know that it is a sculpture made out of a billion…pieces of clay? They say they love you back but they never see your eyes…And you never see theirs.

[*Lights down.* ZAURIEL *and* AZRAEL *are onstage,* ZAURIEL *carries a notepad.* MALE SUBJECT *enters. He looks around, confused, falls to the ground dead.* ZAURIEL *instantly touches the body.*]

Rigor mortis achieved in 0.0007 seconds.

AZRAEL 0.00068 seconds, if you want to be precise.

ZAURIEL If that makes you feel more involved in this process, fine. Reinitialize gestation procedure.

[*Lights down.* MALE SUBJECT *again enters, looks around for a moment, finally addressing* ZAURIEL *and* AZRAEL.]

MALE SUBJECT I…I…I…I…I…am…

[MALE SUBJECT *falls down, dead.*]

ZAURIEL Male Subject Incarnation Number Thirty-Eight Thousand One Hundred Ninety-Six has displayed signs of self-awareness, as well as rudimentary vocalization. We're getting close.

AZRAEL Shouldn't this be going a bit faster?

ZAURIEL We *are* reinventing the wheel here, Azrael.

AZRAEL [*Confused.*] I thought that was Thursday.

[*Lights down.*]

Say, Zauriel? How many of us do you suppose *can* dance on the head of a pin?

ZAURIEL Shut the fuck up, Azrael.

[*Lights down.*]

MALE SUBJECT DAMN YOU! You have NO RIGHT to do this! MONSTERS!

[*He falls dead.*]

ZAURIEL I think we're ready for Archangel Gabriel's inspection.

[*Lights down.*]

[AZRAEL *and* ZAURIEL *sit at a table as* GABRIEL *enters.*]

GABRIEL What have you for me today?

AZRAEL Most Reverend Archangel Gabriel Who Art Second Only to the Divine Father in Command of Our Heavenly Host: We are not worthy of your presence.

GABRIEL I should say not.

ZAURIEL Archangel, the new model humans are available for your inspection.

AZRAEL Which is not to say that your presence is not the shimmering light of our otherwise unworthy lives...

GABRIEL As you know, we've been watching you closely.

AZRAEL One would think that an eternity of living in Heaven would dull one to its pleasures, but the pleasure of your presence remains...

GABRIEL Can you do something about that prattling?

ZAURIEL I could as well ask the same question of you, Archangel.

GABRIEL I don't make personnel decisions, I only live with them, as I suppose do you.

AZRAEL Even as you demean me well within my earshot, I am overcome with joy.

ZAURIEL May I proceed?

GABRIEL By all means.

[*All take their seats.*]

ZAURIEL Bring in the Male Subject.

[MALE SUBJECT *enters, confused but alert.*]

This is New Model Male Subject Number Forty-Two Thousand Three Hundred Eighty-Seven.

GABRIEL I see you've retained the same anatomical structure as the old models...

ZAURIEL We have no mandate for radical change. This is craft, not art.

MALE SUBJECT Um, excuse me...

AZRAEL Bipedal form, that was me, you know, back in the early days...

MALE SUBJECT What's going on here?

AZRAEL A lot of other angels were saying "three legs" but I boldly insisted on two...

ZAURIEL You've never boldly insisted on a damn thing!

MALE SUBJECT Who am I?

GABRIEL You are one of the new models, Male Subject.

MALE SUBJECT The new models of what?

ZAURIEL *Homo sapiens*, or more commonly, human beings. You see, for millennia, humans have been the dominant species of the earth. The prize jewel of creation...

MALE SUBJECT Really?

GABRIEL But we're phasing them out. For a prize jewel they're damned inefficient. They're destroying their planet and taxing the resources of Heaven far beyond the breaking point.

MALE SUBJECT Wait, if I was only just born, shouldn't I be...smaller?

ZAURIEL Racial memory accounts for a great deal of his intuition.

GABRIEL It's true that the old models went through an insanely long period of preparation called "childhood" after which they started to *decompose* for fifty or sixty years...but we've eliminated that in you. It wasn't efficient.

MALE SUBJECT So I'm to be more efficient than the old models?

GABRIEL Yes, if nothing else, you're going to get the opportunity to do far less damage. Your lifespan has been significantly shortened.

MALE SUBJECT By how much?

AZRAEL You're designed to have a lifespan of ten minutes.

MALE SUBJECT What? What are you saying? You're saying I'm going to die? In less than ten minutes? That's terrible!

GABRIEL That's wonderful. It's single-handedly saving this department from financial ruin!

MALE SUBJECT Wait, you've got to reconsider this...please! Ten minutes...it just isn't enough! There's no time for me to do anything, or learn anything! I'm way, way too young to die! It's not just! By any reasonable standard!

GABRIEL And it still has the capacity for logical argument. Cute touch.

ZAURIEL Thank you.

MALE SUBJECT I can't take this emotional pressure anymore! I'm losing my mind! And I only just got it!

ZAURIEL Think of it this way, Male Subject, everything that happens to you from now on will have an enhanced effect. Everything will go by much faster for you, you'll appreciate it more...

MALE SUBJECT If this is what appreciating things feels like, I don't like appreciating things!

AZRAEL Which reminds me, he hasn't reproduced yet!

ZAURIEL Indeed. Bring in the Female Subject!

[*The* FEMALE SUBJECT *enters, her eyes meet the* MALE SUBJECT*'s eyes.*]

MALE SUBJECT What? Are you...

[FEMALE SUBJECT *high-fives the* MALE SUBJECT *and exits.*]
That was it?

AZRAEL Well, we can't have you wasting time.

MALE SUBJECT She's another...like me...in the same situation... She's about to give birth to a child! *My* child! Who's going to be dead in ten minutes anyway! Oh, this is a cruel and incomprehensible universe!

AZRAEL See, he's figured that out already! It took the old models anywhere from ten to twenty *years* to realize that!

MALE SUBJECT DAMN YOU! You have NO RIGHT to do this! MONSTERS!

GABRIEL I see he has retained much of the defiant nature of the old humans.

ZAURIEL It's deeply ingrained in them, yes. It's something I suspect would be very difficult to breed out of them. No matter how much misery is inflicted on them...they still possess the will to live, to fight.

GABRIEL   You almost sound as if you admire them.

ZAURIEL   I consider it…a remarkable achievement.

GABRIEL   You're a romantic, Zauriel. I've always despised that about you.
[*To* MALE SUBJECT.]
Exactly who do you suppose you are, little worm, to talk of rights?

MALE SUBJECT   Why am I here? Why was I created if all I'm going to do is die?

GABRIEL   You are here, as are we all, to serve the purposes of our Creator.

MALE SUBJECT   You'll never convince me to serve the purposes of anyone so cruel.

GABRIEL   Insolent thing! Our Creator loved *us* long before He loved you! From the dawn of time, we have served Him! Oh, but He made this world for you! And He gave you the choice to reject Him! Sometimes I look at you and I wonder if the Fallen One wasn't right…

AZRAEL   [*Standing up, alarmed.*] Have a care, Gabriel!

GABRIEL   I am the Chief Messenger of your Creator. You will kneel before me, now.

MALE SUBJECT   I may only be a few minutes old but I think I've learned something about myself…

GABRIEL   What is that?

MALE SUBJECT   I don't kneel.

[*Enraged,* GABRIEL *punches the* MALE SUBJECT *in the stomach.*]

GABRIEL   Put them into mass production immediately. As for this one, take it back to the lab and let it expire.

AZRAEL   We'll try to breed out some of that persistent defiance, Archangel.

GABRIEL   Don't bother.
[*With disgust.*]
It's the way *He* wants them…

[*He exits,* AZRAEL *follows,* ZAURIEL *helps* MALE SUBJECT *to his feet.*]

ZAURIEL   How do you feel, Male Subject?

MALE SUBJECT   What's the point of that question?

ZAURIEL   I'm not sure. It's considered...courteous to ask.

MALE SUBJECT   Yeah, you've been real courteous.

ZAURIEL   In defiance of the Archangel's orders, I will not be taking you back to the lab. I'm giving you your freedom. You can leave this place.

MALE SUBJECT   I only have a few minutes to live. I won't get very far.

ZAURIEL   The border that separates Heaven from the world beyond is only a few feet beyond that gate.

[*Gesturing offstage.*]

Many of your kind believe that it is better to die in freedom than to live in slavery. A choice your forerunners made long ago...

MALE SUBJECT   I won't go without...her. I feel something for her that...it's not just a desire to mate with her again. Although I wouldn't object to that. But I feel something else for her.

ZAURIEL   What you feel is loyalty. Fellowship. It is admirable. If I had been more capable of those feelings myself...I would have led a different life. But as you wish...Female Subject!

[FEMALE SUBJECT *returns. If she could be visibly pregnant, that would be great.*]

FEMALE SUBJECT   Hello.

MALE SUBJECT   Hi. Um, I know we haven't gotten a chance to get to know each other very well...but I like to think we've made some sort of connection...

FEMALE SUBJECT   You and I are...You are the father of my child.

MALE SUBJECT   Yes. I don't really understand what's going on but I know that much.

FEMALE SUBJECT   I don't understand very much either. All I remember was the darkness, then being told I had to prepare for you. And then for our child. I've had no time to think of anything else... To imagine anything for myself...

MALE SUBJECT   I'm sorry, please understand that's not because of me, it's because of *them*.

FEMALE SUBJECT   I don't blame you for it. I wish we had more time...

MALE SUBJECT   I do too. That's what we both want. More time, more life. Will you give it to us?

ZAURIEL   That is beyond my power to give, but it may not be beyond your power to take.

FEMALE SUBJECT   What does that mean?

ZAURIEL   It means that you humans have always had the power to make yourselves more than what you are. So few of you know that, but I advise you to take it to heart. We angels were created in the beginning... We were created to serve and to see... To see the *order* and the *justice* of divine creation. And we love our Creator for it... But you... *you* He made to see with different eyes. You are capable of seeing what's wrong with this universe. You perceive the *disorder* and the *injustice* in that creation, and that has always fascinated me.

MALE SUBJECT   Yeah, well, it's not all that great a feeling.

ZAURIEL   But don't you understand? Your ability to see what's wrong also gives you the ability to set things right, as much as you can. Your vision is not limited to what is, you can also see what *should* be. Only one of us has ever seen with your eyes... and *he* did not turn out well. I have better hopes for you. But your future is your own.

[*He exits.*]

FEMALE SUBJECT   "Future"? Thanks a lot, you callous, immortal prick!

[*Substitute gender-appropriate epithet if* ZAURIEL *is a female.*]

MALE SUBJECT   You're as angry as I am.

FEMALE SUBJECT   I suppose... But I don't know if that does much good. Perhaps the angel was right, perhaps we do have the power to become more than what we are. That's what I hope for our child at least...

MALE SUBJECT   But still... We're running out of time.

FEMALE SUBJECT   But we have our freedom. That does matter to me.

MALE SUBJECT   If nothing else, I'm glad I can spend these final moments with you.

FEMALE SUBJECT   I'm glad for that too.

MALE SUBJECT   When we mated before...I believe there is more to it than what they led us to believe.

FEMALE SUBJECT   Is that *honestly* what you're thinking about right now? Really?

MALE SUBJECT   It's...among my thoughts.

FEMALE SUBJECT   Mine too.

[*They embrace and kiss.*]

MALE SUBJECT   I don't want to be alone...Stay with me...stay with me, love...

FEMALE SUBJECT   Until the end.

[*Lights down, we hear a baby crying.*]

• • •

acknowledgments

The authors in this collection are the ones who make this book what it is, and they deserve all the credit and thanks for their talent and effort. I would also like to thank all of those who submitted plays that unfortunately weren't selected. The number of good works out there is amazing, a fact that makes the selection process incredibly challenging. I welcome submissions throughout the year and look forward to works from newly produced authors right up to the veteran class.

Thanks always to the folks at Applause Theatre & Cinema Books, especially John Cerullo, Bernadette Malavarca, and Carol Flannery. Thanks also to June Clark, my agent, for supporting this project.

And thanks especially to my recently deceased mom: nobody dies unless they're forgotten.

THE BEST AMERICAN SHORT PLAYS SERIES

2011-2012

978-1-4768-7734-1 Hardcover $32.99
978-1-4768-7733-4 Paperback $19.99

2010-2011

978-1-55783-835-3 Hardcover $32.99
978-1-55783-836-0 Paperback $18.99

2009-2010

978-1-55783-763-9 Hardcover $32.99
978-1-55783-762-2 Paperback $18.99

2008-2009

978-1-55783-761-5 Hardcover $32.99
978-1-55783-760-8 Paperback $18.99

2006-2007

978-1-55783-747-9 Hardcover $34.99
978-1-55783-748-6 Paperback $18.99

2005-2006

978-1-55783-713-4 Hardcover $32.95

2003-2004

978-1-55783-695-3 Hardcover $32.95

2002-2003

978-1-55783-719-6 Hardcover $32.99
978-1-55783-720-2 Paperback $18.99

2000-2001

978-1-55783-480-5 Hardcover $32.95

APPLAUSE
THEATRE & CINEMA BOOKS

AN IMPRINT OF
HAL•LEONARD®
www.applausebooks.com

Prices, content, and availability subject to change without notice.

0414